About the Authors

Don Beville served as president of Rand McNally Fine Books Division then spent fourteen years as a field editor with Pearson Education, working with college professors in developing textbooks in science. He is the publisher of *The U.S Marines in the Gulf War*; managing editor, *Panic Disorder, History of the Boy Scouts of America, History of the USTA Tennis Association, Finishing the Hat: Life of Bill Nelson, Eldridge Bagley: Son of the Soil* for the University of Virginia Press. He has a Master of Science degree from Virginia Commonwealth University, and a graduate Certificate in Neurology from the MIT. He completed twenty-marathons including three Boston Marathons. Today, he loves cycling down hills as fast as he can.

Jonna Ivin-Patton is the founder of *STIR Journal* and writer of the essay, *I Know Why Poor Whites Chant, Trump, Trump, Trump*, which went viral in 2016 with over four million views and was nominated for a Push Cart. She has appeared on NPR, OPB, The Roland Martin Show, and KCRW. Jonna is the author of the books *Will Love for Crumbs*, *8th Amendment*, and *Sister Girl*. Her writing has been featured in *Good Magazine*, *STIR Journal*, *The Establishment*, and *Narratively*. She is currently working on a scripted series of the life story of notorious mother/son murderers Santé and Kenny Kimes and, with Emmy Award-winning All Rise Films, on a docuseries of the same subject.

The Boy Who Broke Records

Don Beville & Jonna Ivin-Patton

The Boy Who Broke Records

Olympia Publishers
London

www.olympiapublishers.com
OLYMPIA PAPERBACK EDITION

A CIP catalogue record for this title is
available from the British Library.

ISBN: 978-1-80074-992-4

This is a work of creative nonfiction. The events are portrayed to the
best of the authors' memories. While all the stories in this book are
true, some names and identifying details have been changed to protect
the privacy of the people involved.

First Published in 2023

Olympia Publishers
Tallis House
2 Tallis Street
London
EC4Y 0AB

Printed in Great Britain

Dedication

To Ry, who has shown me worlds I have never known.

Acknowledgements

No author writes alone. This book would not exist without the encouragement and remarkable talent of my editor and co-author, Jonna Ivin-Patton, who made me write more words even when I didn't want to. She guided me through the telling of a story about the miracles of the human spirit, of which these chapters treat.

Like all authors, I have so many people to thank. To Dr. Nathan Zasler, a genius in neuro-rehabilitative medicine. A man of deliberate preparation and research in providing for positive outcomes in traumatic brain injuries. There were times when he held my hand through my rivers of tears.

I cannot say enough about the staff at Sheltering Arms Hospital for providing a road map for the voyage out of the abyss of a broken brain.

To my many friends who suffered through reading of early manuscripts and providing constructive feedback. Hopefully, this final version is attractive to your eyes, and nurturing to your soul.

I am fortunate to have a network of professional friends who were brave enough to agree to write warm reviews of the book. I treasure them and love that they allow me to be in their orbit. Thank you, Gregory O'Shanick, M.D., David Kitchen, Ph.D., W. Reid Cornwell, Ph.D., and William D. Kernodle, M.D.

It would have been difficult to maintain some sanity through this tragedy if not for the loving community of Notre Dame. My family received support from Father King, Ry's dorm priest; the prayers of Rev. William Beauchamp, C.S.C. Executive Vice-

President; Tim Welch, the Notre Dame swim coach. Tim told me that Ry would always have a place on the swim team regardless of his disabilities. Special thanks to Steve and Charlotte Scott and their family, whose daughter, Haley, suffered multiple crushed vertebrae in a Notre Dame bus accident. Haley and her parents sent loving letters and phone calls that kept me from descending into a darker world.

To Father Don Lemay of St. Edward Catholic Church for his guiding prayers.

To Dennis Michael Stredney and Jack Amos for providing early dust-jacket designs.

Finally, to Laura English, for allowing me to pile stacks of chapters, crumpled pages, and empty wine glasses on her kitchen island. Your love and support make all my days sparkle.

Men go forth to wonder at the heights of mountains,
the huge waves of the sea, the broad flow of the rivers,
the vast compass of the ocean, the courses of the stars;
and they pass by themselves without wondering.

St. Augustine, *Confessions*
Book X, Chapter 8

Advanced Praise For: The Boy Who Broke Records

Don Beville brings the reader along on the most personal of journeys as he describes his family's encounter with the tragedy of his son's traumatic brain injury, the summer after his high school graduation. In combining accurate neuroscientific descriptions with the intimate emotions experienced by a grieving father, his story portrays the essence of the resilience possible in such a devastating test of faith and love. Having spent the greater part of the past four decades treating individuals with such significant neurotrauma, I applaud his articulating what so many parents have experienced in such a thoughtful, candid, and human manner. This is a "must-read" book for every person involved in any aspect of brain injury rehabilitation.

Gregory J. O' Shanick, M.D.

Medical Director, Center for Neurorehabilitation Services
Medical Director Emeritus, Brain Injury Association of America

Bury the memories. Wear that face. Don Beville peels back this façade to reveal the humanity of tragedy. A family struggling to first cope with then adapt to, and ultimately recover from disaster. It is the story of a father and his son, their love and determination, and it ends in the triumph of human spirit.

David Kitchen, Ph.D., Dean

School of Continuing Education

University of Richmond, Richmond, Virginia

This was a very moving and true story about the struggles of a father and his son following the son's traumatic brain injury. I enjoyed the author's elegant and moving writing style. The author is a natural storyteller. It is of special interest to me, as I am a psychiatrist and have treated many patients with traumatic brain injuries. I strongly recommend this book.

William D. Kernodle, M.D.

Tucker Psychiatric Clinic

Author of *Panic Disorder: The Medical Point of View*

Any caring parent should be sympathetic, if not horrified, by the beautiful narrative written in this memoir. The shared path of a father and son is a testament to the strength of character, forbearance, and the love of father and son. At no point does this story become a maudlin expression of self-pity. Rather it is a lesson on how real people can overcome what could be a reason to surrender to their dark angels. As a behavioral scientist, I am struck with its worth as a guide to help make life bearable, when that which you most value appears to be lost. A small masterpiece.

W. Reid Cornwell, Ph.D.
Chief Scientist and Director
The Center for Internet Research

Chapter 1

The Boy Who Broke Records

I remember my grandmother telling me that east is the direction of birth. She would often say it's where the sun lives, and every day our soul emerges from the point where the sun rises. East is where flowers, wheat, and corn orient themselves so they can flourish, and where explorers set out to find the New World. Seeking out the Wild West, ambitious travelers needed to become inspired in the east before taking their first step. The east, she would say, was where each day and each new story began.

And so too, on the East Coast of the United States, in Richmond, Virginia, my family would begin a journey we never signed up to take. At times I would come to feel pushed to follow a path I didn't trust and a light I could not see. In those dark times, I would recall being a child and asking my grandmother on a cloudy day where the sun had gone. She'd laughed and said "Since all of time, man has relied on the sun to rise and bring the light. Even if you cannot see it, know in your heart it is always there waiting to greet you at a new beginning."

Grandma should have known, being patient was not an area in which I excelled.

It was early summer in 1992, the year my son Ry graduated high school and was leaving for his freshman year at the University of Notre Dame as part of the nationally ranked swim team. To say I was in the throes of a pre-empty-nest crisis would be accurate. I don't do well with loss, and although logically I knew I wasn't "losing" my only child, the constant pit in my stomach that had lingered since graduation day felt otherwise.

I was trying to spend as much time as possible with him before he left, so at the sun's rise on one June morning, we headed east toward the creek that ran through the back of our property. The winding stream was more than fifteen feet across with a sandy, pebbly bottom. The banks were overflowing with the blackberry bushes I'd planted ten years before and never managed to cut back enough. The vines were hanging low, covered in shiny sweet blackberries ready to be picked for blackberry cobbler. I had an appreciation for their wild nature. It reminded me of my youth.

Ry and I had embarked on a bold father-son summer project. A hundred yards into the lush forest, we planned to dam up the creek and build a Japanese garden around our newly created pond. Ry had studied Japanese for two years in high school and was now fascinated with the clean, stylized look of Japanese gardens, surrounded by bamboo. As much as Ry had fallen in love with the Japanese culture, he was still a teenager on his last summer before college, and I couldn't imagine gardening with his father was his first choice.

This was my idea, and maybe it was a little selfish, but I was feeling the familiar twitches of panic beginning to fill my thoughts. I had never told him about the loss I had suffered when I was just a few years older than him, a loss and devastation so deep, I had pushed the event into a dark place that I never wanted to visit again. Ry wasn't aware of any of this. He simply thought his clingy old man wanted to hang out. I reminded myself again that I wasn't losing Ry; he was just leaving for college. These words would become my mantra over the next few months.

Ry walked along the banks of the creek, giving no indication he would rather be elsewhere. For this I was grateful. If it was an act, he was doing a splendid job. Maybe it was pity being thrown my way, or maybe there was a part of him that wanted to hold on to his parents a little longer.

I wanted to savor this day and proceeded to take in as many details as possible. The impatiens along the path had come to life, looking like a blanket of confetti. Above us hung the dazzling Virginia creeper vines, and branches supporting chattering squirrels amid the continuous crackling of a dozen different bird calls, some sweet, others loud and annoying. Intimidating spiders hunting their prey clung to the underside of leaves. I marveled at how they never tired of waking each morning to weave their world back together. Orb spiders know when their webs are damaged or deteriorating. They instinctively eat the damaged part, recycling it by digesting it and spinning a new path. It seemed like an exhausting process, and I wondered if they ever felt like just giving up.

I had no idea on that day just how much those orb spiders would come to mind in the next few months. How often I would think of them, gaining inspiration to rise another day and put the web of my life back together, knowing all the while how fragile it all was.

Leaves, their veins bulging with life-sustaining chlorophyll, made a swish as new creatures moved in and out to feed. Even higher, above the treetops, the silent brightness of the sun warmed the dazzling brilliance in the yellow-and-black wings of butterflies. Wars raged between insects, one fighting to take a life while another was simply trying to stay alive. The forest was a reminder that life could simultaneously be beautiful and brutal, and there was no way to extricate the two sides.

Having grown up on a farm, I'd learned early how fragile life could be. My grandmother was fond of saying that there was a thin membrane separating life from death. Her diary was filled with scripture that was testimony to her belief that every day that God let us live was a precious gift. The farm always had a way of reminding us how true that was.

One afternoon, when I was six years old, my grandfather didn't come home for lunch at the usual time, so my grandmother called Uncle Raymond to go out to the fields and check on the old man. I joined my uncle and after walking through the pasture, we saw Grandpa's turned-over tractor in a ravine. With his leg pinned under the big tire, he could not move. Uncle Raymond called for help from the local farmers and after some concerted effort, the townsfolk were able to get grandpa out with minimum damage to his leg. Uncle Raymond told me that grandfather was lucky, because at that time of year, the ravine was dry. In winter, a deep stream would run through it, and my grandfather could have drowned.

"Don," Uncle Raymond said while patting my shoulder, "you need to remember that danger and destruction can hide around each corner, behind every cloud, and surprise you even when you least expect it. You must always be prepared." I didn't fully understand his words and thought maybe my uncle was a bit paranoid. It wasn't until many years later when I was an adult that I understood.

I learned years later that Raymond had faced death as a young navy sailor. On December 7th, 1941, he made his way along the burning runway of an aircraft carrier in Pearl Harbor as Japanese fighter planes dropped bomb after bomb. As an adult, I read books about the bombings that occurred that day, and it became scorchingly vivid the destruction, suffering and loss of life that Raymond must have witnessed. When I recalled seeing my grandfather under that tractor, and the words of my uncle, I never again looked at life the same way. Death was always close.

As we made our way down the creek bed, stumbling over half-rotted roots, I marveled at Ry's muscular body. My son, at the age of eighteen, had a forty-four-inch chest, chiseled shoulders, and a twenty-eight-inch waist. He had a true swimmer's physique, a body he worked hard to achieve. By six, every morning, Ry was in the pool, training with friends, followed by hours in the weight room. He wanted to lower his national times in the one hundred and two hundred meter butterfly, knowing Notre Dame was crawling with nationally ranked swimmers. His goal was to be the best swimmer on the team. There was never an off-season for Notre Dame athletes. Year-round, the entire campus resembled an Olympic training village. Ry knew there was a lot of disciplined work to do and he was prepared for it. My wife, Lynn, and I had raised an overachiever.

We reached a bend in the winding creek and found a place I thought would be the best spot to begin construction. The area I picked was expansive, with a high bank on one side and plenty of small rocks with which to build the dam. Huge green ferns lined the bank. I waded in first, looking around to see if there were some large rocks, we could remove to make the water deeper. Nigel, our black cat, had followed us, claiming residence on top of a large boulder to oversee our labors, like a union boss.

"Dad, I'm not sure I'll have the energy to do more of this tomorrow," Ry said, wiping sweat from his face.

"Why?" I asked, trying not to show my disappointment. The closer it got to his leaving, the more he dashed in this direction and that: dates, friends, practice, and training, so that days like this with just the two of us had become precious to me.

"We have a three-hour practice in the morning—mostly short sprints. The Nationals in Atlanta are next weekend. Tomorrow is our last hard practice. We'll start tapering tomorrow for the rest of the week. The national record holder will be there, but I think he'll be tired. He just swam in a meet at the University of Florida a week ago."

It was amazing for me how Ry immersed himself in his passion, not only with his physical self but also with his mind. He knew all the other swimmers, when they had a meet, what their schedules were. He studied his competition like a stockbroker would follow the markets. "What times are you shooting for?" I asked.

"I want to break fifty-four seconds in the one hundred-meter butterfly." There was a sparkle in his eye that could be read as both confident and cocky.

"That's a bit ambitious, don't you think? It would mean coming down more than two seconds since the meet in March." Ry fell silent and I knew he was mulling over what I had said.

I looked up through the canopy of lush leaves at the top of the trees and peered into the puffy white clouds. Things were right in my life and I felt fortunate. I had a wife and son I adored and who I knew loved me. Everything was right in the world and it made me anxious. I'd lived long enough to know that fortune can swing both ways: good can turn to bad instantaneously. No one is immune to the swinging pendulum of fate. I'd learned from experience that when the pendulum comes back for you it can knock you to your knees. Life moves adeptly through intersections of grace straight into disruption and chaos.

Ry took a seat near the edge of the stream and dipped his handkerchief in the water. He placed the wet rag on the back of his neck, letting the cool water run down his back. "Hey, Dad, there are little fish over here," he said as he looked into the depths of the little pool of water. "I wonder why they don't swim downstream?" Ry seemed to find joy and meaning in the simplest events in life.

"I think we should collect rocks and set them on the bank first. Organize them by size and shape. What do you think?" I was already starting to visualize the dam.

"That works for me, Dad." Ry looked at the large rocks sitting fifteen feet from the bank. Shaking his head, he added, "You know, once we get those big ones anywhere close to the wet sand, they're going to sink before we can move them into place in the stream."

He was right. Without the big rocks, we had no dam. "Good eye, Ry."

"Lego sets, Dad. You don't think I put those together reading the directions, do you?" Ry said with a chuckle. "I got an A in Calculus too. I know a little bit about engineering."

Damn, I had forgotten about the massive Lego sets I had given him for Christmas and for his birthdays, some containing five hundred pieces. He had become a critical thinker like his mom. She too was a methodical problem solver, so quick to articulate the methodology of any scientific article written in her neonatal emergency care journals.

For these reasons, I couldn't understand why he was majoring in Creative Writing with a minor in Japanese. I had hoped he would major in one of the sciences, or possibly architecture, maybe civil engineering. The day my father was handed his engineering diploma from the University of Virginia, the job offers poured in. It seemed the perfect opportunity to ask, "Ry, why did you decide to major in Creative Writing? Have you given any thought as to how you're going to make a living with a writing degree? I love your passion, but..." I trailed off, not sure how to finish. I didn't want to crush his dream, but being a book publisher for twenty-five years, I hired designers, writers and copy editors monthly. Once they turned in their work or provided editing services, they might go months without another assignment. In other words, they were always broke, and I didn't want that for my son.

Ry didn't need me to finish my thought; his answer was instant. So quick, in fact, I wondered if he hadn't been waiting all summer for me to ask the question. I could picture him up in his room, writing out his answer on an index card and committing it to memory, knowing the day would come when I would question his choice. He was certainly prepared.

"Words can seduce you and provide nourishment, like air and water." Ry dug his toe into the mud as he continued, "I want to be a good writer. I want to learn how to write stories with a novelist's eye for detail. I want to learn how to put words on paper that can be a testimony to the tenuous nature of love and life. Maybe even start my own magazine one day."

How could a father possibly argue with that?

Ry had always had a propensity for writing, especially stories about the resilience of the human spirit. In the fourth grade, he penned a story about an American doctor who traveled to Brazil looking to locate a tribe of Indians who may have developed a medicine from a local plant that could cure cancer. The doctor overcame many hurdles before finding the tribe. Ry illustrated the book then created an authentic book by sewing the pages together and gluing them between two pieces of binder's board he bought at a local hobby store. Five hundred years ago, Ry would have been considered a craftsman in the bookmaking trade.

I was happy to listen to him talk all day. What a mind he had! I discovered a secret world of contentment with my son, something natural to obtain and more cosmically thrilling than the promise of land and wealth many believed would bring them happiness. I soaked up the time I spent with him. Many of my friends modulated their moods with caffeine, alcohol, or prescription drugs. My buzz came from interacting with my son. Because of Lynn's career as a neonatal nurse on the night shift, she had to sleep during daylight hours. My job as an editor and producer of trade books was flexible, and I could work from a home office.

As Ry got older, I became his soccer coach, his baseball coach, fixed his breakfast at five a.m. then drove him to his six a.m. swim practices. During those drives we talked about life, what he liked about school, swimming, and girls. I had a front-row seat to his journey into manhood. It was a tremendous privilege to witness his spirituality and courage in the face of enormous setbacks, making one comeback after another. I felt he knew I would always be there for him, just a heartbeat away. A bit of extra protection.

I realized that in a few weeks when he stepped out of the van behind Zahm Hall at Notre Dame, his mother and I would have to develop a new routine in our childless world. I hadn't said anything to Lynn or Ry, but I had purchased football tickets to the Notre Dame home games. At least there would be some weekends when we would be a family again.

Ry and I worked through the late morning into the afternoon building the rock dam. Around three o'clock, he looked at his watch and called it quitting time. He was going to hang out with some friends and then later had a date with his girlfriend, Alexis.

I wanted to protest, ask him to cancel his date and stay in with his mother and me, but I knew to do so would only end in an awkward refusal. There comes the point in every young man's life when they need to go their own way. This was Ry's time to explore a new world. I knew that. My time with him was merging into weeks, then days, and soon it would collapse into hours. A tingle of loss began to rise in me again. I had to shut the door on it.

On the following Saturday, Ry went to the national meet in Atlanta. When he didn't call on the night of his big event, I knew he hadn't broken any records or beaten the national record holder in the one hundred-meter fly. I was proud of him no matter how he had performed but I knew he would be disappointed. When he returned home, I patiently waited for him to talk. I'd learned over the years that if I waited patiently, Ry would eventually come to me. So, I wasn't surprised when a couple of days after the Atlanta event, while we were once again working on the Japanese garden, he finally said, "I didn't get a good jump off the blocks."

We were in the middle of planting bamboo around the edge of the new pond. I stood there in silence for a few seconds. My heart broke for him. I knew how much he wanted to win that event. It would have ended the season on a high and put him in an excellent position on the Notre Dame swim team.

"Do you think you could have taken first if your start had been better?" I asked while using the shovel to dig a hole.

Ry dropped the bamboo into the hole I had just dug and began filling it with dirt. "I don't know, Dad. I felt good. And my taper was perfect. The guy who won holds the pool record, so maybe his pride was on the line." I could see in his eyes he was running through the meet in his mind. Eventually, he seemed to settle on his answer. "He probably tried a little harder. I was even with him on the turn but lost it in the last few meters." Ry pushed a bit more soil around the base of the bamboo. "I can be happy with my second place." Then he smiled and added, "This time."

He didn't mention his Atlanta performance again that summer but continued his twice-a-day practices as the days passed and summer was coming to an end. As a long-distance runner, I knew what it was like to train and not get the results I expected in a race. It drove both Ry and me to work harder. We knew what it was to put our bodies on the line with every practice.

I had run twenty-two marathons trying to qualify for the Boston Marathon and managed to do so only three times. No matter how much I tried to analyze my training leading up to the race, I could never figure out why I ran faster or slower on a given day. The disappointment of failure can be devastating to the soul of an athlete. It can destroy self-confidence. Perhaps by going to two grueling practices each day, Ry could erase some of the pain of failing to win in Atlanta. He also knew he would be competing against nationally ranked swimmers at Notre Dame.

The days of Ry and me spending time together in the Japanese garden started to end. I kept coming up with new ideas and touches to add here and there, but eventually it became obvious even to me that the garden was complete. I sat on the bank with so much pride looking over our creation. The new water flow had slowly chiseled into the soft bank, making our pond look like an overflowing bowl of water. There was a small sandy beach wide enough for several chairs. Twenty feet away, across the stream were dozens of newly sprouting bamboo shoots covering the sides of the bank. We had spent many hours walking up and down the creek, digging up bright green moss and replanting it in a three-by-fifteen area. We moved a few flat rocks next to the moss, and Ry placed some of his favorite bonsai plants on them. Some weekend mornings after his practice, he would wander down and find me sitting next to the pond, reading a book.

"I see you lifted another poetry book from my library," Ry said with a smile.

"Yeah. I will be careful with it and put it back this afternoon. I never read much poetry in high school or college, but I have grown fond of your poetry library. Really enjoy Pablo Neruda and Adrienne Rich. Many of their verses and words appeal to my inner rebellious nature," I said, laughing.

"Be careful, Dad," Ry said as he sat in the chair next to me. "Poetry is about change, and you might be risking yourself by what you identify with and your belief systems of reality."

"Whoa, that's a little deep for me," I said in a somewhat serious voice.

"Poets have their own view of the world, and their voice for change is their poetry. Reading different points of view can give you a different perspective on politics, love, religion, racial and economic realities. You went to college in the sixties, Dad. Didn't protest songs about the Vietnam war resonate with you and give you a different view of the horrors of war, like children who were bombed with napalm? Those songs are considered a form of poetry."

"That's a thoughtful and ambitious way to think about the meaning of poetry. Poetry is kind of a connector of things, like society to one's self. Me to you and you to me," I said as I closed my book. I learned from my son, in those moments we talked, that there are many paths one can take through the human condition of love, loss, and spiritual renewal. Poetry can aid us in the quest for knowing our feelings and our inquiry for the meaning of life. Ry had given me a new perspective of why poetry is important.

For over two years, Ry had traveled to the NPR studios to read poetry and essays on a Sunday morning program that was directed toward listeners who were visually handicapped. People who were unable to read the ink printed on the sheets of paper bound in books. Ry would say he felt that his readings would flow through them like music and would be a new signature to a life they could not witness from their window's view.

I wanted to slow the next few days down, take each moment and press it into my memory bank. It's funny when teenagers are preparing to leave home. We parents want to slow time, but the more we clutch at the minutes and hours, the more the teens speed ahead. So, it came as no surprise when the peace of a Saturday afternoon in late July was interrupted by the heavy footsteps of Ry bouncing down the steps carrying another over-stuffed box of clothes with a stereo balancing precariously on top. He put the box next to the other twenty-something boxes already stacked up against the living room wall. We were two days away from leaving for Notre Dame, and Ry was gathering all his belongings. We had rented a van, which sat in the driveway, waiting to be filled with his worldly possessions.

"Ry, I think it might be better just to buy you all new clothes and stereo equipment when you get to Notre Dame. We can't put five hundred pounds of stuff in the van plus three people. Don't you think your roommates will bring a stereo? Can you call them to ask?" I was hoping I could reduce some of the weight. More importantly, I wasn't ready for every single thing he'd ever owned to be out of the house. Would it kill him to leave a few things behind? The more he packed, the more I worried he wasn't ever planning to visit home.

Lynn and I had spent many nights plotting to sneak some of his belongings out of the boxes and hide them throughout the house. In a few weeks, when he called asking if we had seen his favorite sweatshirt or a particular DVD, we could casually say, "Oh yes, here it is, in the freezer. Can't imagine how it got there. Odd place for an alarm clock. When you come home for Christmas, we'll make sure you don't forget it."

"More books?" I said in a voice two octaves higher than usual. "Don't you think Notre Dame has a library?" I quickly covered my disappointment with a smile before I was hit with the dreaded and soul-crushing teenage eye roll. "Ry, if I knew you were taking your entire bedroom, I would have rented a Greyhound bus instead of a van."

Ry ignored me in that way teens do when parents are loving on them too much or interfering with their independence. He bounded up the stairs once again, calling out over his shoulder, while I played Tetris in my mind trying to figure out how all of these boxes were going to fit in one van. "Hey, Dad, Alexis and I are going to that Japanese restaurant downtown in Shockoe Bottom, you recommended. The one where they cook the food at your table."

"Uh-huh," I muttered, wondering if it was necessary to take both a desk lamp and a floor lamp to a tiny dorm room. "Hey!" I shouted up after him, "This is my hat!" I pulled the black fedora out of a box and put it on my head. After glancing at my reflection in a nearby mirror, I quickly pulled it off and tossed it back in the box. What the hell; it looked better on him anyway.

A while later Ry returned, freshly showered and ready for his date. I noticed he had lifted my expensive imported Egyptian cotton black shirt and my favorite red tie with gold specks. The tie was an impulse buy I sometimes can't resist. It was eclectic, and the salesman at Neiman Marcus said it had been marked down from $125 to $75. Plus, it came with its own designer box to sleep in. How could I say no?

"Please don't spill anything on that tie," I said as I handed him a $50 bill. "Have a good time, but be careful. There is a severe thunderstorm warning for later tonight. Maybe you should make it an early night."

"I'll be fine, Dad," he answered with a confident smile.

"This is supposed to be a bad one," I reiterated.

Ry reached in his pocket and pulled out the car keys. He gave them a spin on his finger and with a teenager's confidence stated, "I've driven in rain before."

With that, he went out of the door and got into the car. Ry and Alexis were spending most evenings together that summer. They had met at the Poseidon Swim Club and were teammates. Alexis was also a nationally ranked swimmer but a year younger than Ry. He would be going off to college but she still had her senior year of high school. Alexis was a sweet kid and I was happy if things lasted between them, but knowing how young love goes, I guessed this would be their last summer together.

I stepped out of the front door, my eyes following the Volvo wagon up the driveway as it backed out. There was a special aura of mutual admiration we shared. Ry was leaving for Notre Dame in seventy-two hours, and cutting my ties with him was nearby. His departure would create uncertainties for both of us. My suspicion was that he was far more up for the task than I. In fact, I would go one further and say he was looking forward to it. Oh, to be young, carefree, and unafraid. His life from now on would be shaped from outside my protection. I wasn't entirely ready to let go but suspected I didn't get much say in the matter. He was going, and I had to accept it whether I wanted to or not.

With Ry on his way to pick up Alexis for dinner, I walked back inside the house. Lynn was in the kitchen, stirring a pot of homemade spaghetti sauce. I put my arms around her, leaning onto her back while she cooked. My wife was my anchor. Feeling her breath rising and falling against my chest told me I was home, I was safe, and I was loved. Lynn and I had been married for nineteen years. Eighteen of those years it had been the three of us, and soon we would go back to only two. I was both nervous and excited to see what the future held. What would it be like to date my wife once again? Would we discover new interests that didn't revolve around being parents?

We had been a childless couple for such a short period after our wedding, I didn't know how we would relate to each other without our world revolving around our son. So much of our life had rotated around being Ry's mom and dad. Who were we without those labels? Of course, we would always be his parents. Still, the days of teenagers traipsing through our house saying things like, "Hey, Mr. Beville," or "Your dad is so weird," after I told a silly joke, those days were over. I was torn between rejoicing in the silence while also being terrified I wouldn't know how to fill it.

Lynn, like Ry, seemed perfectly calm about this new phase in our lives. Yes, she joked about bribing him to come home once in a while but I'd also witnessed her checking out gardening class schedules at the local community college. If she thought I was signing up for couples' tap dance lessons or Thai cooking for two, she could think again. I wasn't ready to become an empty-nester with a bevy of crooked bowls I made in ceramics class.

While Lynn finished the pasta, I threw together a quick salad. We usually liked to sit at the kitchen table for dinner. With all of our busy schedules, each of us running off in different directions, it was the one place we could come together and check in. More and more, as Ry grew up and started spending more time out of the house than in, Lynn and I began a new ritual of sitting down next to each other on the sofa to eat and watch TV.

We finished our dinner while watching one of the many police dramas that filled the airways each night. The weather outside had picked up. Cracks of thunder and flashes of lightning added to the ambiance of our show. "Sweetie, you might want to go save the trash can," Lynn said as she pulled the drapes back and glanced out of the window. "The wind is taking it down the street."

I looked out of the window and indeed the wind was pushing the big can down the street like Texas tumbleweed. I ran out to retrieve it and could feel the wind flowing upward and around my back. The black sky had created a powerful updraft, adding to the strength and severity of the incoming storm. I looked toward the southwest. The dark blue-black clouds were beginning to rotate while flickering lightning streaks illuminated the yellow belly of the storm. I worried about Ry but shook off the thought as overprotective nerves. I was lucky: my son was a responsible young man and I trusted he would be safe.

Back inside, after chasing a wayward metal trash can, we loaded the dishes in the dishwasher and had just settled down with a bowl of ice cream for a second round of murderous TV shows when the phone rang.

"Don, this is Michael, Alexis's father." I knew by the tremor in his voice that I didn't want to hear any more. My hand tightened around the phone, wishing I could slam the receiver down so I wouldn't have to listen to what he had to say. Nothing good was going to come from this call. I could feel it in my soul. The lens to my worldly camera was about to twist.

Michael continued speaking as I remained silent. "Ry and Alexis have been in an accident. I don't know all the details yet. She called from a house across the street from the accident but hung up before I could ask any questions. She's going to call back as soon as the ambulance arrives, and I will call you as soon as I have more news. I'm sure everything is okay."

Hearing the word "ambulance" sent a wave of panic through me. Lynn must have seen the expression on my face. She came over and stood close as I asked, "Michael, do you know if there are any injuries?" His hesitation told me he was holding back. The less he said, the more nauseated I felt.

He avoided my question by reiterating, "I promise I will call when I know more."

I hung up the phone and told Lynn what little information I had. We sat facing each other on the sofa, squeezing each other's hands, waiting for the next call. A bolt of lightning hit a little too close for comfort as Lynn began to cry. I closed my eyes and took a long, deep breath, trying to slow my heart rate. Parents are protected by naïveté, the certainty that life will always be fine. A moment in time seemed like thirty minutes. My uncle Raymond's comments that day we found my grandfather under the tractor pierced my brain, "Devastation can hide behind every corner."

Chapter 2

Jaws of Life

The ride to St. Mary's Hospital only took twenty minutes but it seemed everything was in slow motion. Although I knew I was speeding, I still felt like I could get out and run faster. My hands were sweaty and I reached for a handkerchief in my pocket to wipe them off. Lynn and I rode in silence, both deep in our thoughts as we listened to the tires hit each expansion groove on the Huguenot Bridge. The rain and wind were coming down heavy. Sometimes I had to swerve to miss tree limbs in the road. With every passing minute my foot pressed harder on the gas as I failed to stop at several stop signs. "Will you slow down!" Lynn snapped while white-knuckling the dashboard, "We don't need to have another accident."

After what felt like an eternity, I finally swung the car into the parking lot of St. Mary's Hospital and swerved into the first space I could find. We ran through the parking lot with the rain coming down hard, at times the wind forcing it horizontally. What was I thinking, letting him take the car out? I knew there was a storm coming. I'd even warned him about it. As my feet pounded through puddles all I could think was, *I should have made him stay home.* I berated myself for trying too hard to be his friend. I was his father, and I should have put my foot down and demanded he stay home. I knew my thoughts were crazy, and there was no way I could have made my seventeen-year-old son stay home, but when you are running through the night toward your injured child, being rational isn't at the top of the list of things to do.

We rushed through the Emergency Room doors and to the admitting desk, asking where we could find Ry Beville. The silver-haired volunteer behind the counter picked up the phone and called to the back of the ER. "Mr. and Mrs. Beville are here; who is the admitting physician for Ry Beville?" She listened for a moment then hung up. She gave us a look of sympathy, saying, "Dr. Wilson, a neurosurgeon, will be out to see you shortly. Ry is still in X-Ray."

"Why is he in X-Ray? Does he have any broken bones?" My mind was scrambling with unanswered questions. "Why is the attending physician a neurosurgeon?" The lady could only give us a blank stare and tepid assurances that our questions would be answered soon.

We were directed to a Family ER Lounge down the hall. When we finally found it after several wrong turns, Lynn sat down in one of the hard steel-legged chairs. She patted the top of the chair next to her. "Come, sit down. He's okay. What could happen to him in a Volvo?" She said in a light voice that felt forced. She was grasping at straws, trying to convince herself everything was okay. I immediately took her cue, going along with her logic. *Of course, she was right*, I thought. I remembered seeing ads in magazines showing five Volvos stacked on top of each other. My son couldn't have been hurt too badly in a Volvo. Right? That's why we persuaded him to get one.

It was Saturday night and the ER was overflowing. Patients in the hallway were waiting to be admitted. Down the hall, nurses ran from one curtained-off area to another. A doctor exited one of the rooms with two nurses pushing a patient on a gurney, a tube in his mouth. No doubt a mechanical ventilation machine, I thought. Surreal. Chaos. And somewhere in all this lay my son. My thoughts leapt from one fantasy scenario to another. In one, Ry chatted and flirted with a pretty X-ray tech while checking out an injured wrist. In another, he lay near death, with a team of doctors and nurses swarming around him. I had no way of knowing which of these scenes was closer to the truth, and the not knowing was driving me mad.

"Should we be calling anyone? Your parents, my parents? What should we do?" I asked, feeling like I needed to pace. I stood up but immediately sat back down, feeling light-headed. Lynn was calmer than me. As a neonatal ICU nurse, she had years of experience keeping her emotions in check when dealing with a crisis situation. Whether she was really calm or merely good at faking it, it didn't matter. I envied her all the same. My shirt was soaking wet, and I should have been cold, but I was still sweating. How could she sit there so stoically? I felt like I might pass out, but to look at my wife, you would think she was waiting for a bus.

We sat in the little room for what felt like most of the night, but when Lynn looked at her watch it had only been an hour. "Mr. and Mrs. Beville?" I heard the voice behind me and felt a moment of relief that finally, a doctor was here. But when I turned around and saw a wet police officer with his hand extended, my heart sank. "I'm Officer Shelton with the Richmond Police Department. I'm the investigating officer for the accident involving your son, Ry. Have you met with the doctor yet?" The officer's eyes made a direct line to mine. He had a long face with a flattened nose, like a retired boxer of Irish descent. When he spoke, he tilted his head slightly and led with his right cheek. His big rough hands reminded me of my uncle's. The officer had the same deep lines in his tan hands. Water ran off his plastic raincoat onto the checkerboard-tiled floor.

"We haven't heard from the ER doctor yet. Can you tell me what happened?" I asked, trying to pull my focus away from the puddle of water forming at his feet. I wondered if I should say something. It seemed a terrible fate to come to the ER only to slip in a water spot on the linoleum floor.

The officer took off his raincoat and hat and sat down next to us. He pulled a clipboard out of a plastic bag and wrote on a form. He was unusually pleasant. I stared at his gun, his blue pants, his bright black shoes, and the creases around his eyebrows that gave the impression his life was stressful. Had he ever shot anyone? Had anyone ever shot at him? The smell of imaginary gunpowder made a swing through my nostrils. My mind raced. I could sense my heartbeat and my respiration tapping out a rhythm like a metronome while I attempted to make sense of the last two hours of my life.

He spoke in what felt like slow motion. A swirl of words floated out of his mouth, creating images I never wanted to see. "From what I could gather from witnesses and the other driver, your son ran a red light. The motorist who hit him said the light had been green for a few seconds when he proceeded through the intersection at about 25 mph. His car made an impact on the passenger side of the Volvo, spinning it. The driver's side of the Volvo swung around and collided with the traffic light pole in the middle of the intersection. A witness driving behind your son said tree branches may have blocked the view of the light due to the thunderstorm." He paused and said, "I have no evidence of speeding or alcohol use."

Officer Shelton handed me the forms, scrawled in his messy handwriting, the words alarmingly permanent. The rain had caused some of the ink to bleed, giving the report an ominous feel.

Cause of Accident: Failing to stop at a red light

Injuries: Yes, the driver extracted with possible head and neck injuries

Occupants: Two, one passenger reported no injuries

Extenuating Circumstances: Yes, thunderstorm, rain, wind

Alcohol: None suspected

Car Damage: Extensive, roof removed, rear axle torn from car

"The car is totaled. But it did save your son's life. I've seen a lot of accidents in my twenty years, and people usually come out of crashes okay in a Volvo."

I glanced at Lynn. So maybe the Volvo did save him after all.

My brain fixated around the thought of the rear axle of my son's Volvo, twirling, spinning, speeding, rotating, airborne, down Grove Avenue from the impact of hitting a light pole. I thought about how close he might be to death and the probability of his car being where it was in the universe at the precise moment when another car owned the same space at Grove and Westmoreland. I wanted to be home, with a glass of wine in my hand, sitting in my chair where I habitually sit to watch crime shows, not reading a wet police report involving my son.

I read the report, struggling to take it all in, and stopped at the words "driver extracted." The air in the room suddenly smelled different. The whoosh of being in a freefall washed over me as beads of sweat squeezed through the pores on my forehead. I was too stunned to reply to the officer. I recognized this feeling. I'd been here before and the last time nearly killed me. I could sense the pendulum was swinging back.

The police officer standing in front of me could have been

the priest that stood in front of me twenty years ago, signaling the death of my first wife, Audrey. I was barely older than Ry was now and unable to cope with a loss so great. Was fate testing me again? Where was my guardian angel then when the person I cherished, was suddenly ripped from the earth? I thought I had put the pain of that loss behind me, locked the door securely, but here I was, standing in an ER with scrambled emotions. There was no way I would survive it again.

Twenty years ago, I'd clung to my rosary, rubbed it, put it to my lips, prayed to it, hoping it would bring me comfort. Strange how the brain remembers such things when we are submerged in pain and grief. I reached in my pocket for that rosary but my pocket was empty. It was light years from that day when I had pleaded with God to end my suffering, but I had discovered that faith is just a mystery cloaked in plastic shrines of the Virgin Mary. Faith had not helped me then. I couldn't trust it would help me now.

Everything around me began to swirl with a ringing in my ears. I was being pulled back to a place of painful memories. I couldn't go there. Not when my son needed me. I had to push it away. Push past the overwhelming feeling of helplessness. I hadn't been able to save my first wife; was I now going to lose my boy?

For a moment, I thought I was going down, but, thankfully the admitting clerk entered the room. Hearing her voice was just enough of a break to bring me back to the present moment, where I could take a deep breath and refocus my attention. "Mr. and Mrs. Beville, Dr. Wilson will see you in just a few minutes. Ry is back from X-Ray." The officer shook my hand as he said, "My prayers are with your family tonight." I wanted to thank him (isn't that what we are supposed to do when someone offers prayers?) but I couldn't bring myself to say the words. We followed the clerk out of the room. She pointed to the glass doors with a sign reading, *No Admittance. Hospital Personnel Only.* "Dr. Wilson will meet you at the nurses' station to the left as you go through the doors."

Tremors ran through my body. We walked through the doors and looked down the hall to the nurses' station. I could see a gurney being guided into a cubicle. Dozens of people in green scrubs moved from room to room while IV poles lined the hallway. There was a flurry of activity, and through it all, a tall man walked toward us. He seemed oblivious to the surrounding chaos. His dark blue shirt and stylish tie felt out of place, as if he should be on his way to a fancy restaurant or an evening at the theater. His medical ID nametag read *Dr. Wilson, Neurosurgeon.*

Dr. Wilson's steps were purposeful and measured. He reached out his hand and said, "Hello, I'm Dr. Wilson." His hand grasped mine and locked with a tight vice-like grip. "If you will follow me, I'll take you to see your son. Is it still raining? That was a hell of a storm we had, but we really need the rain."

"Yes," I said, trying to keep up with his long steps. I reached back for Lynn's hand, as she was falling behind. We couldn't possibly be talking about the weather, could we? He was a neurosurgeon treating my son, and we were discussing the need for rain. In what world did this make sense? And then I heard my own wife say, "I think it's still drizzling outside." I whipped my head around to look at her. Who were these people? My entire career revolved around finding the correct words to match any given situation. Not in a million years would I put the word "neurosurgeon" next to the word "drizzle".

Days later, I would ask Lynn how she was able to remain so calm. She reminded me she was a nurse, and there was no way she would ever let a doctor see her cry. It had been drilled into her since her first day on the job. If a doctor saw you cry once, they would forever categorize you as weak. It was a label every nurse dreaded. You could cry in your car on the way home or scream away the pain in your pillow at night, but never under any circumstances did you shed tears in front of a doctor. It was so ingrained in Lynn that the moment she saw Dr. Wilson's white coat, she stiffened into her professional demeanor.

At the junction of the corridor marked "X-Ray and MRI", Dr. Wilson pointed to the right as we rounded the corner toward the ER. The hallway was busy with activity. A young boy in a soccer uniform, sitting in a wheelchair, came out of one of the doors with one foot covered by a newly minted white cast. He looked up at us as we passed. The deep frown on his face told me he was not pleased with his current condition. I couldn't blame him.

None of us wanted to be here. I envied his ability to wear his displeasure boldly on his face. How I wished I could scowl at every person we passed, giving them a visual cue that I wasn't supposed to be here. My son wasn't supposed to be here. We were supposed to be at home, having a casual conversation about how his date went and whether the food was good. I should have been offering my son a bowl of Ben & Jerry's Cherry Garcia ice cream, not rushing to follow a fancy tie-wearing neurosurgeon through the emergency room of our local hospital.

We finally entered the ER through two large doors that opened automatically when we approached. The area contained about a dozen small rooms in a quadrangle. Dr. Wilson led us to the first room, where Ry lay flat on a padded steel table with a small pillow under his head. His long legs extended to the very end of the table. A nurse swabbed his face with a cotton ball dipped in a yellow solution. Ry's face was peppered with cuts, mostly small ones, but one was more than three inches long. Directly above his left eye, a swollen gash was sewn shut with about twenty sutures. The swelling extended from the middle of the temple straight back into the hairline that passed his ear. There were bloodstains on his chin and neck.

"Ry," I said in a soft voice. "Everything is going to be all right."

There was no answer from Ry. Dr. Wilson reached over and lifted an ice pack that shielded his right temple from view, revealing more cuts. "Ry," he said, "this is Dr. Wilson. How do you feel?"

Without opening his eyes, Ry mumbled a few words we could not understand. I thought he said he wanted something for a headache. I stepped next to the table, close enough to hold his hand. Lynn walked to the other side of the table and began to stroke his arm. She whispered in his ear, words I couldn't hear. Trembling, my fingers crossed back and forth over his knuckles. I tried to steady my hand while silently cursing my shaking fingers for showing how scared I felt. The right side of his shirt sleeve was cut from the cuff up past the shoulder, and I wondered if he'd injured his arm, but I didn't see any blood or bruising. As I was looking over Ry's arm, the nurse handed me a plastic bag with a blood-soaked piece of fabric inside. After a long moment, I realized it was my Neiman Marcus tie. Like Dr. Wilson's tie, it too was out of place.

"What's wrong with his arm?" I asked, looking at Dr. Wilson.

Without answering my question, Dr. Wilson looked down at Ry and said, "Ry, this is Dr. Wilson. can you raise your right arm for me?" Ry's wrist, resting on the white sheets, barely moved an inch from the side of his body. His index finger was the only part of his body that demonstrated any sign of life. "Ry, can you move your right leg?" Dr. Wilson said as he gently laid his finger on the top of Ry's foot. No movement. "Ry, try hard to move your leg," Dr. Wilson said, a bit more forcefully this time.

"Can you give me something for my headache?" Ry barely got the words out. He sounded as if he were out of breath. "I feel disconnected."

Dr. Wilson leaned over Ry, placing his hand on Ry's forearm and said, "Ry, you have a large bump on your temple from the accident. This is the reason for the headache. I will ask the nurse to bring you something and then we're going to get you moved to another room." The doctor motioned for Lynn and me to follow him.

I leaned close, whispering in Ry's ear, "Hold tight, son. We will be right back. I will get you home tonight so you can rest in your bed." I rubbed his arm and added once again, hoping it wasn't a lie, "Everything is going to be okay." As a child, he was an escape artist, bolting from my hand in department stores, sidewalks, even across streets in the neighborhood. I couldn't take my eyes off him for fear his little body would meet its end at the front of a car bumper. So many frustrating outings to Sears when I had to go extract him from aisle six, or from power tools. The sight of him fixed to the flat gurney was too much to bear. *I love you, my little escapologist*, I thought as I moved away from my son.

Dr. Wilson led us to a small X-ray viewing room just down the hall from the ER. He pulled the X-rays from a brown folder, jamming them into clamps at the top of a lightbox. Looking at the X-rays of Ry's skull, I recognized his wide-set eyes and the sharp bone lines of his face. Seeing my son's portrait in X-ray form was something I hoped to never see again. When Dr. Wilson spoke, he delivered the words in a monotone, straight-line voice. "Ry has had a severe blow to his frontal lobe and to the side of his head. There are many smaller tissue tears in the top and back of his brain." He pointed to small images on the X-ray that looked like little white spots dotting Ry's brain tissue. Each one was about a half-inch long. "These are the reasons for Ry's partial paralysis."

The word "paralysis" triggered a disconnect within my body and my brain. My ears still heard words, my eyes focused on the X-ray, but nothing was connecting. It felt as if my body was going to float apart, that I no longer had the energy force to hold my particles together. Another moment, and I thought I may fall like sand to a pile on the floor. Poof. Dissolved into dust.

Dr. Wilson pointed to the X-ray as he spoke. "What I'm worried about are the deeper injuries to his brain. These are ruptured vessels that carry oxygen to brain cells. There is a lot of swelling in the region. We need to observe him closely for the next hour and then do another CT scan. If the swelling continues, we'll need to drill small holes into his skull to release the pressure, or additional damage will occur. Sometimes, even more damage can be done to his motor skills if the pressure is not reduced. Do you understand what I mean?"

I did not have the full knowledge of such medical terms, but drilling holes in my son's skull created a fear that moved through my bowels to my brain. Dr. Wilson revealed no distress as I stared at him through the bright light of the X-Ray lightbox. The casual tone of this discussion matched our earlier conversation about the weather. "Is it still raining outside? By the way, we will need to drill into your son's skull." Same tone. Same emphasis. I found it maddening. Perhaps most doctors are this way, learning how to hide painful news from their patients' relatives. They saw so much destruction in the ER every day that they learned how to pass close to other people's tragedies without getting scorched.

Certainly, Lynn must have done this daily, but she left that aspect of her personality at the hospital, where she saved the lives of premature babies. She didn't bring it home, and now I found it jarring to imagine her compartmentalizing her life in this way. Dr. Wilson's words exploded in my head. *We will need to drill small holes in his skull.* I glanced at Lynn. Her face had returned to being passive and controlled. The only giveaway that she was distressed was the tear stains still visible on her cheeks.

I took a deep breath and forced out the words I never thought I would say. "Sorry, Doctor, you can't drill holes in my son's skull." Lynn was silent as she reached out for my hand. I looked behind me for someplace to sit, knowing I was about to vomit or pass out.

I'd recently published a book with a local psychiatrist focusing on panic disorder, so I knew I was in the first stage. Dr. Wilson raised an eyebrow while calmly saying, "I understand how you feel. Ry is on several drugs to reduce the swelling. We'll do another scan in a few hours. Until then, we'll be moving him up to the ICU shortly."

My rear hit the flat surface of the chair as sweat dripped from my forehead. I tried to take a few deep breaths, but it wasn't helping. The room remained stagnant and claustrophobic. "I need some air," I gasped, glancing from Dr. Wilson to Lynn and back. What was wrong with them? Could they not feel the walls closing in? Why were they just standing there, staring at me with those blank, composed looks? Without waiting for a reply, I got up and raced out of the room, past the nurses' station.

I heard Lynn calling after me, "Don, are you okay?"

Running through the maze of halls, I arrived at the ER doors. Rushing past faceless people coming into the hospital, I made my way out. A light mist was falling, and I felt cold, clammy, and afraid. Immediately, I looked for a private place to go, knowing I was going to vomit any second.

Twenty feet out of the door, a sense of vertigo overwhelmed me and I fell heavily and gracelessly to both knees. My face flushed what felt like a deep red rose, and my skin was clammy to the touch. My head spun while my fingers spread out on the ground, like a toad on a rock. My neck thrust forward from my shirt while a frothy liquid burst forth from my throat. It covered my hand and began forming little rivers running outward from the main puddle. Tears mixed with the white mucus that ran from my nose. My face felt swollen.

As I remained on the ground trying to catch my breath, I could sense someone approaching. I looked up to see a woman walking toward me. Reaching in my pocket, I pulled out my handkerchief to wipe away the flow of froth from my mouth and chin.

She was backlit by a nearby streetlight, hiding her face in darkness and shadows, but the glow around her felt angelic. Perhaps I was dying, or maybe I was already dead, and my sweet first wife, Audrey, was greeting me, as we'd always promised each other we would. She would laugh and say, "Promise me, if you die before me, you'll send a sign that everything is okay." I told her I would tug on her toe every night before she fell asleep. We never talked about if she died first.

And then it dawned on me: maybe she was here to meet Ry and take him to the other side. In my altered state, I called out to her, "Audrey?" She was silent but kept walking toward me. I was prepared to tell her to stay away. That she couldn't take my son.

"Do you need some help?" she replied, standing over me and looking down. Away from the streetlight, I could make out her face. She was not my Audrey but she was beautiful all the same, with her deep-set eyes and voice filled with compassion. "Do you need some help?" she asked again. "My name is Sister

Angeline." Maybe it was the trauma of the night or my lightheadedness from being ill, but I immediately sensed I could trust this stranger who'd appeared from nowhere at my lowest moment. She made me feel secure; my panic waned and my senses sharpened.

"Yes," I pleaded, hardly recognizing my own scared and vulnerable voice. "My son was in a bad car accident tonight. He is suffering."

"God will help you and your son. Just pray to him. Every brain trauma is different." She put her hand under my arm and helped me to my feet. Her voice was calming, her hand gentle on my arm. "I will pray for you and your son tonight, but you must do the same." She looked directly into my eyes and I could tell she was checking to see I was okay. When she seemed satisfied that I was alert and present, she added, "Go back inside. Your son and wife need you." With a final pat on the hand, she turned and walked away.

I watched as she left toward the Emergency Room, turning once to face me while raising her hand in a reassuring wave before entering the building. Then the thought hit me: how did this nun know my son had a brain injury? I didn't say anything to her about it. The statue of Mary Magdalene mounted above the ER doors caught my eye and I read the inscription, *Wherever You lead me, I will follow.*

It was a nice thought but one I couldn't commit to. I had put all my trust in faith and God to take care of my Audrey, and where did that get me? If Ry was going to recover, it was going to be based on science and the knowledge of doctors, regardless of whether a kind nun had given me words of encouragement.

Chapter 3

Neurological Intensive Care

After the mysterious woman left, I took some time to catch my breath and calm my nerves. Usually when I am feeling anxious or stressed, I go for a long run, but I thought if the hospital staff saw a man running circles out in the parking lot, they might have me committed. Instead, I walked around the outside of the building for a few minutes. I felt that I had been flayed. I knew I couldn't have my wife and son seeing me in a state of panic. Ry needed me now, so I had to keep it together.

When I returned to the ER, the nurse in charge told me they had already moved Ry upstairs and that Lynn was with him. I didn't think I'd been gone that long but I must have lost track of time. I'm sure my wife was wondering where I was. The nurse called up to get the room number and I quickly made my way to the elevator.

Once I got upstairs to the ICU, the doors were locked. I picked up the phone outside the ward and pushed the call button. "May I help you?" a voice asked from the other end of the line.

"Yes, my son Ry Beville was admitted to the ICU a few minutes ago and I'd like to see him."

The doors swung open to a wide void of darkness, complete with beeping and clicking sounds. I stepped in and waited for my eyes to adjust to the dimness. As I walked by each small bay closed off by white curtains, I could occasionally see monitoring machines flashing vital signs. Nurses and doctors entered and exited rooms like ghosts. It was so quiet. In contrast to the chaos of the ER, the ICU felt like a different dimension. Where was the frenzy, the urgency? Is this how it always is, a mad rush to save a life and then slamming to a stop as everyone steps back, silently waiting to see if life will save itself? I thought again what a faulty decision I had made in letting him leave the house. My uncle Raymond's nugget of advice surfaced, that we are just a thread away from making bad choices that can lead to catastrophe.

"Excuse me," I said, finding myself speaking just above a whisper to a group of nurses behind a large chest-high partition. "I'm looking for my son's room, Ry Beville."

"Yes, your son is in room 2A," one of the female nurses answered from behind the counter. She came around the partition and began walking down the hall as I followed beside her. "I know how scary this must be for a parent, but your son is in the best possible place right now. Everything is being done to help him recover. Follow me and I will walk you down to his room."

"Thank you," I said. It was all the communication I could muster

I don't do well around hospitals and felt I was on another planet, spinning out of control, fearing my situation was not going to improve. A few hours before, my son's laughter and enthusiasm had filled my life. This was not supposed to happen. With every step toward my son's room, my mood began to blacken.

Maybe sensing my despair, the nurse turned back and asked, "Would you want me to have our community priest make a visit to Ry's room?"

"No, thank you." I looked at her nametag: Sophie. How

could I ever explain to Sophie the crisis of faith I was feeling? She wouldn't understand if I blurted out, "I don't trust God to take care of my son. He failed my wife. How do I know he won't fail again?"

It was too heavy a burden to place on Sophie's narrow shoulders, so I left it at, "No, thank you."

She stopped outside room 2A and indicated for me to go in. "If you need anything, I'm just at the desk." I gently pushed the door open, not sure what I would find on the other side. Regardless of what I was about to see, I knew I had to keep my breathing even and slow. Stepping inside the room, I took in sights while telling myself to remain calm. My past had taught me that hospitals were where blindsides occurred. Around every corner, fate waited with the potential to destroy. I knew this to be correct but I could not allow my son to see my fear. Brave face. We parents are masters of the brave face. Even when we are terrified.

Slowly, I looked around, orienting myself to the cards we'd been dealt in the last few hours. There was no option to fold. Regardless of what was in this room, I was committed to going all in. I first noticed a nurse in the room adjusting the drip. She quickly finished up and nodded to me as she left. Lynn was wiping some dried saliva out of the corner of Ry's mouth. I saw the steel rails guarding his body, the IV drip pole, the call button clipped to the pillow like a pacifier tied around the neck of an infant. Slowly, my heart had been looted.

Lynn sat next to Ry's bed, softly stroking his hand. I stood in the doorway for a moment, watching, so taken with the display of a mother's love. Her curly brown hair was piled in a messy knot on her head. Even so, in the soft glow of light she looked beautiful. No, not just beautiful but resilient. The look of determination on her face was the same as when she gave birth. It was a look that said, *one way or another, I brought you into this world. And you will thrive.*

"How is he?" I asked in a low voice.

"Where have you been? I was getting worried," she shot back with an edge of irritation in her voice. It was then I saw her eyes, swollen and red. Lynn, who'd been calm and controlled throughout this entire ordeal, had finally broken. In the quiet of this darkened room, alone with her only child, she stopped being a nurse and allowed herself to simply be a mother. "You've been gone for ages," she said as she wiped her eyes with a tissue.

I wasn't sure how to explain the appearance of the lady who had helped me in the parking lot. Maybe she was an angel. Perhaps I'd become somewhat delusional from the stress? Either way, I didn't know how to explain it to Lynn. And I certainly wasn't going to relive my calling out for Audrey. The thought of it left me feeling foolish and embarrassed. Of course, Lynn knew of Audrey, but now was hardly the time to bring her up. When your son is in the ICU, your current wife doesn't want to hear that you were out in the parking lot, calling out for your deceased wife. I may not have been the most observant husband, but I was smart enough to know this wasn't a good look. Instead, I settled for an old standby excuse. "I needed some air, and my stomach was not feeling right. I am sorry."

I was relieved when she didn't question any further. "Why don't you go home and get some sleep? You look tired," she said, glancing up at me. "Dr. Wilson said he would be back at seven a.m. and would probably take more X-rays. The nurse will bring me a cot so I can sleep here tonight."

"I don't want to leave you alone," I answered. "I'll stay too."

Always the practical one, Lynn rolled her head in my

direction and sighed. "We will have to take shifts, so one of us is always with him. I'm used to staying up nights and watching patients. It's my job." She gave a soft smile and added, "Besides, have you forgotten that we have a dog?" Her facial expression was a shortcut to our intimacy. It was also a shortcut to her getting me to do what she wanted. It always worked.

She was right. I'd forgotten about the dog. The year before, we had adopted a greyhound named Nikki from the Greyhound Pets of America. Our hallway was Nikki's track. At least once a day, a bell would go off in her head, the gates would open, and she would take off through the kitchen, around the dining room table, over the sofa, then back to the den. If she was locked up for too long, without a walk, she went crazy. I could relate to the feeling. It was why I became a long-distance runner.

"You're right. One more hour and I'll go." I pulled up a chair and sat beside Lynn. I put my arm around her and rubbed her neck while we watched our boy sleep. After a while, Lynn told me after I'd left, the officer returned and gave her more details of what had happened with the accident. I listened to her tell the story while focusing on Ry's chest rising and falling with each breath. There were numerous times I wanted to ask her to stop. I couldn't take anymore, but I knew she needed to get it out, so I remained a silent listener.

After gracefully opening her heart, she leaned her head on my shoulder and sighed. "I can't believe this is happening."

When the clock hit eleven thirty, I finally stood to go. I kissed Lynn on the forehead and murmured, "I'll be back early."

I walked out of the ICU, down the hall to the elevator. Staring down the hallway at empty space, my mind replayed the day's earlier events. Suitcases packed, books stacked, a single tennis shoe lingered without a mate, all ready to be loaded in a van headed to Notre Dame. Emotion stuck in my throat and I began to cry. Turning around, I walked back to the ICU. The sharp edges of fear surrounding me were like lightning.

Outside 2A, I wiped my cheeks dry and did my best to compose myself, then opened the door.

"Why are you back?" Lynn asked, surprised to see me.

"I wanted to kiss my son, that's all." I sat on the bed and breathed with him. For a moment, I could taste the air: wild mint. Ry and I had planted it in our Japanese garden. Through all the antiseptic and disinfectant of the hospital, I could still smell the wild mint on Ry's skin as I came closer and kissed his forehead. I whispered for him to get a peaceful night's rest. He did not move. I could feel the fear and panic rise in my gut. His limp, non-responsive body reminded me of a dead person placed in an open coffin, ready for relatives and friends to view. A memory flash swept me back to an arduous journey I took after Audrey was suddenly ushered to the afterlife. I reached across the bed and touched Lynn's hand. I needed to feel the warmth of her skin. I needed to know she was here with me.

Holding my wife's hand while looking over my son felt like the perfect moment to pray. So many times, I was told as a child, sitting in the church pew week after week, year after year, that prayer can change a life. Counting the times I had said prayers would be in the thousands, but no epiphanies arrived, at least not one that I could feel in my heart. I wanted to have faith. I wanted to believe that a power greater than myself could restore my son and bring him back to me, but it wasn't there. Faith had slipped away over the years. Audrey had taken it with her to an invisible realm on the other side. I was on this side, where fear and uncertainty lived. As much as I wanted to count on a miracle, all I could do was try my best to stay strong and listen to his doctors.

For now, I would place my hope in science, not rosary beads.

Leaving the hospital, I drove my car into the night, not entirely sure where I was headed. Soon, I was at the corner of Grove Avenue and Westmoreland Street, standing in the middle of the road. A traffic light dangled above me—not just any traffic light but *the* traffic light. I looked up at it, feeling betrayed. Twisting in the wind, it had failed to protect my son. And now it was still, switching from green to yellow to red in perfectly timed intervals, completely unaware of the damage it had done. I wanted to take a bat and smash it.

Staring out into the intersection, I replayed every excruciating word the officer had told us about the accident. I needed to reenact each detail in my mind to try and make sense of it all. If I could understand what had happened, maybe the tremendous guilt I was carrying would be alleviated. I was his father. It was my job to protect him from storms and accidents. I stood at the intersection, imagining over and over how the evening's events had unfolded.

Ry had been heading west on Grove Avenue, approaching Westmoreland Street as the thunderstorm passed over. I imagined the wind snapping tree limbs, blowing them across the street. The windshield wipers couldn't have kept up with the torrid rain. Approaching the intersection, Ry could not see the stoplight turning from yellow to red. As the Volvo entered the intersection, a massive Lincoln hit the passenger's side, pushing the door in and sending the Volvo into a vortex-like spin. The driver's side of the car slammed into a light pole with such force that the impact severed part of the rear axle. All four tires went flat from the sudden change in the direction of the air inside them.

The same inertia that blew out the tires caused Ry's brain to slam against one side of his skull. According to one of the EMTs, the seatbelt must have failed to engage. His face hit the side door window, breaking it and sending dozens of pieces of glass deep into his flesh. Alexis escaped severe injury and got out of the car, running to a stranger's house to call 911.

A short time later, first responders were on the scene and the rescue squad cut Ry out of the car with the Jaws of Life. It was the only way the EMTs could get Ry out. Shards of glass peppered his tanned face; his strawberry blond hair was matted with blood. Inside his skull, blood slowly seeped from damaged brain tissue. His brain began to swell. He sat motionless. It took more than twenty minutes to cut through the roof struts, retract the roof, and extract Ry from the front seat.

I wanted to walk over the grit on the street where my son had left his blood. *In the midst of life, we are in death,* Episcopalian priests say at burials. My eyes explored the pieces of glass and oil residue beneath my shoes. I found a part of the front amber signal light and slipped it into my pocket. It was a landscape of sadness I replayed over in my mind. I could nearly convince myself I'd witnessed the events.

It was time to go home.

Back at the house, Nikki met me at the front door, tail moving in a circle like a propeller and her body making twirls like a ballerina. I grabbed the leash for a quick walk. Once I returned, I walked through our home, turning on all the lights. I thought light over darkness would help keep me grounded.

Memories came flooding back as I walked from room to room. For most of his years, I had been blessed with meeting my son's needs in this house. I fixed his lunch on the first day at school in this kitchen before walking him to the bus stop. He was five and did not hesitate to walk up the steps of the bus. The truth was, I had been sad he wasn't more reluctant. I wanted him to miss me, at least a little bit, but that wasn't Ry. Up the stairs of the bus he went without a glance back—the curse of the independent child.

I juggled my job as a book publisher and managing editor so I could attend his soccer games, baseball games, and swim meets. Within these walls were the recorded memories of our lives, and now the house felt too still, too calm. I walked upstairs and sat in his bedroom. On the wall hung the paintings he'd created over the years. As I looked over them one by one, I wondered, *how long would his room be silent?*

I'd been preparing myself all summer for the quiet to come. I knew that when teenagers left home, the silence was the first thing to descend. It is often greeted like a long-lost friend with a sigh of contentment. The funny thing about silence is that when it is gone, we often don't realize it. It is only when it returns that we understand we had missed it all along. *Where have you been for so many years*, bewildered parents often ask the nothingness filling a room. *Where did you go?* We sit down with a book, or a long overdue project and drink in the sound of nothing. *It's been eighteen years since I sat with you*, we say, as if welcoming an old friend.

But this silence felt different. It carried with it a dark and ominous feeling of dread. Turning all the lights on had helped a bit, but it wasn't enough to smooth over the angst I was feeling. For the second time in my life, I felt alone in the world. There is a myriad of ways in which fear and grief can enter the body and can pile on like cement blocks. The mind is a tricky territory and when faced with waves of fear, it can push a person to self-destructive impulses. I'd been in this place before and it slowly wore me down. I needed to prepare myself for the worst to come.

In some ways, I had been preparing for the worst most of my

life. Ever since Grandpa's wreck with the tractor and Uncle Raymond's solemn words, I learned about death and suffering before I was ready, and it instilled in me a sense of foreboding. Yes, there was beauty and joy too, but it was always doing a slow dance with an end.

On the farm, life was about routine. Every morning at five a.m., my alarm clock went off. My chores began with following my grandmother to the pasture, where we would herd the cows to the barn for their morning milking. As my grandmother tended to the cows, it was my responsibility to feed the chickens and fill their watering containers. I was a child and made the cardinal mistake of loving those chickens. Farm life can be lonely for a little boy. There were no other children around and so the chickens became my only friends. I would feed them from my hand and they would follow me around, their little heads keeping the beat to a silent song.

The joy the chickens gave me was shattered when my grandmother would walk through the chicken house and randomly pick a chicken for slaughter. The first time it happened I cried for days. Eventually, I learned that when she came out of the house and walked toward the coop, I would run as fast and as far as I could. There was nothing I could do to save my friends, but I could not stand the pain. I had to flee. This would not be the first time I would run from death. Years later, when Audrey left me, I would once again find myself running to escape the pain.

But my pain was my grandmother's blessing. "The Lord shall provide," she would say as she served up one of my beloved birds for dinner. "Don," she would say in her soft voice, "always believe the Lord will take care of your needs. Every day is precious. Be thankful and have faith that the Lord will never give you more pain than you can bear." How could I explain to her that killing my friends was more than I could bear? I prayed hard to God to save the chickens, but my grandmother must have prayed harder for food on the table. It made little sense to me then and not much more as an adult.

After walking through my own house, leaving all the lights on and the memories of dead chickens in the past, I entered the kitchen. I poured a glass of wine and downed it in a swift gulp, then went back upstairs to do something I never do — take a bath versus a shower. I put my feet in and sank into the warm water. The wine made me woozy. After a short time, I got out of the bathtub and, without drying off, walked down the steps to the kitchen, pouring myself another glass. I followed the wet marks on the floor back up to the tub. I wanted to sleep without the taint of a thought in my head. The warm water on my skin felt safe, like everything had gone back to normal. I was in an altered existence. And although it felt nice, it was fool's gold.

When the water finally went tepid, I climbed out and got ready for bed. As I lay my head on the goose-down pillows, I knew sleep would be difficult. One corner of my brain insisted on pushing thoughts inward through a tiny hole in my consciousness. Ry's peppered face raced before me, along with a continuous stream of panicked thoughts. *Every hour that passes, he's changing, shedding memories and abilities as his brain swells. When I return in the morning, will he know who I am?* I tried to force the images and negativities out of my mind but it was a losing battle. *Would he swim again? Walk again? Remember the poetry he used to recite? Climb in the fully loaded van and head to Notre Dame? Would he remember his dreams? His ambitions? Would he even remember who he is?*

Chapter 4

Burr Hole Trephination

I awoke at five a.m., jolted from a horrible dream. In it, Audrey stood at the shallow end of the pool while Ry swam toward her. I struggled in the deep end, water washing over my face. Each time I screamed for him to return to me, a strong current pulled me under, and water filled my mouth. I awoke, gasping for air, unsure of where I was. Was Audrey trying to end Ry's suffering by bringing him to the other side?

Freezing, I went into the kitchen to adjust the thermostat. An empty bottle of wine sat on the counter, no doubt the reason for my headache. Outside, the sky was streaked with the first pink rays of sunlight. I liked to enter the day in gradually developed steps: make coffee, feed the dog, walk the dog, bag the poop, read the paper, check phone messages, go for a run, then shower and shave. On this morning, I fed the dog, walked the dog, and shaved. I kept telling myself to focus as I dragged the razor across my jaw, but my thoughts kept drifting to my endless list of things to do: call Notre Dame, call the dorm priest, call Notre Dame swim coach, tell my parents, call the neighbors, call Ry's swim team manager, contact my office about the dozen manuscripts that needed proofing.

I wanted to leave this behind and not deal with any of it.

As I approached the exit for the hospital, I felt a twinge in my gut and blew right past it. I drove on the state highway for miles, not sure what to do. I thought about Dr. Wilson and the rest of the staff at St. Mary's Hospital, daydreaming of someone there working magic on Ry and putting him back together again. I imagined showing up to the ICU, finding Lynn and Ry awake and chatting, laughing at what a *close one that was* I fantasized about a script where Dr. Wilson explained it was an overnight miracle and Ry was free to go home. It was all wishful thinking, but sometimes lies are easier to digest.

Driving east on Hull Street, I came to a desolate shopping mall. Most of the buildings were boarded up. Men stood on the corners, talking and passing a paper bag to each other. A man was sleeping on a bus stop bench with a balled-up newspaper for a pillow. A pang of sadness struck me as I thought, *He was someone's little boy once.* How did he fall this far? What would happen to my son if Lynn and I died today? Would he be sleeping on a bench one day? What if Ry could never care for himself again? What if he needed a full-time caregiver? I am going mad.

Once those thoughts started, I couldn't stop them. They just kept crashing into me, one after another. *What needed to be done to convert the house into a handicapped one? Who will take care of him after we are gone?* He had no siblings. *Why didn't Lynn and I try to have more children? How could we leave him alone?* What if I rolled down the window and screamed, "Damn you, God!" right into the morning air? *Would He hear me? Would He care?*

The sky was now covered in thin clouds, crisscrossing like jet streams. It was like the sky had been cut apart and stitched back together. Maybe it was a sign that all things can be mended. Maybe I was just desperate for signs. I was sitting in an abandoned parking lot, hoping clouds would give me answers.

Fifteen years ago, this had been a busy mall—a popular

hangout for teens and a place where families came on weekends. The old Walden Bookstore was still here, though its sign was faded and barely legible. When Ry was in middle school, I'd bring him here once a month. We had a special deal: I'd buy him books if his report card had A's and B's. Ry loved it—he loved coming here, browsing the stacks of books and trying to choose which ones to take home. I should have known then a burgeoning writer was in the family.

Once, his fifth-grade teacher sent home a note asking me to meet with her. She was in her sixties and skeptical of everyone. During the meeting, she told me she had caught Ry cheating on a test. She'd wanted to fail Ry, but I knew that would crush him. After a few minutes of negotiation, I persuaded her to give him an "incomplete" for that quarter, as punishment, and make Ry write her a paper on the importance of honesty. She agreed.

On the way home from that meeting, I'd told Ry that I loved him, but he could never cheat again. He was embarrassed, and I could see that he was ashamed. With a lot of children, one gets the feeling they are only sorry they got caught, but with Ry, his pain always showed so clearly on his face. His wounded eyes and slumped shoulders told me he was truly sorry for what he had done.

Lynn would have been furious if I'd told her—she would have grounded him for a month, and I saw no benefit in that. So instead, we made a deal: if he promised to never cheat again, I wouldn't tell his mother. Though I was being lenient, the negotiations worked. The next quarter, Ry got all A's, and I began bribing him to continue with the promise of books. For me it was a win-win. He never again had trouble with his studies, and he developed a love for literature. By the time he was fifteen, I had put two huge bookcases in his room to hold all the novels and poetry books he treasured. Some kids collected CDs; Ry collected poetry, sci-fi, and graphic novels. He could have opened a public library in his room.

Staring at the boarded-up book store, I didn't want to go back to the hospital, choosing instead to stay in the past, where my son was safe. The idea of Ry lying motionless in that bed had me frozen. I didn't want to be trapped in that tiny room, watching machines and drugs to keep my son alive. He was in the ICU, my wife had sat by his side all night, and yet here I was, driving around town, doing anything to avoid going back to that place. Guilt tore at me. An eerie feeling sat on my chest, whispering that I should go back or something awful would happen. But what could I do besides sit by Ry's side? What could I really do to help him? I simply couldn't bring myself to face the truth this had happened. This was *still happening*. I wanted someone—a doctor, a psychic, anyone—to tell me what this all meant, why it was happening to my family.

I needed someone to tell me how to get through this.

After leaving the mall, I drove to my office. Lynn would be wondering what was keeping me, but there was one person who I thought could help me. Although it was Saturday morning, I knew my co-worker, Frank, would be in his office. A graduate of Notre Dame, Frank was friendly, with a positive attitude. He was a straight shooter and always had a level head. I needed someone to talk me off the ledge and get my head on straight.

While Ry was applying to Notre Dame, Frank had been quick to point out that high SAT scores alone would not get a student in. Prospects had to sparkle. They had to demonstrate through community volunteerism that they understood the meaning of bringing comfort to the less fortunate. Frank would often say an education at Notre Dame gave you a sense of place on earth. He was one of those people who said, "Everything happens for a reason." I wanted to know what meaning he could find in all of this.

Just as I'd expected, his car was alone in the parking lot. Frank put in more hours than anyone, because he always said an honest day's work kept a man honest in his heart.

Our building was usually like a beehive, but today it was quiet. Frank's office was on the second floor, in a wing that had a bank of floor-to-ceiling windows. His door was open, just as it always was.

"Good morning, Frank," I said wearily while sinking into the chair next to his desk.

"What's up with you?" he asked. He looked concerned, like he could tell something was wrong.

"Frank, I have horrible news." I looked up at the ceiling as the tears arrived. "Ry was in a car accident last night and can't raise his right arm or leg. Doctors are afraid he might have some paralysis and a brain injury." Once the words were out, I couldn't stop the tears from spilling over my cheeks.

Frank got up and put his arm around my shoulder. "How did it happen? Where is he now?"

He listened as I filled him in and then said, "I'll call Father Malloy at Notre Dame and we'll get a prayer network going this morning. By tonight there will be thousands of people praying for Ry."

"Thank you, Frank." I wiped away my tears with the back of my sleeve, embarrassed. "It's good to know so many people will be thinking of my family." For the next few minutes, I found a small bit of composure to give him the details of what I knew so far. Frank told me to go buy a writing journal to record my thoughts. That it would help with the stress. He also said to pray, just like the mysterious nun had told me the night before.

Everyone kept telling me to pray, as if that were the only solution. But they didn't know how I'd prayed in the past—how I'd begged for a life to be saved and God had ignored me. Down on my knees I had cried, pleaded, begged, and offered to give my life instead, and still my wife was taken. It seemed God wasn't satisfied taking my darling Audrey; now he wanted my son too. What good was prayer? Why did everyone seem to think this was the answer? Prayer had never helped me, and the more people told me to pray, the more helpless I felt. I just couldn't bring myself to do it. Our future was uncertain, but I was done putting my faith in a God who never helped me.

"Thank you, Frank," I said. "But I should get to the hospital."

Walking out of that building, I still could feel anxiety lurking, stalking, ready to pounce. I now felt a sense of urgency to go relieve Lynn.

Twenty-five years before, on hot August day, I'd walked to the middle of the Huguenot Bridge, where a hot kettle of intention burned in my stomach. It was the day that grief had caught up with me. A loss so painful, my heart was cracking open. I had just lost my best friend. The person I thought would be my life's companion. My hippie wife, who I was going to grow old with and sit in rocking chairs when we were ninety, holding hands. Gone. She was gone and I didn't want to see another sunrise.

My belt buckle had pushed up against the metal guardrail as I leaned over and stared down into the gorge. The James River was five hundred and fifty feet below me, churning and tumbling its way toward the horizon. My arms dangled over the metal railing, pulled downward by gravity toward the hole in the earth.

I closed my eyes, feeling the pull of gravity, leaning down towards the river. Soon, the sound of the rapids quieted to a faint whisper, as if luring me down to the water. It would be so easy to let go, to give in. I imagined the cool water pulling me under, and my mind became calm in the promise of death. Death's door opened and closed for Audrey. Would it open for me?

Death brings an end to our suffering. We don't have to answer to anyone any more. No more sensory images of what a day might look like with our loved one leaning on our shoulder, sipping tea as we laugh or read a poem together. Death didn't arrive on time and I backed away. The white noise of passing people asking how I was doing, saying hello, was a form of intimacy. Maybe it was a passer-by who smiled at me, like Audrey did a hundred times a day. I backed away but retreated into a shell to hide.

I could not hide now. I had to face the fact that I might have a handicapped son. Back at the hospital, I went to the cafeteria for coffee. As I stood in line to pay, people all around me were stirring cream into their coffees, eating their breakfast, putting jelly on their toast, as if this were just a normal morning. Plates, silverware, and trays clinked above the low din of their chatter.

How did these people act so normal? Did they not know there were people on other floors clinging to life? Above them were teenagers whose futures may have been altered forever in a single moment. There were fathers lost in a sea of strangers, struggling to make sense of this chaos. Could they not see it? Were they so selfishly engrossed in their own worlds they couldn't see some of us were dying inside? I wanted to scream in rage. I wanted to pick up a chair and throw it through a plate glass window while shouting, "Notice me! Notice my pain! Please!"

Suddenly, I realized someone was talking to me. The cashier

was asking how I wanted to pay for my coffee. Handing over my card, I saw in her eyes that this was not the first time she had dealt with a distracted loved one. I looked around and it occurred to me that someone could, at this moment, be watching me buy a cup of coffee and wondering how it was that I could act so normal. When I looked closer at the sea of faces, I saw the sadness in their downturned mouths, the confusion in their eyes. These were not selfish people. These were people who were suffering and distracted, just like me.

As I walked down the hall toward Ry's room, I heard someone behind me call my name. "Mr. Beville," a voice said. In a moment, my heart stopped. I didn't want to turn around. Turning around meant facing whatever terrible news was coming my way. I froze, thinking of Audrey, of that horrible day. This couldn't happen again. It simply could not. I was not ready for another doctor or priest to tell me that my loved one had passed.

A hand came down gently on my shoulder.

Dr. Wilson. He'd been standing next to the nurses' station. He gave me a slight smile and said, "How are you doing?"

I wanted to cry. "Not too well." My lungs felt empty of air. The ground beneath me started to give way. Silently I pleaded, *don't say it. Don't say it.*

"I understand how you feel," Dr. Wilson said. "I have a new CT scan from a few minutes ago. Would you like to walk with me to the viewing room and I'll show it to you? Is Mrs. Beville here with you?"

My son was still with us. I took a deep breath, feeling myself relax a bit. "Yes, she has been here all night," I answered, ashamed I'd taken so long to get here.

As I walked to Ry's room to get Lynn, all I could think was how grateful I was to have my Lynn in my life. How could I possibly have managed this alone? I was falling apart, but my wife was a pillar of strength. Or so I thought. I was so wrapped up in my own feelings, I failed to see the strain on her face. I kissed her on the forehead. "I love you. I missed you. Thanks for being here all night."

A few minutes later, Lynn and I were with Dr. Wilson in the viewing room. The CT scans showed seven areas where the tissue had been damaged. Cerebral edema with acute subdural hematoma.

"What's the worst-case scenario?" I asked.

Dr. Wilson did not mask the truth. He told us that there was no doubt that the extent of the injuries would cause some deficits in motor skills, causing delayed muscle movement in the right arm and leg. It might affect Ry's speech, and he'd likely have problems with his short-term memory. The hematoma had increased the pressure on nearby healthy tissue. This pressure would reduce blood flow, killing healthy cells.

"I would like to do another CT scan in the early afternoon," Dr. Wilson said to the radiologist. "Mr. and Mrs. Beville, we still have a good option here. As I told you earlier, it is called Burr Hole Trephination. We can drill tiny holes in the skull over the affected areas of the hematoma and suction out the blood through the holes."

It was bewildering. Ry had been through so much in his life. Multiple surgeries to repair his foot and lengthen his leg. A dog attack at the age of five that required two surgeries to repair his eyelid. Having his appendix removed a week after our family doctor misdiagnosed Ry's excruciating pain and vomiting as a stomach virus—the ER at the Virginia Commonwealth University Medical Center revealed a mass of jelly-like tissue that was once an organ. This all felt like too much for one kid to bear. It was unfair, and I was growing increasingly angry at an unjust world that would put my boy through so much pain.

"Traumatic brain injury is always a complicated medical issue," he said. "Some symptoms don't show up for weeks or months after injury."

I wanted to say to Dr. Wilson that my son was not just another medical case. He was a nationally ranked swimmer, volunteered to read poetry to blind listeners at PBS. He loved bonsai plants and wanted to be a writer. He tutored younger students with their math skills. But I remained quiet.

Lynn was crying, in shock. My wife, who'd remained so calm and brave the night before, now appeared fragile and broken. She told me once that she never cried in front of doctors and other hospital staff as she would be seen as weak. She'd managed to tamp down her feelings every day in this hospital, and now it seemed she couldn't hold emotions at bay any longer. Seeing her this way tore at my heart. Her face sagged with exhaustion and something became quite clear: I must put my own sadness aside and support her.

Taking her hand, I did my best to convince her that everything would be okay. It didn't matter if I wasn't confident. It didn't matter if I didn't believe my own words. I needed her to believe that we could do this together. "I love you, Sweets. We will get through this. We will nourish him back to where he was. He is a good kid; maybe God has plans for him." Religious scholars speak with authority, but I would never be a scholar. I had nothing but scorn for religious doctrine, but my world had become a crucible, and perhaps I felt the need to open a crack in my thinking.

I was not ready to pray the Rosary, but I was hoping that my words would bring some comfort to my wife. It was like Albert

Camus said, I told her, that to live in this irrational world, we must believe God exists. I spoke the words because I knew she needed to hear them. But the words rang hollow in my ears, because to me they weren't true any more. All I could think was, *where is this God everyone keeps telling me to pray to?*

Dr. Wilson invited Lynn and me to have coffee with him in the doctors' lounge, but I wanted to stop by Ry's room first. He'd been moved from the ICU up to a private room on the sixth floor while we'd been looking at the scans. Lynn and I stepped onto the elevator and pushed the button for the sixth floor. It felt like the longest elevator ride of my life.

"You must be exhausted," I said, putting my arm around her shoulder.

"I am," she sighed. "I plan on going home after I check on Ry again."

Again, I was hit with a pang of guilt over the bottle of wine and the bath. "How was he last night?" I asked.

"He didn't move for most of the night. Around six a.m., he opened the one eye that is not swollen shut and asked where he was. I sponged some of the dried blood off his ear and from under his chin. His hair is…" Lynn choked on her words as her eyes welled up. "It's so matted with blood. It'll be a few days before we can move him to wash his hair." She covered her mouth to stifle a sob, "His beautiful hair."

"I love you," I said, leaning over to hug her. I kissed the top of her head and moved to her cheeks in a futile attempt to kiss her tears away. "Don't cry," I whispered, squeezing her hand. "He's in the best hospital in Richmond. Dr. Wilson said it was important for us to know that the EMTs got him here in less than forty minutes from the accident. That's the golden hour in treating brain injury." I felt as if I were reciting a medical journal, but I was desperate to convince us both that our paralyzed son was going to be okay.

The elevator chimed and we came to a stop. The doors opened and two men and a woman, wearing white coats, entered. Immediately, Lynn stood straight, dried her eyes and nodded, as if the last few minutes had never happened. I could hug and kiss her and whisper words of encouragement, and she hardly reacted at all. But the sight of a white coat transformed her and she was all business, like a soldier reporting for duty.

Ry's room was small, with just enough room for a chair by the window and a little TV mounted high in the corner. Outside the window was a view of the parking structure. Two machines clicked and hummed, displaying vital signs. Green cords were connected to patches on his chest. Bright lines zigzagged across the monitoring screens. IV drips from bags of Decadron, Klonopin, and antibiotics ran into both of his arms, which were taped to support boards attached to his bed. He looked peaceful, even with part of his forehead covered in bandages. One eye was bruised and swollen shut. The bridge of his nose had a jagged cut leading across the edge of his eyelid, extending through his eyebrow. I counted a dozen sutures. It was hard to look at my beautiful boy this way, so broken and bruised. I gently placed my hand on Ry's chest, wanting to feel his heartbeat.

We all pick roles in these situations. Lynn was the stoic, calculating as she did every day as a neonatal nurse. I cast myself as the good father, thinking that if I researched his injuries, managed them, and directed his treatment, eventually I would fix my boy. I would help him through physical therapy. Be his cheerleader.

I can fix this, I thought. I can fix him. With or without God's help.

After Lynn said good-bye to Ry, I walked her out and kissed her goodbye, and she disappeared through the elevator doors. I felt lucky to be married to my wife. She had been steady and reliable for me for over twenty years in our marriage. She had changed my life by supporting me in most everything I did. I always felt I could do anything as long as she believed in me. I was in awe of Lynn, who knew about any number of things by constantly reading and educating herself. It was not unusual to see her place clippings and journal articles about her medical field into the plethora of notebooks she kept around the house.

Lynn was the most organized person I knew. When we traveled and checked into a hotel, I used to watch her unpack. She placed blouses in one drawer, socks in another. She grouped her makeup and lotions on the bathroom counter, all in a neat row and evenly spaced them out by product category. By contrast, I'd leave everything in my suitcase and live out of it for a week. She never complained, because she accepted that I was wired differently. Her system worked for her, and mine worked for me.

When it came to Ry's injuries, I was going to have to take a cue from Lynn and get organized. If I was going to help her and Ry too, I'd need to dedicate myself to learning everything there was about traumatic brain injury. I would become an expert in all things relating to the recovery of my son. Everyone else could tell me to pray, but I needed to take control. I needed to take action.

I would put my son back together again.

While Ry slept, I studied his face like I hadn't done since he was an infant sleeping in my arms. As our kids grow, an invisible wall forms that keeps us parents at bay. My head understood it: children need independence to develop. They need to go out into the world and explore, make decisions, and take it all in. It's hard to do that with a parent right up in your face twenty-four-seven. So, we step back. As much as it breaks our hearts, loving parents give space.

Now was my time to break that invisible wall. Alone in that hospital room, with the bleeps and tics of machines, the dripping of IVs, and the air that didn't move, I took in every aspect of my son's face. I looked past the cuts and bruises and saw the boyish smile he flashed just before leaving the house for prom, or having his arms raised when he set another pool record. I smiled when I thought of the last day, we spent in our newly created pond just a week ago. So much joy watching Ry push bamboo shoots in the sand. We were having so much fun that our grasp on time kept merging into endless hours of laughing, talking about his new journey going to college, and me sharing memories of my childhood with him. My Ry was still in there, deep inside.

I just needed to help him get out.

Chapter 5

Wrap Myself in the Tubes

There would be no drilling into Ry's skull.

Dr. Wilson called and said Ry's scans had improved and he had decided against the Burr Hole technique, unless the intracranial pressure increased. Although Ry's vital signs were normal, he remained in a semi-comatose state. It was good news, I thought, but he looked worse every day. The nurses told me this was normal. The worse he looked, the more he was healing. Some of the swelling had slowed over his eye but the bruising increased. Staring at Ry's face reminded me of the pottery class I took many years ago at Virginia Commonwealth University. All my bowls were slightly off, more askew than smooth and round. His eyes were not in alignment with his forehead.

Dr. Wilson's new assessment was to continue the steroid IVs. He gave us some pamphlets to read (in a hospital, pamphlets were handed out like tissues at a funeral) and I made it my full-time job to absorb their content. In just a few days, I'd learned new words and how to gauge the meaning of critical, stable, guarded, and how those terms applied to my son's brain injury. I took the words from the doctors home with me every night. Before placing my head on the pillow, I opened the drawer to the bedside table. There at the bottom lay my abandoned string of Rosary beads, waiting to hear the voice of someone who needed to pray. Would it be the words of science or the words of prayer that helped my son? Each night, I shut the drawer and turned off the light without an answer.

Being in a hospital is a transition to another world. The antiseptic smell greets you at the front door. The hanging paintings on the yellow walls made no sense. The constant ringing of the phone at the nurses' station. The clatter of the food cart wheels. Visitors talking in the next room. My fitful sleep on the hard hospital cot next to Ry's bed. I was going mad.

There were days I wanted to skip going to the hospital. His personality was morphing in front of my eyes. Sudden outbursts—"Where am I?"—while trying to pull himself up. When he failed, his fist slammed against the guard rail. It was unnerving to see my gentle, kind son turning into an angry, rageful man. I had always admired his swimmer's physique, but now those powerful shoulders and muscular arms which glided him through the water had turned into battering rams.

In contrast, some nights were quiet, and I would sit by his hospital bed, watching him breathe. In the silence, there was peace. I could see my son as a little boy once again. A child who needed my protection. I didn't want to admit it, but it had been a long time since my son needed my protection. Much like the orb spiders I'd witnessed in the Japanese garden; my son didn't know how to quit. No matter how much debris life threw his way, he always rebuilt.

Ry was born with a birth defect where his foot was turned ninety degrees to the right. There was a clinical decision made to manipulate the foot weekly with splints. Watching my infant son scream in pain was by far the most heart-wrenching thing I've ever witnessed. At some point during this straightening procedure, it was decided that further casting would be unsuccessful; therefore, surgery was required. The curved bone was removed, which caused Ry's leg to be approximately two inches shorter. For the next ten years Ry needed to have a special shoe made with a two-inch lift.

Corrective surgery was performed at the age of eleven to lengthen the leg by two inches. The pediatrician had to sever the tibia then stretch the leg with a mechanical device by a few millimeters several times a week. After the bone was lengthened two inches, surgery was performed again to insert a section of cadaver bone. A steel plate was screwed over the tibia and a cast was placed on his leg for four months.

Ry was eleven when he had the leg-lengthening procedure, requiring him to stay in a children's hospital for four months. The new bone had to heal, giving the old bone time to grow in to it. He wore a leg brace for a year. When it was time for him to finally go back to school, he was on crutches. There was a bully, who would walk behind Ry as he was going up steps then grab the bottom of the crutch, causing Ry to trip and fall. Not only was this cruel but it was also incredibly dangerous. A hard fall could cause another break requiring additional surgery and more time in the hospital.

Had Ry told me about this I would have been livid. No doubt, there would have been phone calls, meetings, and a lot of shouting on my part. But Ry said nothing. He did what was in his nature: he thought about it and formed a plan. One day, he asked Jason Snead, his best friend, to bring some fishing line from home. On the bus ride home that afternoon, Ry proceeded to meticulously tie the bully's backpack to the bus seat. It must have taken the entire trip. When the bus stopped, the bully was unable to get out of his place. The driver noticed that no one had left their seat to get off, so he shut the door and tootled off down the road. Needless to say, the boy's anxious mother, who was left standing at a corner waiting for her missing son, was not amused when the bus took off with her son banging against the window.

After the school principal summoned me to the office, Ry confessed why he did it. There certainly was some yelling but it didn't come from me. Instead, I sat in a chair getting an earful from the bully's angry parents. It took everything I had not to start laughing. Not only was I not angry with Ry, I was proud of him. He settled the situation without violence while also showing the bully he wouldn't be pushed around. I spent a portion of my afternoon in the principal's office, defending Ry's actions. Only when I threatened a lawsuit should Ry need another surgery due to a fall did the other kid's parents take their son by the hand and march him out of the office.

On the way home, we stopped for ice cream and I tried to explain to Ry that in the future, if he had a problem, he could come to me and I would help him solve it. I was his father; it was my job to protect him. He nodded and licked his ice cream, all the while pretending we were in agreement, but of course the next time a problem arose I would only hear about its weeks after it was solved.

Once again, sitting in a quiet hospital room, watching his chest rise and fall, I was left wondering how I would fulfill my duties as a father and protect my son.

Occasionally, his eyes would open and scan the room, darting to the ceiling, then at me, and back to the ceiling. What he was seeing, I couldn't say. And he didn't tell me. Getting him to talk was difficult. When nurses came into his room to replenish his IV bags, he would mumble incoherent words. I'd lean over a few inches from his face, as if looking into a well, but there was no response. I was desperate to see any sign of my Ry, and I wanted to breathe in any word that might pass his lips.

Say something, son. His voice was hiding deep down inside of him and I couldn't get it to come out. No matter how much I spoke to him or how many times I laid my hand on his leg, he never seemed to know I was there.

This went on for days. When I'd leave his room, hours would glide by in a haze. Start the car; drive away; stop for some fast food; pass Lynn on the road; flash hopeless smiles at friends who came to see Ry and me. I hadn't even told my parents yet. The stress was destroying my mind, just as Ry's hematomas might have destroyed parts of his brain. Everything was gray. Food had no flavor, life had no color, and the days rolled one into another, with the night sky and daylight break my only clue of time's passing. If there were such a thing as purgatory, I had to imagine it resembled the sixth-floor unit of a hospital.

Four days after the accident, I met Dr. Wilson once again in the doctors' lounge. He reached into a cabinet and handed me a big blue coffee mug. The words printed on the cup read, "Bon Secour Hospital: Helping You Get Well." On the opposite side was the inscription, "And when the centurion which stood over Him, and saw that He so cried out, and gave up the ghost, he said, truly this Man was the son of God... Mark 15:39"

This hit a nerve. Why did God create this earth, where so much pain rages? Where so many little children have cancer? Others writhe in pain from disease, war, starvation, hatred, birth defects. My son did nothing to deserve this. Like Voltaire states in *Candide*, "If this is the best of all possible worlds, then what are the others like?"

"Would you like some cream or sugar?" Dr. Wilson asked as he filled my cup.

"No thanks," I said, staring at the black coffee.

We sat down at one of the large dining tables next to the

window that looked out over a small garden. Water lilies filled a large fountain's basin adjacent to a stone statue of Mary Magdalene. In the small rock garden, bright green moss grew in circular patterns around tiny ponds filled with vibrant-colored orange and red carp. Strawberry-red pots, filled with impatiens and purple lobelia, were singing to the sun. Swallowtails and bumblebees danced in the wind. For a few blissful moments I forgot where I was.

Dr. Wilson opened Ry's chart. "Don, the initial CT scans revealed multiple bilateral areas of hemorrhage involving a relatively large area in the high left parietal region and contusions in the left front temporal area."

The peaceful feeling from the garden vanished. "What did you mean the other day when you said Ry's injury might change who he is as a person?"

Dr. Wilson pulled a notepad out of his coat pocket and began to draw a skull with interconnecting lines to little circles, which he said represented the areas where Ry's brain had been injured. "There are billions of nerve cells in the brain which transmit bits of vital information to the body. When the brain is injured, cells may be too injured to produce, release, or absorb the neuro-transmitting chemicals. Even with CT images, we don't know the extent of the damage."

"Can you speak more to the personality changes?" I had worked for three years in a psychiatric hospital to satisfy my college clinical fieldwork. I was aware that physical deficits like motor and balance difficulties can be corrected with wheelchairs, leg braces, and physical therapy. However, mood instability, word recall, cognitive functions, and psychosis can only be improved with lifelong psychotropic medication. As a father, it would be difficult to approve of the invasive procedure of using drugs. I felt Ry's body, one way or another, would be put back together. It was his mind I was concerned about.

"Don, let's wait another week and we'll do another CT scan measuring the effects of the pharmacological agents we've given him. Within the next month, Ry will be entering a rehabilitative phase. Our hospital has a great staff of caring rehab specialists. They'll meet with you and Ry to develop a neurobehavioral assessment program and coordinate a care transition plan. I want you to meet Dr. Benoit soon. She specializes in rehabilitative medicine. She's consulted with me on Ry's brain injury and will be actively working with our case workers."

I'd had dozens of questions when our meeting began. Now only one mattered: would my son ever live a life? Would I see my boy's luminous face again or stare into fixed irises of impacted matter and skin the color of faded copper? The shape of his face was becoming rounder, caused by the steroids being pumped into him. I had to believe that one day Ry would feel joy again. Right now, he seemed to feel nothing at all.

"Over time, the brain will begin to repair the cell damage. New cells will branch out and form links through and around the dead cells. Electrical signals will be restored. But some deficits might never be resolved."

Loss of cognition. Short-term memory loss. Ry could have severe problems for the rest of his life. TBI patients could read a magazine article and not remember the story ten minutes later.

My son had worked his entire life to get accepted into a prestigious university and now he might not be able to remember what day it was.

I thanked Dr. Wilson for his time. I needed to go home and be with Lynn. I needed to eat and sleep. I needed a glass of wine. I needed a hug, the kind that surrounds your body so you can't get hurt by anything. A while back, I'd watched a documentary where a herd of elephants surrounded a baby elephant, defending it from a predator. I wanted that. I wanted to be surrounded by community, family, friends, anyone I could get, to protect myself and my son from harm.

"Don, you must have faith," Dr. Wilson said as he walked me to the door. "Circumstances can change. The brain has remarkable plasticity and will adapt to sensory loss by growing new cells. Ry will adjust, but you too must adjust with him by accepting a new reality."

It wouldn't take long to discover that I was completely fooling myself. This was never going to be a fast fix. But in that moment, I felt like I could do anything.

For the next few days, Lynn and I took alternating shifts at the hospital. We sat in a chair next to Ry's bed and watched the monitors.

Seeing my son in this way was shattering. I had always viewed Ry as if he were in *fast idle*. He was like a race car sitting at the gate, ready to jump on every opportunity that came his way. He was so enamored with the mysteries and magic of life, it was difficult to keep up with his curiosity.

For eighteen years, I had fooled myself into believing I'd provided him with a safety net. That was my job, wasn't it? Keep the children safe.

Now, I wondered if any of our children were ever truly safe. Perhaps it is random fate that allows one child to come home safely from a date and another to end up in an ICU bed. What was the point of personally driving my son to every swim practice and after-school event? Why were parents coordinating all our children's activities with pickups and drop-offs, rushing from one place to another, and packing in the days of the calendar? Maybe I should have spent the last eighteen years throwing caution to the wind and given Ry his ultimate freedom. Maybe I should have bought him a bike and set him loose in the world, the way my parents did for me. What if no one is ever fully safe, no matter how much you try to protect them?

Ry's monitors bleeped in a hypnotic rhythm, and I could not fathom what kind of God would want to derail an eighteen-year-old boy.

Ry groaned, and I realized I had dozed off.

Pulling my chair close to his bedside, I said, "Ry, I'm here. Your mother just left for work. How do you feel?"

My son struggled to find his words. "My head... gyrating. Blackness in my eye."

"Do you know where you are?" I asked in a soft voice.

"Home?" Ry mumbled.

"You're in St. Mary's ICU," I answered in the most soothing voice I could muster. I had to remain calm so as not to spook him. This was the first time he'd been awake in days and the first time he'd spoken. I knew he would be confused and disoriented, but my heart began to beat faster. Maybe the God I had believed in all my life had finally heard one of the prayers I had been saying ten times a day for the last week. Was my exile from my son over?

"Your eye is swollen closed, and you have a bandage covering it. That's why you can't see."

It was the same statement I had made the previous day and that I would make again in a few hours and a few hours after that. I wasn't aware that a brain injury could affect short-term memory this way, but Ry couldn't remember simple things I told him from one minute to the next. It was troublesome for me to grasp. In a short seventy-two hours, it appeared his brain function had deteriorated. Three days before, he was asking questions. Today, he was having trouble with word recall, his sentences breaking off before I knew what he was trying to say.

I didn't know how much I should tell him about the accident, his injuries. It would upset him, and then he'd forget, and I'd have to tell him again.

"Headache," he mumbled.

"Ry, you were in a car accident, coming home from dinner with Alexis. You hit your head on the steering wheel or the side of the door. Alexis is okay. Just bruises from the seatbelt."

"I can't find... words. Floating. Words float."

"Ry, you have a bad concussion that's causing the confusion in your head. It will go away in a few days."

"Arm hurts," Ry said.

"There is some paralysis in your right arm. A few days of physical therapy, and it will be fine." I reached over and touched his right arm to reassure him that he would be okay. But the truth was I had no idea if any of this would ever be okay. It felt like lying, and it made me feel like a terrible father. I had never lied to Ry. Honesty was the cornerstone of our relationship, and now I was down playing his injuries, feeding him a steady drip of lies.

I wanted to tell him everything and at the same time nothing. What did it matter if I told him things he would forget within minutes?

"Why is my arm tied down?" Ry said, his uncovered eye looking out into dark space.

"You have slight paralysis on that side. It just feels like it's tied down." How else could I explain the paralysis? I'd been a steadfast parent and been his cheerleader while protecting him from the world's toxins. I pushed back in the chair, feeling a wave of panic.

My heart sped up and I was overcome with a sense of vertigo. The ground under my chair began to sway, as if I were on an ocean liner. I could feel the back of my mouth salivating, telling me I was going to be sick again. I braced my hands on the arm of the chair and focused on my breath.

I couldn't have another episode like that first night here in the parking lot. My son needed me, and I was determined to fight through this. I would not jump up and bolt out of the room. As much as my body was screaming for me to run, I had to stay. I took several deep breaths and picked up Ry's hand. Breathe and focus. Breathe and focus. It became my mantra until I could feel my own pulse slow as the panic subsided.

"Untie my arm," Ry said, in a slow release of each word. His voice was hoarse. He was agitated.

"Ry, your arm isn't tied down."

Ry moved his head slightly, his one open eye trying to look around. "Black. My eye. Black."

"Ry, it is nice to hear your voice." There were moments the first few nights that I thought I might not hear his sweet voice again.

"Where am I, Dad?"

"You are in the hospital," I said. "But only for a few days."

"No."

I reached for his hand. Was there a small pocket somewhere in the untouched parts of his brain that knew he had been in an accident? The look on his face was blank.

It went on like that all day. And the next day. Over and over, the repeated questions. In between he would sleep, but his confusion was never alleviated. Eye, head, arm, leg. He'd ask about each one then start again in varying order. Head, leg, eye, arm. Eye, arm, leg, head. Blackness. Words floating. Tied down.

Most of the time, I'd answer his questions simply and directly, but one day I tried another approach. My son had always loved writing and playing with words. He was a poet, so one afternoon, I said, "Ry, I want you to think about a poem and all of its parts. Your body and brain are like the poem. Its lines have repetition and cadence. Think of every word in the poem like a cell in your brain. For the poem to work, every word has to be precise and fit with the voice in the poem. Remove one of those elements, and the poem doesn't work. Your brain, because of the concussion, has cells that are not working. That's why you're having some trouble speaking and moving your arm."

As much as Ry was struggling to remember and understand what was happening, I was too. He looked at me for a moment, blinking his one good eye, and I thought perhaps I'd finally broken through.

"Untie my arm," he muttered, before closing his eye.

He drifted off to sleep again, and I lifted his hand to my lips. "Son, your mother and I will be here every day to help you heal. You just need to sleep and not worry about tomorrow."

Leaving Ry to sleep, I walked through the hospital lobby, past the gift shop, where people were buying flowers. Every electrical impulse in my brain was saying to put one foot in front of the other and not look back — out the door, across the parking lot — not stopping my feet until I was safely home. I wanted to lie down in the bamboo garden and roll my exhausted body into the pond. It was our little world we'd created that summer. What world did my son inhabit now?

Chapter 6

Dr. Jeanne Benoit, MD

Along the sidewalk at St. Mary's, the crepe myrtles were covered in cicadas, announcing another hot, humid day in Virginia. It was seven a.m., and I was waiting to meet Dr. Benoit in the Department of Clinical Psychology and Rehabilitative Services. The plaque by the door read, "Everyone prays in their own language, and there is no language that God does not understand." Every hallway, every elevator, every room, and the nurses' station had framed plaques with Catholic quotes. Some asked for the Blessed Mother's intercession. Prayers by saints, some on earth, and saints in heaven. *Hail Mary, full of grace. The Lord is with thee.* I felt I was back in Bible school. A patient at St. Mary's might wake up and think they had become Catholic. The hospital could be a guide for converts, reverts, and anybody wanting to brush up on their beliefs.

Dr. Benoit's office had a wall filled with framed degrees and awards. She held a B.Sc. in Biology and a B.A. in Theology from Notre Dame, a master's degree in Biochemistry from Johns Hopkins, and a medical degree from the Yale School of Medicine. There were dozens of certificates for research articles published in various journals: "Recovery of Cognition After Brain Injury" from the *Archives of Physical Medicine and Rehabilitation*; "Neuropsychological Rehabilitation After Brain Injury", *Johns Hopkins University Press*; Recovery of

Communication Functions After Brain Injury and Stroke, *Scandinavian Journal of Rehabilitation Medicine*. She had also been a research assistant and a professor at the Harvard Medical School in the Department of Neuroscience. This woman, I thought, had lived a life of research. I was impressed by her accomplishments.

"Good morning, Mr. Beville," a calming voice said from behind me.

I turned to see an athletic, six-foot-tall, beautiful woman in a white coat. She had a familiar face and I swallowed hard as I realized where I'd seen her before. She'd come to my aid in the Emergency Room parking lot, the night Ry was admitted. I'd begun to think I had imagined the whole encounter, but here she was—taller than I remembered, but when you're on your hands and knees hovering over your own puke, it's hard to gauge a person's height.

"It's you," I said in a surprised tone. "You helped me the night of Ry's accident." Now I understood how she'd known about Ry's condition that night.

"Yes, that was me," she said with a warm smile. "You seem to be feeling much better."

"I never had a chance to thank you," I said.

She waved her hand, "Please, it was nothing. God sometimes puts us just where we need to be." Dr. Benoit walked over to her desk and picked up a file. "I've been checking Ry's progress every day, and I think here, in the next week or so, we can move him to Sheltering Arms Rehabilitative Hospital. They have a brilliant rehab team there. I talked to Dr. Wilson yesterday and he's in agreement."

It was what I'd been hoping for, but once she said it out loud, I began to have doubts. "I don't see how that is possible," I stammered. "He is barely moving and has difficulty speaking."

"I know, but I do see signs of improvement. When I visited Ry, I tried to get him to articulate his thoughts. Although he does not always respond, I can tell by his body language that he's comprehending some things. Your son is a special kid, Don. Students who get accepted into Notre Dame are not only smart, but they sparkle. There's something that makes them stand out from the crowd."

I had never used the word "sparkle" when describing Ry, but it fit. There was a certain sparkle or electricity I felt when he walked in a room, but I thought as his father I was biased.

Dr. Benoit leaned against her large desk, crossing her arms in front of her. "Right now, his mind is silent and not processing much, so we need to keep reminding him that his caregivers love him and that he will recover. His brain is figuring out how to repair itself, and it will. He told me yesterday it felt as if his brain was on fire. It's good he can articulate feelings to me. Have faith in our Lord and pray for his recovery. It will happen, but it will take time."

She said this matter-of-factly, and I felt hopeful by her calmness. Dr. Benoit appeared to be in her late thirties or early forties. Her face was smooth and white, like it had been polished. Her curly black hair fell in tight ringlets. She had bright green eyes, delicate eyebrows and lovely thin lips, which gave her face a look of weightlessness.

The wedding band on her hand told me she was a bride of Christ. *Ego te sponsabo*. A ring engraved with two hearts pierced by a sword. Her fidelity was sealed. She was more beautiful than I'd realized that first night. I marveled at how she could be dedicated to both God and science. How was that possible? I had grown up in a deeply religious family, listening to repetitious

Catholic prayers. My grandmother had a book full of verse and would recite them to the cows as she milked them, filling one tin pail after another. It was hard for me to develop any inward sense of faith.

I prayed to God for Grandmother to spare the lives of the chickens I had befriended. All the while, she prayed to God for food on the table. How could the same God honor both our prayers? My heart broke each time one of my friends was offered up on a platter, and I came to understand that God was definitely on Grandma's side. Or at least not on mine. It was then that I began to have an interest in science. Science was real. Data and math didn't lie. Faith was elusive.

As if sensing my gaze on her, Dr. Benoit looked at me. She didn't say anything for a few seconds and I could feel my face growing flush. She smiled politely and asked, "Who is Audrey?"

The question stunned me and I could only stare at her, words stuck in my throat. How could she possibly know about Audrey?

Reading my look of surprise, she said, "The night outside the hospital you said her name as I approached."

I cleared my throat and stammered, "Um, she... she died a long time ago. She had black hair too." It was all I could think to say. I wanted to tell Sister Angeline that I had married Audrey impulsively when we were young college students. I wanted to tell her how Audrey's father was in a rage when he found out we'd run off and tied the knot and how he had driven halfway across the country to try and talk his daughter out of making a huge mistake. I wanted to tell her that the same man had held me in his arms as I wailed in agony after her death. Instead, all I could come up with was, "She had black hair too."

After a long pause, Dr. Benoit said, "Oh, I see. I'm very sorry. Loss can make us feel helpless."

"Yes. I struggled to recover from that loss. The pain was hard to put behind me. It was a time in my life when everything seemed right. Why does it seem that the Universe sends the worst pain when things are good?" I looked up at a cross hanging on the wall behind her desk. Jesus hung his head in what must have been excruciating pain. "Is God only happy when we are suffering?"

"I don't think God takes pleasure in our suffering," she answered, with compassion in her eyes.

It was too painful to look into her soulful eyes and I looked away, changing the subject. "I've been reading the TBI pamphlets about behavioral changes, inappropriate behavior, and aggressive anger."

Dr. Benoit was not ready to let the topic go. "Don, the loss of someone we cherish can keep us on a depression treadmill. Healing and renewal are not out there somewhere. It is not in a shrine or a church. Salvation lies within. Don't have a relationship with doubt. Have a relationship with your faith. Every day is a new story of your life."

I wanted to believe her. I did. But I was afraid to trust. I was afraid if I let down my guard I would be blindsided by grief once again. Audrey's death nearly killed me. If Ry were to die, I was done. "All of what you say makes sense." I said, "I'm just numb right now. I don't want to lose my son."

"I don't believe you will lose your son," she said. "The symptoms noted in those TBI brochures are just a list. Sometimes they show themselves, but I think with an individualized targeted rehabilitative program we can limit the severity of those symptoms. We have to be creative, persistent, and willing to experiment. Every brain injury is different. Outcomes are different. The beautiful thing about the brain is its ability to adapt to change. With habituation, new pathways through the brain will develop."

"I've not had a chance to see Ry this morning. Do you know of any changes since yesterday?"

"Well, he did allow the nurses to sit him up so he could get a bath. Getting him in a wheelchair was a no go," she said with a laugh. "His face is still puffy, but that's normal from the steroids he's taking. Your son has the biggest shoulders I have ever seen. I believe Dr. Wilson said he is a swimmer? What stroke?"

I was surprised and pleased that she was interested in Ry's swimming. "He's a butterflier," I said with pride. "He started swimming at age eight."

"Dr. Wilson said he holds some national records."

"Yes, he swam on a relay team that tied the national record this year in the four hundred-meter freestyle. He's currently number one in the state in the one hundred-meter butterfly."

She smiled and nodded, returning to her reading. How was it possible for her to be so comfortable with this silence? I interrupted her reading once more and said, "I am worried about him swimming at the same level. His ability to walk, do homework. Live a normal life. I have a long list of 'ifs'."

Without looking up, she answered, "Yes, but maybe not at a collegiate level." Then she quickly added, "What has Dr. Wilson told you about Ry's injuries?"

"A lot," I said. "But I don't always understand all of the details."

"I can help with those details," she said as she walked over to a table behind her. Picking up a plastic brain, she set it down on her desk directly in front of me. "As you can see, our brains have two hemispheres. Both hemispheres talk to each other." She pulled the two sections apart, exposing a dark area sitting at the middle-bottom of each sphere.

"This is the *corpus callosum*. This is how each hemisphere shares information with the other. Think of blue Christmas lights on one side of the tree that are plugged into white Christmas lights on the other side. They share electricity through the cords that cross back and forth through the tree. In the brain, there are billions of cells carrying information back and forth from one hemisphere to the other. Working together, the two regions help us perceive the world around us."

I nodded my head like an enthusiastic student on the first day of school. Why was I so desperate for her to like me? Perhaps it was her likeness to Audrey or her connection to spirituality. Could a nun working as a neuroscientist have an in to the world of fate? Was it possible my son's future lay in her hands? Or was it simply that being in her presence brought me great comfort? Her beauty, her peacefulness, her intelligence, made me feel, at least for a moment, that everything was going to be okay.

Dr. Benoit continued with her lesson as I eagerly hung on her every word. "Our right hemisphere controls the left side of our bodies and vice versa. Since Ry's left side of the brain is bruised, it's affecting signals going to his right arm and leg. Thus, the paralysis. Cognitively speaking, the right hemisphere lives in the moment. It senses tastes, smells, and sounds. It allows us to know what's in the space around us." Dr. Benoit placed her palm over my hand as she continued. "When I place my hand on yours, sensors in your right hemisphere are immediately presented with a sensation of touch."

"Dr. Benoit, you have an appointment with your staff in thirty minutes," said a voice from behind me.

Looking up, Dr. Benoit answered, "Yes, Margaret. Thank you," she said to her receptionist, before glancing back to me and removing her hand. "Mr. Beville, is this helping?"

"Would it be okay if you called me Don?"

"Of course."

"I know you have to go, and I'm grateful you spent this much time with me, but may I ask you about the risks of seizures?"

She cleared her throat and said, "With a traumatic brain injury, seizures can be brought on by certain spectra of light, blinking lights, music, and drinking."

"That's great," I said. "A college freshman trying to avoid blinking lights, music, and alcohol. Is there anything we can do to reduce the probability of seizures?"

"There are drugs, and then there's neurosurgery. Don, it's too early for us to know how Ry will respond to rehab. I would say to you over and over, have faith."

There it was again. Pray. I wanted something concrete. I wanted advice based in science and facts, but of course she was a nun, so a suggestion of prayer was to be expected. Was it wrong that I wished she would touch my hand again?

I loved Lynn dearly, and would never cheat, but being with Dr. Benoit was filling me with a sense of nostalgia. Just for a moment, I wanted to feel the young love I had with Audrey. Lynn and I had a mature, grown-up love. We'd built a life together. We shared mutual respect and love. We had adult conversations and worked through our troubles with compassionate conversation. I loved our marriage. I loved our life together. And yet, for one moment, when Dr. Benoit touched my hand, I had a reckless, impulsive surge of young love rush through me. It was pain and suffering and angst mixed with exhilaration, adrenaline and risk.

It was time for me to go.

"Thank you, Dr. Benoit. Will you still be working with him once he's transferred to Sheltering Arms?"

"Absolutely. Don, put your hands inside mine," she said, holding out her hands to me. I did as she instructed, and she began to speak. "I will embrace your grief and take it away. Rejoice with me, because God will heal Ry. Weep with me, because I will weep when you suffer. God loves you and I believe he has a plan for Ry. Ry may not fully recover, but I know that God has work for Ry to do. I believe that. He will reveal it in time."

In a soft voice, next to my ear, Sister Angeline began to pray. I allowed her healing words to wash over me, although I was struggling with my faith every time anyone mentioned God.

For the first time in days, I felt a sense of peace. As I walked back down the hall to Ry's room, I considered Dr. Benoit's words—*God has a plan for Ry*—and felt maybe she was right. I just needed to be patient.

When I opened the door to Ry's room, I walked in on Alexis and Lynn washing Ry's hair. They were using an unused bedpan as a makeshift sink. The sight of them was so beautiful, it took my breath away. Two lovers, one a mother, whose blood ran in his veins, and the other as wide-eyed as only young love can be. From the doorway, I watched quietly as they gently lathered his hair and rinsed away the bubbles, using only a small cup. Seeing Alexis care for my son brought a lump to my throat

I knew what it was like to be young and watch the person you loved suffer. I knew what it was like to feel so afraid, so vulnerable. A stabbing pain filled my chest, and all of the hurt came rushing back. The whole world felt like it was shifting beneath me, and I did the only thing I knew that would stop it.

I ran. I ran down the hall, down the stairs, and through the big double doors of the hospital. It wasn't until I got to my car and drove away that I felt like I could breathe again.

Chapter 7

Audrey the Butterfly

A few days later, while Ry was in physical therapy, I chose to get out of the hospital for a while. It was a beautiful fall day. The air outside was crisp, but the sun was shining and warm. I found a bench visitor's garden retreat and took a seat, opening a book of poetry I'd brought with me. Off in the distance, I saw a woman in a white coat coming my way. I immediately recognized that mass of dark curls.

"Good morning, Mr. Beville. It's a nice morning for reading," she said as she came closer.

"Yes," I replied with a smile. "I enjoy poetry. It brings a sense of lightness to my world. And please call me Don."

"I do too," she said, and then to my surprise and delight she took a seat on the other end of the bench. "It opens new worlds, and we get to experience foreign views from the poet's eyes."

For a moment, I watched her face moving up and down so sweetly. I always thought I had good skills for social encounters. I usually found conversations with others comfortable and enjoyable, but sharing a bench with a nun who was also my son's doctor, that was somewhat intimidating. Without warning I blurted out, "Why did you become a nun?" I immediately regretted asking such a personal question.

To my surprise, she didn't hesitate to answer. I could only assume it was a question she was asked frequently and was used to answering. So much for my originality. "Well," she said, looking straight ahead, "my mother was an alcoholic and my father was an army doctor. We moved a lot to different bases around the world. They got a divorce when I was eleven and my father decided I would be happier at a Catholic boarding school not far from where he was stationed."

I was taken aback by her direct honesty. In my experience, it was rare for people to be so open, or maybe that was just me. Dr. Benoit turned her head and looked at me as she continued her story. "You see, I needed love, and the nuns gave that to me. They were kind, and their dedication to helping others really stuck with me. There was a space in my heart left behind when my mother went out of my life. The nuns helped to fill it, and I decided early, maybe at age fourteen, that I wanted to be like them, and I also wanted to study medicine."

"I worked in a hospital when I was in college," I said, not really knowing why I wanted her to know that. It was a lifetime ago. Maybe I just wanted her to see we had something in common.

She raised an eyebrow with interest and asked, "Did you study medicine?"

"No, I liked psychology and occupational therapy. But that was another life."

Dr. Benoit focused her gaze on me and for a moment I was able to hold eye contact, but then I had to turn away. I looked down at my poetry book, digging at the corner of the book cover with my nail.

"Can I ask you something?" she said then quickly added, "And please, if I am too intrusive, just tell me."

"Yes, of course," I said. "Ask me anything."

"I understand what you and your family are going through is

very traumatic, and of course you are concerned about your son, but when I look into your eyes, I can't help thinking there is something else weighing heavy on your heart. If it is none of my business, say the word and I will never mention it again, but…" she said, as she reached over and patted my hand, "Should you wish to speak to someone, I am here." Dr. Benoit sat back, leaning against the bench while turning her body toward mine. "Something tells me we aren't speaking of Ry at the moment."

I shook my head, no, unable to bring myself to look at her.

"Audrey?"

I nodded.

We sat in silence for a moment and I knew she was giving me a moment to compose myself. "Would you like to tell me about her? It might ease your burdens to get it off your chest."

I hadn't openly spoken of Audrey in nearly twenty years, although the memories of her floated through my mind often, reminding me of the crazy, sweet days we sang to each other, sitting on a blanket by the James River. Lynn knew about her and knew that I'd been married before, but we never had any deep discussions regarding her. Conversations of dearly departed wives and husbands felt better suited for the elderly crowd. So, my previous life with Audrey was carefully tucked away, like a dusty memoir on a stranger's shelf. But there was a part of her inside me that had never died, infinite, eternal.

Audrey and I had met when she was eighteen and I was twenty-one. I'd felt grown up enough to be married back then, and now, when I looked at Ry and his friends, they seemed like babies. No wonder our parents had been so upset. I would have strangled Ry if he were to get married now.

We were impulsive. Crazy. We'd gotten married after dating for only a few months. We had a mutual friend who had introduced us at a summer party. I'd just finished my first year of college and was working at a psychiatric hospital. She had just graduated from high school and was headed to the University of South Carolina.

I wasn't sure how to speak about Audrey. She had been locked away for so long, it felt strange to bring her into the present world. Looking at Dr. Benoit brought back Audrey's face, so I started there. "She was the most beautiful woman I'd ever seen, with pale olive skin and long black hair. Her eyes were wide and green, and every time she looked at me, I thought I might just die on the spot. At that age, every feeling, thought, and desire was so intense. It was a different time. Life was wild. Life was so simple: we were either making love every chance we had or getting high."

I immediately regretted the words as soon as they came out of my mouth. I was speaking to a nun, and my face instantly turned red at revealing too much.

Picking up on my embarrassment, Dr. Benoit laughed it off and said, "I wasn't always a nun. I remember the passions of youth very well. I just never followed through with them, but yes, they were there."

I laughed, remembering what a pair Audrey and I must have made. "She towered above me at nearly six feet to my five-eight. We were young and full of life, so of course we never thought it would end, but God had different plans. He stole her from me, and I don't think I can ever forgive Him for that." I felt tears coming but managed to block them.

"She was a special person, so young. I wish I could have met her."

I shook my head and added, "I'm sorry. I haven't thought about Audrey in years. Ry doesn't even know I was married before his mother."

"You never told him?" she asked, as a wrinkle formed along her forehead.

I shrugged, feeling a bit silly. "I don't know why I never told him. At first, he was young and there seemed no point, but then so much time passed it always felt strange to bring up. Also, and I know this sounds selfish, but as a parent, we give everything to our kids. Maybe I just wanted to keep her to myself, have that small part of me before I became a dad." I took a deep breath. "The other day, I walked into Ry's room and his girlfriend Alexis was washing his hair. Something about seeing Lynn and Alexis brought the memory of Audrey all flooding back. There were times when Audrey was very ill and I would carry her to the bath and wash her back and long hair. There was something so intimate and sensual. Every night, we would stretch out on the bed and take turns reading stories to each other. Short stories, poems, magazine articles."

"I can see you loved her very much," Dr. Benoit said. "When we experience a shock to the system as you did with Ry's accident, it can bring up past trauma, much like PTSD, especially if we never really dealt with the previous event. Sometimes, acknowledging our anxieties and fears, talking about them, can help you release them. Prayer can help you do that."

I sighed heavily, tired of being told to pray. "Dr. Benoit, I'm going to be honest with you. I have reached the middle of my life, and my Catholic upbringing has been a burden to me. I turned to Mary for her intercession, praying the Rosary, attending confession every Sunday, but my journey through Catholicism is ripe with skepticism. I don't think I can ever make my way back to the church again. Even hearing the word 'God' makes me uneasy. Now I sit here before a nun, who has taken an oath to

Him, struggling with the thought, is the fate of my son in God's hands? I'm sure you've read Ry's medical chart. One serious illness and injury after another. Why would God put this burden on the backs of children? Should I believe God will heal my son or believe in medical science?" I immediately wanted to apologize for my frankness but decided to remain quiet.

"Oh my," Dr. Benoit said as she gave a slight smile. "I have a true doubter before me. Don, salvation lies within. The focus of our belief is put on us to discover the true identity of God. I'm not going to be able to convince you today that my God exists. In time, the Holy Father will reveal his identity to you. I understand your misgivings on the mystery of God. It is not a sin to have them. Do not let your anger over the loss of Audrey blind you to the salvation that God can bring to you."

She pushed her curls away from her face and added, "I have no conflict between my faith in God and the scientific disciplines. God does not seek out children and make them suffer. Injuries, diseases, and other human calamities, I believe, are a normal course of nature. God guides us and gives us the strength to weather these events. I believe in my heart that God wanted me to be a doctor so I could provide aid and comfort to the sick and to understand how science can heal your son. Faith and science are a complex relationship. A patient who has faith that God is guiding my hand and my skills responds more positively to healing therapies. *Credo in Unum Deum.*"

I let her words sink in, desperately wanting to believe them, but the doubt continued to nag at the center of my soul. How could I trust God to save my son when he'd turned his back on me so many years ago?

"Don, it's about faith. God will give you a path. It might have detours, but follow it. I am pleased that God allowed me to find you and Ry. Let's talk some more in the coming days. By the way, Ricardo Reyes Basoalto is my favorite poet."

"Who?" I asked.

"Pablo Neruda is his pseudonym," she answered, tapping my book.

I smiled. She was full of surprises.

Dr. Benoit stood to leave but then turned back and recited Neruda.

"Something started in my soul, fever or forgotten wings, and I made my own way, deciphering that fire and wrote that faint line, faint without substance, pure nonsense, pure wisdom, of someone who knows nothing, and suddenly I saw the heavens unfastened and open."

"That was beautiful, Dr. Benoit, but Pablo was an atheist," I said with a grin.

"Yes, I know. But God loves all his children, even the non-believers."

Chapter 8

The Deep End of the Pool

I knew I was going to be writer and a runner. Sometimes, writing and running were the only things that could clear my head. In the fourth grade, Mrs. Winfield told me that she liked reading my stories during writing period. She said that I had a special gift for content. I fell in love with her. I also liked to run during lunch. My friend, Francis Baugh, and I would leave the back door of Dinwiddie Elementary, scurry across the baseball field and disappear on dirt trails in the woods. I don't know how far we ran. It didn't matter to us. We just ran until we heard the exterior bells announcing the end of lunch period. My life was built on routines. I had a new routine centered on doctors' visits and small updates on Ry. "He asked for water earlier," or "He looked around for a bit." The information took up space in my memory.

I needed a break, and the only way for me to empty my thoughts was to run. Years before, running had become my greatest stress reliever. I decided to take a break from the hospital for one day. I missed my wife, her tender touch, her kiss. She was going to be home soon, so I left her a note.

You, beautiful lady. I have gone for a run. I skipped the sick ward today. Need break. Let's get lunch and drink.

I laced my shoes and disappeared on the black asphalt, under puffy clouds. I don't know how long I ran. It didn't matter. I just ran. My neighborhood this time of year was beautiful. Green yards with multicolored flowerbeds. Everyone took pride in their homestead. Neighbors waved as I went by, unaware of the drastic changes that had occurred in my life.

Over the past few weeks, I had been thrown into a new world with different rules, and running was the thing I could count on to never change. I understood running. I knew how to pace myself and what to do if I grew tired. It was the only thing in this upside-down world that still made sense. I understood the pain that came from running miles along with the rush of endorphins. Running rarely surprised me. In some ways she had become my comforting mistress.

The bistro was on Cary Street, just a few minutes from St. Mary's Hospital. It was one of the few places that served breakfast and lunch all day. A delicious aroma of coffee and freshly baked cinnamon buns filled the air as students from the University of Richmond crowded the large tables. The bistro was alive with the energy of young people. When I arrived, Lynn was just being shown to our table. I caught up with her and gave her a kiss on the cheek. She recoiled from my sweaty face and grimaced. "You're all sweaty," she shrieked.

We sat down and the waitress was kind enough to bring me a clean hand towel to wipe my face. I may have been hot and sweaty, but it was the first time in a long while I felt normal. Lynn and I both needed this break. The day in and day out of hospital life was taking its toll. I needed to hold Lynn's hand and look into her eyes. I needed to connect.

I ordered black coffee with a salad and two hardboiled eggs, while Lynn settled for chicken and a bowl of fresh fruit. When the food arrived, I drowned my eggs in pepper.

"Why do you do that?" Lynn said with a look of disgust on her face.

"My taste buds are getting old and I can't taste things the way I used to. They're my eggs and I can do whatever I want to with them." I could tell she was annoyed, so I stuffed an entire egg in my mouth and gave her a big yolky smile.

"Sometimes I want to change my last name," she said with a laugh. Hearing her giggle sounded beautiful. I could hardly remember the last time one of us had laughed or even smiled. We had started sniping at each other, something we'd rarely done before but now seemed inevitable. We were tense all the time, worried about Ry, and we were taking it out on each other. The previous week was in slow motion. Moments crawled.

I reached into my back pocket and pulled out one of the TBI pamphlets.

"Are you learning anything?" Lynn said, taking a sip of her café con leche.

"You want to know everything or the Cliff Notes version?" I motioned for the waitress to come over and asked her, "Could I see your wine list, please?"

Lynn's eyes widened in surprise. "You're going to drink this early in the day?"

"Why not? It's technically afternoon. Afternoon is close enough to evening."

Lynn gave me *the* look. The one that told me she did not approve of the alcohol. I had to agree. She cared about my health. Twenty years ago, it was about drinking and weed. But I was no longer that person. The sixties and seventies were gone. No more long hair and wild beard. No more turning on, tuning in, and dropping out. I was a respected member of our community. I was a husband and a homeowner, a boss, a publisher of national trade books and, most importantly, a father to an amazing young man who needed me. Lynn's look was a reminder to stay focused on all the things I held dear.

I wasn't sure where to begin the grim story in the pamphlets. When my wine arrived, I took a big gulp, hoping that the alcohol would help me gravitate toward honesty.

"I've read all of these. Some, I just don't want to open again. It's grim," I said in a solemn voice. I took another sip of my wine.

"Please take smaller sips," Lynn said, "or I will have to drive you home."

"I still had hope that he would be able to head to Notre Dame in a few weeks. It is not going to happen. Even going to Notre Dame is going to be a long shot. The chances are high that he will have short-term memory issues." It was a horrific prediction, and the look on Lynn's face told me she felt it too. It was a staggering thought.

"We are so not prepared for this," Lynn said. "When are you going back to work?"

"In a few days. My boss told me not to even think about coming in, but I have some big clients I need to check on." I had been working on producing a coffee table book for the Boy Scouts of America. My designer and his team had gone through hundreds of boxes and scrapbooks of photos and come up with the best ones for the book. It was just a matter of doing a preliminary layout with the text and then getting approval from the Scout Committee to complete the book. I knew my designer would prepare a lovely mock-up for me to take to the national president of the Boy Scouts.

"We'll have to learn as we go," I continued. "Dr. Wilson said yesterday that Ry might be moved next week to a rehabilitation hospital. I'll be thrilled when he's out of bed, even if it is in a wheelchair. Maybe we can take him out in the sun for a few minutes?"

"Yes, that will be nice," Lynn said, and then her eyes began to well up. She quickly brushed the tears away. "No, I will not cry today. Just one day without tears. That's all I want."

I reached across the table to grab her hand. "How about another cup of coffee? I could use another glass of vino." I didn't wait for her to answer, just ordered her a cup as the waitress refilled my glass. "You know, we have no idea what the outcome of this will be," I told her. "He just might get up tomorrow and walk out of the hospital with his memory patterns intact, no deficits, and no seizures." I knew it was a desperate plea, but I wanted my son back, and I wanted to say something to comfort Lynn. She squeezed my hand, letting her fingers brush across my knuckles.

"I love you," she said as she pulled my hand toward her face and kissed it. Then she sighed and added, "There is so much to do. Where do we start?"

"We start in the east," I answered. "Grandma always said the east was where new beginnings started. Each day the sun rises and our soul begins anew."

Lynn smiled and kissed my hand again. "I'm glad I married you."

"I'm glad you married me too. You make more money than I do."

Chapter 9

Tweaking the Script

Telling my parents would need to be a good performance. I did not want to tell them everything. But what details to leave out of the story was troubling me. Hope is a good thing, and I wanted to give them the impression that, in time, everything was going to be all right. At the same time, I didn't want to give false hope in the event Ry never fully recovered.

The last week had been tough. Little sleep, bad food, hospital visits, and anxiety about the work sitting on my desk. I had transitioned from a prized middleweight fighter to a thin featherweight. My mother would notice the weight loss. She always did.

My parents lived in Petersburg, Virginia, almost an hour's drive from the hospital. They loved their grandson. They had cheered him on during his swim meets from the time he was eight and would take him to church whenever they were in town for a visit. Taking Ry to church was no easy task, as he had a difficult time sitting still.

The interstate was quiet for a Saturday night and I was making good time. But it was a trip I didn't want to be making. I wanted to be on a plane, going someplace nice. A plane filled with happy people reading books, wearing tennis shoes, a drink on the pull-down tray. I wanted to look out of the window and watch the plane lift up from the tip of one continent and settle back down hours later on the other side of the world. I didn't care where. Paris, London, Athens would work. But I wasn't. I was in the next chapter of my life, and I didn't like the opening paragraphs. A Robert Frost quote became my mantra: "Life goes on." Anywhere but the center of my chest. Ever since Ry's accident, my heart rate had significantly increased. Maybe it was the stress. Maybe it was the bottle of wine every night. Maybe it was missing my ten-mile-a-day run.

I knew my father would be sitting in his big recliner with the TV flipper in his hand. He loved watching the news, reading papers, really anything to do with politics or world affairs. He could quote Roosevelt and was quick to tell you that Lincoln started the Grand Old Party. My dad had a kind heart, but he also came from a generation that kept their emotions tightly in their pocket.

He'd served his country in World War II by joining the Army-Air Force and had likely witnessed horrible things while stationed near Berlin. No matter how many times I'd asked him, he rarely spoke of his stint, only mentioning once that he'd handed out chocolate bars to kids in Poland. He no doubt had a dusty memoir tucked away somewhere in his soul, full of dark, uncomfortable moments. His plane was a B-17 Flying Fortress. Its mission was dropping bombs on enemy railroads, munition factories, bridges, and on occasion, food drops for our troops. It was a hastily made aircraft that had major flaws, from bad landing gear to poorly designed instrument panels. By the end of the war, over sixty percent of pilots and crew had died in plane crashes or became prisoners of war.

My father and mother had started an elderly daycare center in Petersburg, Virginia, in an abandoned church several years before. Dad sold hot dogs at the Little League games and stayed late to count the money. It made me happy that my dad and mom went on missions to improve human dignity.

Both my parents had grown up on a farm. My dad had nine brothers and sisters. My mother was one of fourteen children raised in a house without running water or electricity. How does a family of fourteen do that? I asked my Aunt Ethel that question once. "A Bible and strict discipline," she said. "Plus, we were cheap labor." My grandmother pulled water up out of a well with a bucket. She milked a cow and then churned the milk into butter. I still remember eating fresh biscuits cooked on the wood-burning kitchen stove. Sweet butter and blackberry preserve on a fluffy biscuit used to start my day. No one knows what a fresh glass of buttermilk tastes like today.

My mother would tell me that growing up on a farm was like nothing else in the world. "You got to work with your family every day. You raised and learned how to support animals, and you knew where your food came from. Your playground," my mother would say, "is wide open spaces as far as you can see."

My imagination ran wild when I sat next to my dad on a tractor. A little pressure from the toe and the beast would take off. By age ten, I'd learned to drive the tractor and helped plow the weeds in between the tobacco rows. I watched my grandfather cry once when a July hailstorm tore through the tobacco field, punching holes in the big-veined leaves. He knew it meant lost revenue. I learned that if you don't feed and water it, it dies, be it plant, livestock, pets, or people. Care of living things comes first.

When there was not enough money or time to fix a problem, you learned to use your brain and figure it out. You understood and witnessed death, and you experienced new life. I had a healthy respect for both. Those early childhood experiences stayed with me as I grew into adulthood, started my career in book and magazine publishing, and became a husband and father. My parents, aunts, uncles, and grandparents all taught me in tough times how to stay focused. They taught me how to shine a searchlight on my problems and find solutions

When I pulled into their driveway, I was sweating. I was not prepared for this. My mother and father would grieve for Ry, just like I was doing. They had always been there for Ry during his other injuries, but this was like nothing any of us had ever imagined.

"Hi, Mom," I said, opening the front door to their brick rancher. She stood at the kitchen sink, cleaning up after dinner. It is what was expected of women of her generation. They fixed the man's meal and then cleaned up. I gave her a hug and asked if she was almost finished.

"What are you doing over so late? Where is Lynn?" She hung up her dishtowel and followed me to the den, where dad was sitting in his big chair.

He got up to hug me, which he liked to do every time I visited. My dad believed in giving me generous amounts of physical affection and loved to ask me analytical questions to keep me on my toes and to see what I knew. He wanted to know how I felt about things. You could say I'd borrowed a few parenting techniques from the old man. I was proud of the way my father had raised me and was happy to engage with my son in the same way.

I sat down on the old sofa that had been in this same room for twenty years. "Dad, would you mind turning off the TV for a minute? I have some news."

"What's wrong?" my mother quickly said. "Did you lose your job? Is someone sick? I knew you looked thin."

"No, Mother. I wish it was that easy." My voice quivered. My dad turned off the TV and the room fell silent. I was on stage. Though I'd stopped smoking years ago, I wanted a cigarette. I looked down at my hands and cleared my throat, looking for the right words.

"Is it a divorce?" my mother wanted to know. She always jumped to the wrong conclusion.

"There's no easy way of saying this, but last week, when Ry was coming home from a restaurant with Alexis, his car was hit by another car at an intersection. Ry's car was spun into a concrete telephone pole. Ry suffered some head injuries."

"Oh God, what kind of head injuries?" my mother asked.

My tongue was stuck to the roof of my mouth. How much should I tell them? Should I mention Ry's black-and-blue face? His eye swollen shut? The eleven sutures across his nose and eyebrow? My dad was just a few feet away, and I reached over to grab his hand.

"Ry is paralyzed on his right side, and he has a serious brain injury."

My parents didn't flinch at first, but I could see the cauldron of emotions building in them. They were like children having just fallen on the floor, the screams from their lungs not yet reaching their vocal cords, a moment suspended, waiting for the shock to pour out as emotion. My dad was the first to break down and sob. Tears fell from his blue eyes and spilled down his cheeks.

My mom wanted to hold hands, and we did. She said a prayer, and I kept my eyes wide open. "Oh Lord, be with us in this time of great need..."

Where do prayers go? Where was my mother sending her prayer and by what means of energy? Would God ponder the request and forward it to one of His angels? Is God like Amazon.com, handling millions of requests per second? Outside, heat lightning streaked across the sky, just over the long green grass of a golf course situated across from my parent's house. A powerful thick fog had rolled into this room, one that made me feel nauseated and my skin hot.

A memory struck me, as fierce as a bolt of lightning. I was a boy, leather reins in my hands, riding my pinto horse, Dusty,

113

across the field. Guiding a horse was my art back then—an essential skill for a kid growing up on a working farm. I joked with my grandparents that I had mastered the tongue of my horse and spoke to him as we would ride through the tobacco rows.

There was a lot of contentment and suffering living on a farm. One's livelihood depended on the rain, the heat, no hail, and plenty of hired help when the crops matured. I loved the hard work, because at the end of the growing season we got paid in cash for our goods. It was about renewal of the family unit. It took the entire family to make the farm work and we helped one another to succeed in our chores. It reminded me of the books I had read about the frontier. But it also made me think of when you are in trouble, turn to your family for help. We were a good herd.

A farm was never without its suffering. And now this farmhouse would have more.

I laid my hand on Dad's shoulder. His tears had soaked through his shirt, leaving spots. His heart had come to grips with the news, but he looked paralyzed with shock. The deeper the love, the greater the grief.

My mother's words of a "merciful God" did loops inside my ears. What was merciful about any of this?

"He has suffered so much in his life. Why can't God give him some peace?" My father said with anger in his voice. "I'd like to extrude the pain Ry has suffered in his short life and into a big bowl and present it to God."

"Amen to that, Dad."

That night, my parents and I sat for a long time, talking about Ry's accomplishments. It was good for them to focus on happy memories, I thought. My dad told stories about his swimming skills and how he was placed on a traveling swim team at age ten, how his swim coach would say, "He can feel the water move over his skin."

"He loved baseball," my dad said. "Ry could play any position but liked first base best."

After a while I said, "I really need to get back home." Lynn was sitting with Ry and the dog needed to be fed and taken for a walk. There was so much to do, all the time now.

"When can we see him?" my dad asked.

"I don't know yet, Dad. Give me another day and I'll ask his doctors. I know he's supposed to be transported to a rehab hospital early next week. I'll call you at the end of the day on Monday." The truth was, I didn't want them seeing Ry until at least some of the bruising and swelling had gone down. I wished to save them the shock of seeing their grandson in such a state. All of our lives were about to take a drastic turn with no foreseeable end in sight. The least I could do was prevent them from carrying around the mental picture of Ry's damaged face. Every time I closed my eyes it was all I could see. If I could save my parents from having the same pain, I would.

A couple of hours later, I drove home with mixed feelings. I was relieved to have finally told my parents about Ry. I'd felt guilty keeping them in the dark, but now it was real. People knew. That cemented Ry's condition in reality. I could no longer pretend this was something that would clear up in a few days. We were now on the path of recovery and there was no turning back.

Chapter 10

Flying Food Tray

As I approached Ry's hospital room, there was a loud crash. My heart sank and I slowed my pace, afraid of what I'd find. An orderly came out of the room with a large white trash bag and walked in my direction.

"What's going on?" I asked him.

"He just used the wall as a backstop for his lunch tray. The food is bad here, but not that bad," he said with a slight smile.

I appreciated him trying to make light of the situation. Embarrassed, I looked at the bag and saw what looked like a smear of mashed potatoes and possibly peas. I gave the man an appreciative nod then continued into Ry's room to find another staff member wiping a splatter of what appeared to be milk running down the wall. Her face was calm, as if this happened every day.

A loathsome string of obscenities was flying from my son's mouth. I'm no shrinking violet, but it was shocking to see him behave that way. Who was this horrible person who'd taken up residence within my son's body? At any moment, I expected his head to spin around and green soup to pour out of his mouth. He shouted at the top of his lungs, his face red. Once I was able to regain my senses, I rushed to his bedside and placed my hand on his shoulder.

"Ry, calm down," I said as I caressed his shoulder.

Thankfully, at my touch, he collapsed back on the bed and the dramatic outburst was over. A fraction of a second later, he looked up at me and said, "Hi," as if nothing had happened. A minute later, he was fast asleep.

We were now close to two weeks from the accident and Ry was becoming more aware of his hospital environment. From what I'd learned about traumatic brain injury, or TBI, hallucinations and aggressive behavior were expected. The doctors had told me this repeatedly, but it still shocked me each time Ry acted out. I was glad Lynn wasn't there. She had dedicated her life to saving babies. Now her only child had disappeared inside the body of an angry man.

Lynn had returned to work since Ry was out of the danger zone and on his path to a long recovery. With outbursts like these becoming more common, she'd begun to disappear into her work. All week she'd been calling me throughout the day to check in on Ry, but had left me alone to deal with the daily routines. She still came to visit every night after her regular twelve-hour shift to hold Ry's hand while he slept, but the exhaustive schedule was taking a toll on both of us. How would we ever cope with this behavior in the long term? Within a day or two he was scheduled to go a rehabilitative hospital. Who knew how long the rehabilitation would take? A couple of months? The rest of his life? The doctors could only guess and leave it up to fate.

Ry's room smelled like sweat and old urine. The trunk of his body lay on his bed like a giant felled oak. During the last two weeks, my son had fallen from an enviable state of physical grace into the awkward dependencies of childhood. No longer was he an elite athlete with national rankings and records and daily four-hour practices. Now he resembled an overgrown child, innocent and flushed in sleep. This was our new reality. One moment he had the rage of a grown man, throwing a tray of food, and in the next he was sleeping like an infant. His grasp of reality had slipped away as the blood had dripped down his chin on the night of the accident. I stood at the end of his bed, a warrior, unarmed and totally unprepared for a battle I didn't know how to win.

With the mess cleaned up, the room fell silent. I settled into a chair by Ry's bed as a nurse came in to crack the curtains, letting a few rays of sunlight creep along the wall at the far end of the room. I scooched my chair closer to Ry and began to read. He liked poetry, so I read some Sandburg, and then a Rilke poem while he napped.

The Panther
From seeing the bars, his seeing is so exhausted
That it no longer holds anything any more.
To him the world is bars, a hundred thousand
Bars, and behind the bars, nothing.
The lithe swinging of that rhythmical easy stride
Which circles down to the tiniest hub
Is like a dance of energy around a point
In which a great will stands stunned and numb.
Only at times the curtains of the pupil rise
Without a sound… then a shape enters,
Slips through the tightened silence of the shoulders,
Reaches the heart and dies.

Throughout the day, I tried to get him to sit up and eat or say something. For most of the morning, as the sun rose higher in the sky and cast a bright swath of light across his face and body, Ry lay motionless.

The days become monotonous. Ry needed no watchman, no father, no mother, no God. His body was a sundial. The light was time. The normal rhythms of light and dark that govern waking and sleeping were irrelevant. He slept; I read. He slept; I took a piss. He slept; I ate pizza. He slept; the physical therapist manipulated his limbs. He slept; I uncorked a bottle of wine and drank it when the nurses were not around. The sun's rays touched his skin, seeping into his pores yet never awaking the joyous energy he'd always relied on, never penetrating inside his pupils nor his brain, nor his soul, nor his heart.

I decided I had a choice to make. Either see a psychiatrist or stop coming to the hospital. I had flashes of seeing him in our Japanese garden, pushing rocks through the sand and laughing. But staring at him in this condition, that person, my son, no longer existed in my universe. He might as well have died, been put in a coffin and slept under six feet of porous soil, yet there he lay in the flesh right before my eyes. I ordered breakfast for him off the hospital menu. When it arrived, I put the tray on my lap and ate his over-easy eggs with bacon and hash browns.

Under normal circumstances, it would be a horrible thing to eat your child's breakfast while he slept. But, nothing about this was normal and I felt no guilt, because Ry wouldn't eat it anyway. If he were awake, an undeserving and underpaid orderly would just be cleaning it off the walls. Better I eat it and save us all the grief.

Time lay on Ry as weightless as air. He was somewhere else. For days he spoke only a few words at a time. "Where is the urinal?" "I need meds." "I want to go home." "I feel disconnected." "Shut the damn curtains." "Get out!" My heart ached for a conversation with my son. Instead, I got grunts and groans and the occasional, "Leave me the fuck alone," shouted at an innocent nurse, whose only crime was trying to adjust his bedding. I would cringe and shuffle and stare at the shiny marble floor, trying to become invisible as I mumbled apologies.

Dr. Benoit had said he would have a hard time processing information. She said I should talk to him slowly, look into his eyes and make some motions with my hand or body when I spoke, because his eyes were not working normally. If I didn't, Ry might not know I was in the room. He might not even understand a question had been asked of him. The thought of my son trapped in his own mind, not even knowing his mother and I were there was almost too much to bear. I was desperate to reach him, to connect in some meaningful way. I would gladly have given up television for a lifetime, never eaten a bite of breakfast again, for just a single sign that my boy was aware of my presence.

On the table next to Ry's bed was a shaving kit. I pulled out a pair of scissors and reached down and snipped a lock of his curly strawberry-blond hair from the back of his head. I had read somewhere that when an elephant encounters the dry, white bones of its kind, it pauses, as if in silent respect, feeling the skull with its trunk. Sometimes, on making such a discovery, the elephant will pick up one of the bones or tusks and carry it around for a while. Biologists didn't have an explanation for this, but I liked to think it was an animal burial ritual. We take the remains of our loved ones, put them in metal boxes and lower them in a hole. An elephant chooses to walk around with his loved one for a while.

I rolled the curl of hair between my fingers for a few seconds, smelling it, then gently pushed the tufts of hair down inside my shirt pocket. I decided to carry it around for a while. Maybe the elephants knew something we didn't. Reducing herd anxiety. At this point I was willing to try anything.

***

At the end of each day when Lynn would relieve me, I would go home, walk the dog, shave, shower, take off my contaminated clothing, fix a grilled cheese sandwich, fill a glass with red wine, make some phone calls to neighbors and friends to update them and let them know when they could come to visit. Then I'd take a nap, wake up and start the car for the trip back to the hospital. Some days I wondered if I had any value. My dreams were gone. There seemed no point in thinking about a future I could not plan. Life was on autopilot for all three of us. The bowl on our kitchen counter began to fill with wine corks. Hangovers became common.

Some days, I would sit on a bench outside the hospital and call my loving, funny, fiery, straight-to-the-point, red-headed Catholic mother. "Mother," I would sing into the phone. "I need some serious insights on how to live my life. I am just hanging on. I want to get in my car and point it west. Mother, I am homesick for peace."

"Don, don't let this event grind you up. I know he has the best doctors. Slow down. Have you or Lynn called your priest?"

I sighed, "No." Again with the advice of prayers.

"We want to see our grandson," she said, changing the touchy subject.

"Mother, I love you. He is being moved to a rehabilitative hospital, and you and Dad can come as often as you like." I hung up the phone, not feeling any closer to being a grown-up.

I thought Ry's recovery would depend on me standing by his bed, stimulating his broken brain. Instead, I was a spectator. A lowly bystander watching from afar. If I was the caretaker of his neurons, the taskmaster, I gave myself an "F," because I saw the same body, the same stone face every day. During the hours I spent in a chair next to him, my eyes had traced his face and body thousands of times. Some nights I would capture his image and then create in my mind an animated figure in a Walt Disney movie feature. I would replay the movie over and over. He became alive in my scenes.

In reality, he lay like a police-chalk figure on a sidewalk. Some nights I would massage his legs, giving extra attention to the paralyzed limb. Before the accident, I wanted to hug him every day but didn't. Now it felt natural to touch him, lay across him, cry on his back. Each morning, I awoke with a positive outlook, remembering what my grandmother said. "New beginnings start in the east." I would convince myself that it was a new day while I sipped black coffee and hoped for a miracle, but by nightfall I became prey to despondency. I just want to go home and pull the cork out of another bottle.

It was in the quiet moments while Ry slept, and Lynn was still at work as the sun began to drop on another day, that the sadness crept in. I allowed myself to think of her, my Audrey. It had been so many years since I'd let her memory creep back in. I'd forced myself to move on, make a new life. Now, as I sat there in the quiet darkness of my son's room, I gave in and reminisced. I let her ghost sit beside me and guide me back to the past, when our life was so rare, with moments of continuous laughter. When we were holding hands or sleeping, I felt I was in a holy place, a place of peace and beauty.

Audrey had always been frail. She towered over me in height but was slight and thin. With her frame, I never thought much of Audrey turning down sweets and candies. It was only after our quickie wedding that I found out about the diabetes she had been hiding from me. When I stumbled across the needles one afternoon, my mind went to the worst-case scenario, heroin. After I confronted her, she finally broke down and told me the truth. She'd been hiding the daily insulin shots for fear I wouldn't be interested in a relationship with a "sick person."

Nothing could have been further from the truth. I loved her so deeply and completely that there was nothing that could chase me away. I felt confident that between the two of us we could handle it. I was going to get my young bride through every obstacle, even if it meant I carried her. Two years into our marriage, when the diagnosis of breast cancer came, it only offered another challenge we would beat. We were young, madly in love, and nothing would stop us. Or so I thought.

One afternoon, I was relaxing in our apartment, smoking a joint and reading a book. Audrey came home with tears in her eyes and told me she had a lump in her breast. I didn't understand much about it. I was too young then to know about the warnings. In my world, she was a fairy princess and I was her knight in shining armor. That was the narrative that played in my head. I had a young man's arrogance telling me I was invincible. In truth, I was woefully ignorant of the ways of the world.

In the coming weeks and months, I was exposed to new terms: oncology doctor, tissue sample, lumpectomy, axillary lymph node dissection, micrometastases, and systemic chemotherapy. What was not in the doctor's narrative were the risks of chemotherapy. Cancer affects the lining of the blood vessels. Add the effects of chemo and dying cancer cells and you get thrombosis, a blood clot. It ended up being the real villain we never saw coming.

At the fifth or six cycle of Audrey's treatment, I drove her to the hospital. Her black hair was gone and she had taken to wearing long flowing scarves over her head. It didn't matter to me; she was still magnificent in my eyes. Over the weeks, we'd become accustomed to the hospital routine. One day, as they were draping the bags over the IV poles, I gave her a kiss and said, "I need some food. I'll be right back." I made my way down to the hospital cafeteria for a Coke and a sandwich. I couldn't have been gone more than half an hour, but when I got off the elevator on Audrey's floor and walked by the nursing station, a man with a Roman collar stepped toward me. "Mr. Beville?"

"Yes," I answered, hoping he wasn't going to hit me up for a donation to some charity. Audrey and I were already broke, and now with her added medical bills we were bordering on destitute. Luckily, a lawyer who had helped us with a rental dispute had put us in touch with some of his wealthy clients, and we were staying afloat by selling Maui Wowie to the upper echelons of Richmond's finest lawyers and dentists.

"I'm Father Nicolas. May I walk with you down to the lounge so we can chat for a few minutes?"

I really didn't want to get into a conversation, but at the same time I didn't want to be rude, so I followed him. He indicated for me to sit down and then began to speak.

I could never remember much from that day. It was like a black space in my mind. I heard the words "blood clot," and then I heard, "The doctors did everything they could, but she passed away." At that, I dropped my cup filled with leftover ice from my to-go Coke. As the pastor continued talking, I watched as the small cubes of ice melted, leaving little puddles on the linoleum floor. It was a small detail I would forget until twenty years later, when a dripping-wet police officer would leave similar puddles on another hospital floor as he explained my son's accident.

One moment I was kissing my young bride on the forehead and the next she was gone. I never had the chance to say goodbye. The curtain came down on my life. No more dancing naked across the bedroom, no more touching our wine glasses on the deck overlooking the beautiful campus of Virginia Commonwealth University, no more reading poetry to each other while sitting in a warm tub filled with bubble bath. In the cruelest flash, the life I knew was over. The cogs of my life had sputtered, stopped, and now were in reverse. How could I ever trust again?

Sitting alone, across from my son hooked up to IVs, I thought about what Dr. Benoit had said, about one trauma triggering another. I'd spent over twenty years pushing the memory of Audrey out of my mind. Every now and again, over the years, she would pop up, but I would immediately refocus my attention on Ry or Lynn. Hell, even our dog. Anything to keep the ghost of young love out of my mind.

I was beginning to see why I often had a physical reaction to uniforms. Priest collars, police uniforms, and doctors' coats were consistent deliverers of bad news.

There were times I wanted to talk to Lynn about how Audrey had begun to consume my thoughts, but it felt wrong somehow. The timing felt off. I knew the amount of stress Lynn was under, and to dump my feelings over my first wife onto her felt selfish. I kept my thoughts of Audrey to myself. In hindsight, maybe that was the wrong decision. Maybe I should have included Lynn in my inner world, but I didn't. Instead, over the next few days, when she would catch me gazing out of a window or pushing my dinner around my plate, and she would ask, "Where are you?" I would lie.

"Here, my love," I would answer as I patted her hand. "I'm right here."

***

At eight p.m., a nurse entered Ry's room to ask if Lynn was going to want a cot. "I know your wife usually does the night shift with your son."

"No, thank you," I said. I didn't want Lynn to stay at the hospital. I wanted to her to come home early with me. I wanted to spend an evening with my wife. Lynn had brought me back from the years of grief hanging over me, and I would be forever grateful to her.

"If you should change your mind," the nurse said, "just push Ry's call button and I will bring one. Will you help me roll him?"

"Sure," I answered. The morning nurse had showed me how to roll him earlier that day, to keep him from getting bedsores.

Ry moaned and briefly opened his eyes as the nurse rolled him on his back. Then, as usual, he fell into his deep, habitual sleep. I lightly rubbed his forearm but he was impenetrable. The nurse quietly pulled the curtains across the window, in case Ry awoke early. "You might not know that brain-injured patients are very light-sensitive. Some of my patients have told me bright light gives them a sensation of a wildfire burning in their brains. The cells can't handle that much stimulation."

"I remember reading about that," I said. A few minutes later, Lynn walked in with a cheeseburger. She brought biggie fries and a Diet Coke. What a blessing. I was starving, and the idea of eating in the cafeteria again was making me nauseous. I'd been downing about a dozen Rolaids to eat the hospital food. I kissed Lynn and said, "I have never loved you more."

She laughed and replied, "Not even on our wedding day?"

"Nope," I laughed, "This sandwich is the greatest gift."

Just as I was about to sit down and dive into my meal, there was a tap on the door. Father Gooch, our local priest, entered the room. He was a gentle and kind man with graying hair and a rounded face. We got the hugs out of the way first, and I set my food down on the table as my stomach rumbled. The three of us talked for a few minutes about how Ry was doing while I mentally prepared to dig into my food. Father Gooch walked over and stood over Ry's bed. I knew what was coming, and with a heavy heart and empty stomach, I remained standing. With his hand on the back of Ry's shoulder, Father Gooch began to pray. "Dear Lord, I ask you to turn this weakness into strength, suffering into compassion, sorrow into joy, and pain into comfort."

I moved to sit, but Father Gooch turned to us and said, "I'll recite a paraphrased version of James 5:13–16. Then I'll place my hands above Ry's head, asking the Holy Spirit to help his body heal itself. This sacrament is about healing. The grace will be with you, Ry, during this time of trauma, during therapy, right up to the moment of recovery. Finally, I will gently rest my hands on the top of his head then anoint his forehead and the palms of his hands. Once the anointing is complete, I'll invite all of you to be quiet for a minute and feel the peace, love, and presence of God."

There was no way those fries were still going to be hot by the time he was done. No way.

For such an unassuming man, Father Gooch was an accomplished orator. The prayer was long. Incredibly long. Lynn stood by the bed, stroking Ry's arm. The nurse stood on the other side, her head bowed at a slight right angle and her lips moving as she repeated some of the priest's words. For a moment, I thought she might actually kneel to the floor in a moment of profound meditation. I stared at my food and wondered if it would be rude if I just took a quick bite.

If God had entered Ry's body, I could not tell. He remained sleeping, and after the prayer we all stepped out into the hall. I picked up my food and held the bag close to me. I was not going to share. We stood in the hallway, silent for a moment, until I could no longer stand it. I put my hand out to quickly shake Father Gooch's. "Thank you so much for stopping by, Father. Please visit again." I knew I was being short with Father Gooch, and I did really appreciate his visit, but I was truly getting weak from not eating all day.

Finally, after what felt like an eternity, Lynn and I sat quietly in the hospital lobby, eating our cold dinner. The lingering smell of hospital disinfectant filled the air. Lynn giggled and said, "I thought for a second you were going to shove Father Gooch out of the door."

I joined in her laughter, finally feeling better now that I had some food in my system. "I love Father Gooch and want him to come back. I hope he didn't feel rushed, but Lord Jesus, I was really feeling weak in the knees."

After a while I said, "Your garden is beautiful." I desperately wanted to have a conversation that didn't include sleeping patterns, medications, and violent outbursts. "All the dogwoods are in bloom. The white kousa dogwood has so many blooms, it looks like it's covered with snow. Have you had a chance to walk through the Japanese garden that Ry and I created?

"Yes, I love all the bamboo plants you and Ry planted. They're thriving. I think we should make a trip to the greenhouse this weekend. Maybe see if they have any late summer sales."

Lynn was the full-time flower gardener in the family. There were flowerbeds on both sides of the house as well as the front and backyard. You name the flower and it was planted somewhere. She tended to them, watered and fertilized them, made sure they were in the right bed for full sun or partial shade. There was always something blooming from May till frost. She was happiest when she was outside planting. On vacation, she'd get homesick for her plants. When she told me the hole for the new bush had to be two feet deep and one foot wide, I learned not to stir her indignation by not complying. My wife brought her measuring tape and measured in millimeters, not inches. She didn't tolerate mistakes in digging. Her art was precise.

"I'm looking forward to spending a quiet night together. Maybe we can get into a nice bottle of Caymus and forget the day," Lynn said as she put her hand on my shoulder.

She was right. We needed to create a sanctuary for us. A safe place where we didn't carry the memories of the day inside. If this was going to be our new normal, we were going to have to adjust. I'd resigned myself to accept that this might be the best it was going to get. I would always push and hope for more but was mentally preparing in case this was it. Only time would tell.

Chapter 11

Dr. Nathan Zasler, MD

Saturday was a rare day when Lynn and I could be at the hospital with Ry at the same time. It was approaching three weeks since the accident, and Ry was still sleeping for most of the day. When he was awake, he barely spoke unless it was to articulate some need, adjusting his pillow or wanting water, something like that. Otherwise, it was silence. When we tried to talk to him, he still had issues with word recall. He would become frustrated and shut down. Physical therapy had improved his right leg and arm movements, but it was his mental state that concerned me the most.

Dr. Benoit stopped in on her rounds, as cheerful as ever. "Good morning, everyone. How is my favorite patient doing today?" She sat in a chair next to Ry's bed and smiled at him.

Ry gave a small wave with his good hand but remained silent.

"Well, he had an outburst yesterday and threw a tray of food against the wall," I said, feeling like I had to confess a crime on behalf of my son in case Dr. Benoit heard about it from the nurses.

"Are his medications causing these outbursts?" Lynn asked. I could tell from the look on her face that she felt as I did. We kept trying to come up for a reason for Ry's behavior, because this wasn't his personality. The Ry we knew was kind and friendly, and we felt like we needed to convince everyone that this was not the real Ry. *Ry would normally never throw food across the room at home. You understand, right? Our son is a good kid.*

Dr. Benoit shook her head. "No, it's not the medications. His brain is healing and it does not know how to react to stimulation. I'm recommending he be transferred to Sheltering Arms Rehabilitative Hospital. He's getting only one visit a day from our PT staff. Since Sheltering Arms is a full-time rehab facility, Ry is likely to be seen three to four times a day." She handed me a card from Sheltering Arms that read, *Dr. Nathan Zasler, Rehabilitative Neurologist, M.D.*

"Well, I don't know how Don is feeling," Lynn said, sounding defeated, "but Ry responds to you, and I think he would be disappointed to be moved to another hospital."

I agreed. Were we were being punished, or worse, given up on? Having Ry discharged and sent to a rehab facility was a punch to the gut. It felt like the staff at St. Mary's was telling us, *Sorry, your son is a lost cause. We're tired of his shenanigans, so off you go. There's nothing more that we can do. He's your problem now.*

Of course, this was not at all what was happening, but sometimes, what is actually happening and how we *feel* about what is happening doesn't precisely align. I knew about Sheltering Arms. In 1989, I had worked with Anne Lower, who was on the Board of Directors, to produce and edit a history of the hospital. I toured the facility and met many of the nurses, physical therapists, occupational therapists, and a brilliant staff of medical psychologists. Sheltering Arms was the best, but still, I couldn't shake the feeling of abandonment.

Dr. Benoit immediately tried to reassure us. Taking hold of

Ry's hand, she looked into my son's eyes and promised, "I'm not leaving my favorite patient. I would never do that to you, Ry. We plan on getting you back to Notre Dame. I want to hear about those swim records you're going to break. I'll still come over and work with your new doctor." She smiled and said, "You're going to like Dr. Zasler. And guess what they have there?"

"More doctors and nurses," Ry muttered.

"Yes, more doctors and nurses," she replied with a hearty laugh. "But they also have a pool."

Hearing that, Ry smiled briefly before closing his eyes and drifting off. It still amazed me how fast he could fall asleep. We followed Dr. Benoit out of the room. Out in the hall, Dr. Benoit said, "I don't know if he'll remember the conversation about the pool at Sheltering Arms, so you might want to remind him later today. I think we can put together a more aggressive recovery program there, especially since the physical therapists are accustomed to working with TBI patients and the disruptive behavioral consequences an injury of this type can cause."

The more Dr. Benoit spoke, the more my enthusiasm began to grow around the idea of an aggressive physical approach to Ry's recovery. He's an athlete and had been injured before. Because he understood the process of physical therapy, maybe Ry would attack it the same way he had in the past when he was injured. I imagined my son making a miraculous recovery once he got into a gym, growing more confident each day as the strength increased in his arm and leg. Lifting weights, being on a treadmill—these things were as natural to Ry as breathing. I could only hope that returning to this environment would be like coming home for him. Maybe it would trigger something in his brain to bring him out of the fog.

So far, he had not been responding to any attempts of

physical therapy. The physical therapist tried to work on his forward mobility and standing with the support of a walker. The hospital staff also attached ropes to the trunk of his body, holding him upright as he walked along a raised walkway in the therapy room, but it had been a struggle for the PT team to even get him out of bed. He just did not want to cooperate. Was it depression? Anger? Disappointment? Whatever it was, something had to change. The staff kept reminding me, this was typical TBI behavior.

The last three weeks of watching my son slowly disappear into himself reminded me of the years I worked in a psychiatric hospital. In my mid-twenties, I did three years psychoanalytic training working in a maximum-security psychiatric ward. What did I learn as I calmly sat next to patients every day as they stared through me? I came to understand their perception level of fear and could see the pain in their eyes. Their fear was that they were not going to get better, and I had to change that by reassuring them that they had within themselves the ability to make small gains every moment of the day.

There was also the self-stigmatization that by having to be confined in a mental hospital, they were somehow a mentally weak person. I worked every day to rebuild their self-esteem. I coaxed them to articulate their successes in the past and assured them that their current situation was a small setback in the whole scheme of things. Medication opened the door to recovery, but with every session with them I focused on laying out the idea of having enthusiasm for living in the moment. With kind words, I spoke of making small moments in their lives a celebration. "Celebrate the wind blowing through the trees; celebrate each dinner you have with your wife or child; celebrate singing church hymns."

After Dr. Benoit left us, I returned to Ry's room and pulled a seat up to his bed. I was glad to see he was once again awake and staring up at the ceiling. "Ry, I know this situation has knocked the breath out of you. But you have been knocked down before." My experience at the psychiatric hospital had taught me to keep Ry's emotions and reactions in check. Talk it out. Talk it out.

I helped Ry sit up, raising the back of his bed. "It's just you, me and your mother today, Number One Son." A smile came to his face.

"Dad, I feel weak," he replied. "Close the…" The word for blinds eluded him, so he pointed toward the window saying, "Too bright."

Lynn closed the blinds just enough to reduce the glare. "Going home and getting you back in the pool is everyone's goal," she said, while keeping a smile on her face to focus on the positive. "Dr. Benoit let us know that they will be moving you tomorrow morning." Lynn continued to nod and smile. It was the same smile she had when she was trying to convince me of some new health kick, she wanted us to try. I had to admit, it usually worked. I would start off with a no, then another no but in a short time would find myself enthusiastically going along with a plan that included giving up wine and swallowing a handful of horse pills with a thick, green, grassy-tasting concoction three times a day.

I left Lynn to work her magic, hoping that by the time I got back, Ry would be chomping at the bit to be transferred to Sheltering Arms. I made my way down to the lobby of the hospital and called my mother from a payphone.

"How is he?" my mother asked before I could even say hello.

"They are moving him tomorrow to Sheltering Arms

Rehabilitative Hospital. They have a pool there, and the staff, I've been told, work with brain-injured kids and adults all the time."

"Can we come over to visit tomorrow?" she asked with a shaky voice.

I suddenly felt sorry I had called. "I think it would be okay, but let me check with his new doctor tomorrow." I quickly got off the phone and leaned back against the wall. I knew they wanted to see their grandson, but I hated hearing my mother sound so nervous. It made me feel like a little boy and right now I needed to be a father, not a scared son.

I knew the only way to get through this was to continue to move forward, but leaving the hospital was scary. It felt final. That was all they could do, and now we were on our own. I could only hope Ry had it in him to dig deep. This would be the biggest fight of his life. I knew he could do it, but did he?

The next morning, Ry was taken by ambulance to the inpatient rehabilitation center. Lynn had been called in to work a shift on a day she was supposed to have off. I was on my own to drive over to Sheltering Arms to begin the next phase of our lives. It was only five miles from the hospital, but it felt like it was a world away. I was nervous, excited, and completely unprepared. I had just gotten used to the routine at St. Mary's, and although it was tedious and dull at times, at least I knew what to expect.

I'd read up on Sheltering Arms and knew it had an impeccable reputation, but still I couldn't stop my mind from replaying the horror stories you read about: places where patients sit in the hallway for hours with no one coming to help. Would I need to stay by Ry's side twenty-four hours a day to make sure he wasn't forgotten, sitting in a wheelchair, staring into space in some far-off corner of the rehab center? My mind was wild with all the possibilities of what could go wrong.

By the time, I arrived at Sheltering Arms, I was shaking with anxiety. I'd convinced myself I'd agreed to send my son into the bowels of hell but, thankfully, I couldn't have been more wrong. Approaching the complex, I began to relax. Although the building was old, the grounds were vast and shaded with beautiful hundred-year-old oak trees. The historical architecture reminded me of an elite east coast university.

I entered the main doors and saw expansive halls with green walls. The nurses and staff were friendly as they passed me, and I didn't see a single neglected patient wandering the corridors.

A nurse showed me to Ry's room and I entered to find him peacefully sleeping. The drive over had probably been hard on him. I took a seat on his bed and within moments there was a sharp rap on the door.

"Hello, I'm Dr. Zasler, head of the Neurological Rehabilitation Center here at Sheltering Arms. How are you, Mr. Beville?" He didn't wait for an answer as he flipped through Ry's chart and continued talking. "I spoke to Dr. Wilson and Dr. Benoit this weekend. They'll be consulting with me on Ry's case but I'll begin treating him here."

"Good morning," I muttered, looking at him for some enthusiasm in his body language. "I have heard good things about this hospital, and they have a pool." Ry opened his eyes and looked around the room at the sound of the word "pool."

"Why don't we go down the hall to the conference room so we can chat about the treatment plan for your son?"

I cleared my throat, glancing at Ry. "No," I said politely. "I think you should share your thoughts with both of us. The treatment plan is about him."

"That's fine," Dr. Zasler said, glancing over at Ry and then sitting down in a chair facing us.

Based on Dr. Zasler's appearance, I guessed he was a Hollywood plastic surgeon. Maybe that was an unfair stereotype, but he looked like he was straight out of Beverly Hills, sporting designer Gucci shoes that I imagined he wore on his yacht while popping bottles of Dom Pérignon. He had a round face and a thick moustache and was deeply tanned, as if he had just returned from a week on an island. The three top buttons on his silk shirt were open, exposing a thick triangle of dark black hair. I expected to see a gold chain dangling from his neck.

His shirt's floral pattern reminded me of the large aromatic flowers that bloom in the Amazon jungle. My wife could have identified the species. An intoxicated person might have been tempted to lean into one of the flowers and inhale. Maybe he had just dropped in from playing a round of golf. *Damn,* I thought. *My son's future is in the hands of a golf pro.* He moved his hands to emphasize the importance of his words and spoke with a New England accent. Maybe Boston? This was the guy Dr. Benoit spoke so highly of? The anxiety I had just released was creeping back. My palms began to sweat.

"Dr. Benoit said that you were a book publisher. Anything I might have read?"

"Probably not, unless you like reading sports books or coffee table museum art books. I also teach a writing seminar at the University of Richmond."

"The reason I ask, I have just finished writing a book on brain plasticity after severe concussion."

Was he seriously pitching me his book proposal in the middle of my son's treatment plan? I stared at him blankly, not knowing what to say. I expected he would move on when I didn't respond, but he didn't. After an awkward moment, I finally said,

"Let's talk later. My company does the editing and printing of several medical books for Lippincott." That seemed to please him and he nodded and looked back at Ry's chart.

Looking back up he said, "I think I remember seeing your son's photo in the paper last month. He set a new state record in the butterfly when the championship meet was held here in Richmond."

"Yes, that's correct," I said, feeling impatient. That event had vanished from my memory, and I didn't want to explain my family's history to another stranger. He was trying to be courteous, and a good doctor is one who takes an interest in your whole life—but I wanted our lives back. For two weeks, I had listened to so many plans to speed Ry's recovery. Now I was going to have to listen to another one. I tried to keep my brain on a short leash and be polite, but I wanted honesty. "Have you had a chance to review his X-rays or CT scans?" I asked, pressing the doctor to get to the point.

"Are you sure you don't want to walk down to the conference room to discuss Ry's prognosis? We can stop by the coffee shop."

I looked over at Ry, curled up like a cocoon, his beautiful body drained of all its energy. For eighteen years, his mind had been blessed with electrified biochemistry. Now, the electrical dance of energy grew dim. What physical mechanics no longer worked? Had his ability to generate language and thoughts and understand his emotions been compromised? The richness of his life lay in the hands of this rehabilitative hospital and the flashy doctor standing across from me. I wondered if Dr. Benoit would keep her promise to continue working with him.

"When do you think he might be able to leave the hospital? When will he get the movement back in his arm and leg? What about cognitive functions?" I wanted all the facts in their raw unpleasantness. I didn't want any more elusive medical jargon.

Dr. Zasler began to speak, and I sat staring at Ry as anxiety whipped through my brain. Two weeks ago, I was content with my life. I had purpose and a son who broke records. My only concern was how I was going to navigate the silence filling our empty nest. Now the sound of my son not speaking made me want to scream.

This was not a blue mood or the everyday doldrums. I recognized this as depression and could no longer deny it. My body and mind had been trained to run 26.2 miles in twenty-two different marathons, including three Boston Marathons, and I could still run across the finish line. But grief—well, grief is exhausting. Grief is a stake in the heart. Grief is pure pain. I didn't want to move. For the last two weeks, my mind had been clicking in the fast mode, trying to figure out what to do next. Every time I thought I had things organized, there was another bump in the road. Another piece of bad news. Another string of decisions to make.

I could hear Dr. Zasler talking but his voice became muffled, as if he were speaking to me from a long distance. They were all words I'd heard for weeks. They echoed off the walls of my inner ear: *paralysis, personality changes, memory loss, no internal time clock, unable to make an analytical decision.* There was a hopeless chasm between Dr. Zasler and myself, and my mind would not let me jump to the other side of it. I glanced out of the window, where all the trees were brown from the drought. My life felt like the leaves on the dogwood tree, curling and dying in the late summer heat.

The relationship I had created and nurtured with my son was dissolving. Would Ry remember our Boy Scout trips, the outing at the beach each year, the stories I read to him each night? Would he remember the garden we'd built together? Instead of basking in the light of my son's life, I was about to become a caretaker to a perennial child. Was I now relegated to the sidelines, left to watch other people's kids live healthy, full lives? Go off to college and mature intellectually? No one could tell me anything good or noble would come from this type of suffering. My despair was something to carry around with me, like the elephant bearing the bones of his kind.

Years ago, I walked into my grandmother's room at the Medical College of Virginia, where she was being treated for advance-stage cancer of the abdomen. I was told that the cancer had spread to most of her organs. There was nothing more they could do except keep her medicated with morphine. I could still remember the nurses walking around her bed with their rubber-soled shoes that made squeaking noises on the tile floor as they hung more bags of fluids and painkillers on the IV poles. I stood there, watching my beloved grandmother slowly pass away. I sat across from Dr. Zasler, feeling that same black numbness. Helpless. Alone. Fearful. A heart pounding out of my chest day and night. As I began to sob, Dr. Zasler leaned over and put his hand on my shoulder. "I will make sure he goes to Notre Dame.

Still our future felt grim. I glanced over to Ry and discovered that his eyes were wide open and looking up at the ceiling. Could his brain even process the meaning of Dr. Zasler's words? And even if it could, would he be able to retrieve what he was hearing in a few days, or a few hours? How long would he be devoid of word recall to make complete sentences? I put my hand on his leg and rubbed it. I wanted a sign from Ry that he wanted to hear what Dr. Zasler was going to say. I wanted some signal, maybe a glance or a grunt. *Ry, I can't make these decisions alone. I wanted*

*him to speak about what he had just heard from Dr. Zasler. He
had to realize how dire his recovery was going to be. He had to
be a part of this process.*

I had not had a migraine for years but when I closed my eyes,
I saw patches of wavy lights that resembled jagged butterfly
wings floating across my vision. My temples felt like a vise was
closing on them. This flood of information had overloaded my
sensory receptors. I thought of the poem I'd read to Ry in the ICU
by Ranier Maria Rilke.

It's possible I am pushing through solid rock
In flint-like layers, as the ore lies, alone:
I am such a long way in I see no way through
And no space: everything is close to my face.

I shook my head and the white-and-blue zigzagging lines in
my vision disappeared. "What is your prognosis for his
recovery?" I asked, looking at Dr. Zasler while fearing I was on
the verge of a panic attack.

"He's telling you I'm fucked for life," Ry announced while
still staring at the ceiling. The sound of his voice startled me. Dr.
Zasler's eyebrows shot up, I could only guess he was also
surprised.

I immediately had to stifle a laugh. It was the most beautiful
thing I'd ever heard. Usually Ry's angry outbursts rattled me, but
this time was different. His use of the word "fuck" strangely
made me feel more energetic. It was beautiful and poetic,
considering Ry's condition. What muddled information was his
bruised brain intercepting? Maybe the word "fuck" had a new
ritual meaning in his mind. Or perhaps it just meant he felt
fucked. Either way, Ry comprehending that Dr. Zasler was telling

us he was fucked gave me hope that perhaps he wasn't totally fucked after all.

He was alive, like a child yelling into the spaces of a deep canyon to hear an echo. He was proclaiming his existence, his self, even if it was an angry self. In the middle of Grove Avenue and Westmoreland Street in Richmond, Virginia, in a few short seconds, the course of Ry's life had changed forever. If he had been going just three miles per hour faster or slower, he would be swimming at the Rolfs Aquatic Center at Notre Dame. My grandmother told me once, after our best milking cow suddenly died, "Happiness and sorrow ripen on the same vine." Happiness is vital for our survival. Happiness leads to enthusiasm. The Greeks called enthusiasm *en theos*—a God within. Did Ry still possess a God within? Feeling fucked was about right.

"I know this is difficult for everyone in your family," Dr. Zasler continued, graciously ignoring Ry's outburst. "Starting tomorrow, you'll meet the team that will help Ry with his recovery. We'll do some diagnostic neuropsychological evaluations to test his memory, attention span, and perhaps an IQ test if he'll allow it. Dr. Hays is our neuropsychologist. "He has been on our team for twenty years."

"So, there is no magic dust here, I suppose?" Without an alternative, I had to put all my faith in this man with the laidback appearance. Dr. Benoit told me he had published several peer-reviewed articles in scholarly journals on neurological recovery after brain trauma. Maybe he could do magic. Please do magic.

"No, there isn't any magic, Don, but there's a creative team of people here that will help him realize his dreams of going off to college one day."

"How long will you keep him on steroids? I've heard about a lot of negative side effects." Ry's face was already swollen and

142

his mood swings more pronounced.

"Drug therapy is essential in this early stage. The brain is a complex biochemical factory and the quicker we can restore normal stasis, the faster the recovery will be."

Dr. Zasler got up to leave, shaking my hand as Ry struggled to push himself up. Dr Zasler reached over and put his hand on Ry's leg.

"Ry, here is what I am sure of. I know your pedigree. The athletes I have treated do well with aggressive physical therapy as well as cognitive sessions. I am going to be honest though. It requires motivation on your part too. Work with me and the team. You will go home soon. I want to walk into this room in a few days and see a new person."

Ry came into the world a full-throated exuberant. Full of excitement in everything he did. He skateboarded, he swam, he hiked in the Boy Scouts, he wrote poems and short stories in elementary school. Now, as I looked at him, I didn't see my outgoing, vivacious boy. His body movements were slow. Would he ever reach the same level of conditioning again? Ry's recovery would be long, and maybe he was right, maybe he was "fucked," but as long as my son wasn't giving up, I wouldn't either. We would have to take one painstakingly slow step at a time, and I vowed I would be there for him for each and every one.

Chapter 12

New Brain Patterns

"What is two plus two?" Dr. Hays, the neuropsychologist, asked Ry.

"You've got to be kidding me," Ry shouted back. He was also fuming about the new bright red plastic band on his wrist that read "FLIGHT RISK."

He had been moved to a locked neurobehavioral ward with twenty-four-hour surveillance and a locked elevator. It wasn't unusual for brain-injured patients with displays of psychosis or aggressive behavior to be placed in a protected ward like this one. I had cheered the decision, as trying to get Ry to do simple tasks had become an exhausting battle. Every request from a staff member was answered with angry sarcasm.

"Why?"

"I don't want to."

"How does that help my leg?"

"Since when are you my boss?"

"Mom, Dad, get me out of here."

It went on like this daily, making me miss the days when he silently stared off into space. At least the atmosphere was peaceful.

I was sitting across the room in a very uncomfortable chair that had been worn down by other parents watching their kids go through this process of daily PT, OT and cognitive functioning tests. I was oblivious to what was happening outside these walls as I listened to the repeated commands of Dr. Hays. The room was stuffy, with no air movement.

"Ry, I am sorry to hear about your accident," said Dr. Hays. "I saw on your chart that you are going to Notre Dame."

"Was," Ry said.

I waited for a sentence to float through his lips. I was disappointed.

"The reason for this simple test is to give me a baseline on where we need to concentrate your therapy. You have had a solid blow to the left side of your head. Do you remember any details of the accident?"

"No."

My son was not a cooperative patient. Although I kept telling myself that progress was just around the corner, the truth was I could not see the finish line. "Thank you for being so patient with him," I said to Dr Hays. Ry glared at me. He hated it when I apologized for him.

"I was on the UVA. swim team," Dr. Hays said. "I knew you were a swimmer when I walked in the room. You don't get shoulders like that from riding a bike," he remarked, smiling.

"What stroke?" Ry was reluctantly showing a bit of interest in the doctor.

"Well, mostly backstroke, but occasionally I was on the eight hundred freestyle relay team. Ry, I would like for you to count backwards from ten. When you get to zero, I want you to stand, and I will help. Take both hands and walk your fingers up the wall, like a spider slowly moving upward."

"I am tired. Can I sit and rest?" Ry asked. "I really don't want to do this."

"Ry, my job is to assess what barriers you might have in

getting back to swimming. Getting to Notre Dame. Okay? You work with me, and the minute I think you are ready, I will take you down to the pool myself. Now, count backwards from ten, and when you get to zero, stand and put both hands on the wall, and walk you fingers as high as you can."

As Ry began slowly counting, "Ten... nine... seven..." I looked down at Dr. Hays' open chart on the chair next to me. At the top of the page he had written, "Cognitive Remediation," and below that line, "Identification of Treatment Barriers."

After taking more than thirty seconds to count ten, Ry finally stood up with my help and began the gradual movement of his fingers up the wall. The right hand made it less than a foot up the wall. I did not know if that was progress. At least he had complied.

Ry was on a new path now, and so was I. Everything had to be re-examined as we entered an unknown realm of challenges. My sense of urgency to get Ry's brain and body working again became a hunger. A quest. I was good at becoming obsessed with things. You have to be a little obsessive to run twenty-two marathons. As I stared out of the window, I saw my face reflected in the glass. And in my face, I saw Ry.

I realized Ry was good at living life intensely and passionately too, or at least he had been. He needed to get that back, but how? What could fire that spark in him? He was a gifted world-class swimmer who had put his body on the line twice a day in the pool for the past ten years. He knew how to push through pain and injury, but how hard would he have to work to overcome a brain injury? This was a different type of injury.

We needed to work together as father and son. We had to face reality and rearrange our lives into new patterns. We still had two weeks to play with the timeline for leaving for Notre Dame.

Or should we not push? Let his brain heal and set our target for January? His dream, well, my dream too, was for him to be accepted into a rigorous academic program and swim on a national ranked swim team. Notre Dame provided both. Oh my, what do we do now?

This journey had to be momentous, a spiritual and physical pilgrimage. I had to help him search deep inside himself to restore that hunger to compete, to thrive, to find his dance of energy. How could I help him reconnect with his personal destiny? What Ry needed was a task-relevant focus. The hospital had a pool—but how would I get him in the water when I couldn't even get him to sit in a wheelchair for a ride to the cafeteria? Ry intrinsically loved the activity of performance and winning. He needed to feel the water on his skin again, and soon. Even when he was six and dove off the blocks in a neighborhood swim meet, his exuberance for winning fueled his achievements. He always wanted to swim a few more laps in practice than the other kids.

The next day, the therapists were focused on getting him to move his legs. The atmosphere in Ry's room was tense, and I waited nervously for Ry's creative swearing to begin.

My son did not disappoint. No matter how many times I apologized to his caregivers, I still felt mortified by my son's offensive language. These people were trying to help him, and yet he cursed them to pieces. Could he not see they were on his side? Cathy Armstrong, one of his occupational therapists, told me it was a typical response for brain-injured people, as they have poor impulse control.

Each day, rehabilitation team members would divide their time between physical improvement and cognitive improvement. They would wrestle Ry out of bed and help him to walk down the hall with a walker. Therapists would ask him to count backward from a hundred by six. It was a difficult task on an average day for anyone, but for him it was even more frustrating, as the cells controlling logic had been damaged. On this particular day, Ry's performance was a D plus.

After multiple attempts to get past ninety-four and on to eighty-eight, Ry had had enough. "I have to piss," he shouted. "I want everyone to leave my room!"

"Ry, that is rude," I said gently. "These people are here to help you." I fidgeted, raising my body up and down on my tiptoes in a nervous motion. It was my way of trying to stay calm.

"Ry you are going to be fine," Cathy Armstrong says in a calm voice. "Tell me how you feel?"

"How do I look?"

"You have some bruises."

"So I am not well. I feel worse."

"You are Ry Beville and you are going to Notre Dame to swim?"

"I was."

"You are going to stay with us for a while. This is a good place for you to be right now. You ok with that?"

"Yeah."

"Do you know anything about Sheltering Arms?"

"Nothing."

"Do you want to know about what we do here?"

"I don't care."

I could not be calm about how this was going. Not in the slightest. I wanted to walk over to his bed, jerk him up and shake the ever-loving shit out of him. As soon as that thought appeared in my brain, I suddenly felt guilty. My son has a brain injury and I knew he had little control of his emotions.

One of Ry's treatment team members, Stephanie, seemed to

realize I was about to explode with anger. She gave me a gentle smile and asked if I'd walk outside with her. "Maybe we should go on a quick tour of the hospital, Mr. Beville. We can stop by the cafeteria and get some coffee."

Why was everyone always offering me coffee? Didn't these hospital people ever drink anything else?

As soon as we were out of the room, I muttered, "I need to be on meds." That statement was a carefully calibrated revelation. I knew I was getting depressed and my current alcohol consumption didn't help. The evolution of the malady was making stirrings in my brain. I wanted desperately to seek counseling for my deteriorating condition, but where was the time? My son was not getting any better that I could see, and the obligations at work were pressing me like a vise. Clients were calling me daily to ask me about the progress of their book projects.

"Good morning, Don. This is Richard at the Virginia Historical Society. I was wondering when we might be getting our printing quote for the *Virginia Westward Movement* book?"

"Good morning, Don. This is Beverly at the University of Virginia Press. We need to see the corrected page proofs for the Eldridge Bagley art book."

"Good afternoon, Don, this is General Taylor at the Marine Corps Association. We're ready for you to produce another fifty thousand copies of the *Guide Book for the Marines*. Can you come up to Quantico tomorrow?"

I would call them back from, trying to buy more time and making flimsy excuses as to why I wasn't in the office. I kept Ry's accident a secret, afraid that if they should know the truth, they might feel I wasn't up to the task and go elsewhere. The last thing I needed in the face of everything going on was for my business to go south. To say I was stressed was an understatement.

Stephanie was perky and young, which immediately irritated me. What could she possibly know of such things? With a cheery smile she said, "I know you feel this life event is impossible to cope with, but it's not. You need to give up the idea that Ry will not recover. Let go of that idea. By letting go, you will be free. Dr. Benoit says to give one hundred percent of your concentration to being in the moment."

Great. I was dealing with the Yoda of the rehabilitation world. Just what I needed: someone telling me that everything would work out fine if I could only breathe in the good and exhale the bad. How do you exhale out an automobile accident that flipped our lives upside down? Didn't she understand that if I could have done that I would have by now? I would have exhaled myself inside out if it would heal my son.

Mediate. Pray. Breathe. Well-meaning words by well-meaning people, but they made me twitch with frustration. I wanted fix-it words. I needed action words. Where were the words that were going to help me figure out how to tape my son back together? If Stephanie had some of those words, I was all ears.

Still, I had nothing better to do on our way to pump more caffeine into our systems, so I figured, why not make conversation and humor her? Being polite had been drilled into me as a child. I excelled at it.

"What do you mean?" I asked.

"Well, we're walking right now. Give one hundred percent of your body and mind to this act."

I gave her a sideways glance, letting her know I wasn't convinced. She chuckled and added, "Just try. You will feel alive, and you will get joy from the act of your steps moving you forward."

I stopped walking and looked at her. "I don't know... it all seems a bit..."

"If you don't feel any better, we can always go back to Ry's room and clean his latest meal off the wall," she said with a little grin.

There wasn't much for me to lose, and I couldn't imagine feeling worse, so I tried to concentrate on her suggestion. I turned and took my first step while trying to push any thoughts away. *Just walk.* I took another step. *Focus on walking.* I wanted to relax but my mind was in a gallop. It felt impossible to slow all of the thoughts that swirled in my head. I thought back to my younger years, before I had become a father and a provider. I remembered the way Audrey and I would sit across from each other on the floor after smoking a joint. We would place a hand on the other's chest and close our eyes, listening to the beating of each other's hearts through our fingertips. It was some real hippy-dippy shit but it always brought me peace.

Breathe in, breathe out. Breathe in, breathe out...

Damn, I thought, *it's actually working.* There I was, walking down a long hallway, practicing acts of mindful thinking. I wanted to reach out and grab her hand to thank her for giving me the relief of a few moments of peace. My thoughts shifted to the past summer, and I saw Ry's quick smile, the warmth and energy in his actions. I missed my son. I wanted him back.

"Don," Stephanie said, "life can be like thunder sometimes. And at other times it can be as peaceful as the sound of a distant river. How you think will determine which you hear. I noticed on Ry's chart that he's going to Notre Dame."

"Yes, he *was* going."

"He *will go* in time," she reassured me. "My cousin went to Notre Dame and he would send me the most magnificent postcards of the Golden Dome. He used to tell me it was painted in fourteen carat gold. Is it?"

I had misjudged Stephanie, something I was doing a lot of in my constant state of exhaustion and irritation. She had a relaxed, graceful manner, and it did put me at ease. "I don't know about the fourteen carat gold," I said with a smile, "but it is beautiful. The building sits high in the city skyline, and there are spotlights on it at night. It's the first thing you see in the dark when you approach South Bend on the interstate."

"I would love to see it," she said.

"I think most people think of Notre Dame for its sports, but there's a long tradition of scholarly inquiry and social service participation. Each semester, every student must perform community volunteer work."

"That's excellent. I admire people who can be sympathetic to the less fortunate and offer their skills to make the community a better place." Stephanie looked so young but she spoke beyond her years.

"Ry did a lot of volunteer work this summer. Twice a week he went to a local hospital and read the daily newspaper to patients." I was growing more excited talking about Notre Dame. So much so, I almost forgot where we were.

"My cousin said he was shy and that his community work at Notre Dame helped him with his self-confidence and self-esteem. I think helping others makes you feel better about yourself and helps you have a positive view of your life," Stephanie added.

Not long ago, my life felt simple and seemingly boundless. My book-publishing career had offered me the opportunity to interact with two presidents and afforded me the position of having lunch with generals in the Army and Marine Corps. I had a framed letter on my wall from General Colin Powell, the Joint Chief of Staff at the Pentagon, congratulating me on the coffee table book I had produced on the Marines in the Gulf War. My picture had been in the newspaper with famous artists and I was making more money than I could spend. Life was good. My family was still together and I had enough free time in my life to pursue my passion of running.

Now I was moving down a corridor of a rehab center practicing mindful walking. Outside the cafeteria, I looked around and took in the people around me. All walks of life, all shapes and sizes, with one thing in common. They were all fighting to get their lives back. There was no way to know what those lives were before; some may have been better than others. Some I may have envied, some I may have pitied, but it didn't matter. They were *their* lives, and whatever they may have looked like, they were worth getting back to.

Tears came to my eyes as one child with a bent hand slowly pushed his chair, one slow turn at a time. He smiled at me when he crossed the threshold to the cafeteria. I worried that this was going to be my son, struggling for every small victory that most of us took for granted. Would I resent others for staring the way I stared now? Would I forever feel compelled to explain to every passing stranger, "You should have known my son before, he was something special."

I knew these were wounded individuals who had lives and futures, just like Ry. Their lives had been changed in an instant, just like Ry's. These were the walking wounded, and the sight terrified me. How was I supposed to be my son's greatest cheerleader, his biggest fan, his inspiration and supporter, when I was crippled by the fear of what the rest of Ry's life might be like? And yet, I had no choice. We had to move forward in our new life.

Sometimes it's the "have-tos" of life that are the only things pushing us forward. I never thought I would survive the loss of Audrey, but the have-tos kept me pressing on. Now it was the same. Each day I awoke with a list of have-tos. I had to check on Ry. I had to call his doctors. I had to try and get him to sit up. I had to… I had to… I had to… It felt like it had been ages since my have-tos and my want tos had merged into a single task. They used to all the time, and I regretted not appreciating it more in the past.

I could hear the chapel bells from the nearby church, and I counted twelve for twelve o'clock as we made our way into the dining hall. I felt emotionally paralyzed, frozen in my spot. The best I could do was push one foot in front of the other. Maybe that's the best any of us can do?

Inside the cafeteria, brightly colored posters hung from the ceiling, displaying sumptuous-looking fruits and vegetables. Beautiful young people adorned the food art, happily sipping their soup while sitting at a sunny window. One young woman sat with a cat curled up in her lap and gazed into the distance with an expression of peace and serenity. I thought the New Age art display might have some significant practical utility in improving the psychological wellbeing of the damaged minds sitting in the room. It was relaxing and made me want to close my eyes and forget everything that had happened in the last weeks. This journey was testing my endurance and my capacity for sheer misery.

Against this cheerful backdrop, thirty large round tables sat suspended from the ceiling by metal poles. At first, I didn't understand and thought an overly ambitious interior designer had made a peculiar artistic choice, but as I looked around it dawned on me—this configuration allowed wheelchairs to park at the tables with patients' legs comfortably fitting underneath.

I nervously massaged my wedding band out of habit. The suspended tables instantly made me think about all the changes we would have to make to our home. If Ry used a wheelchair, we would need a ramp to our front door, new furniture, and possibly a van to move him around town. We would have to remove some walls and widen every doorway. Would he want his room downstairs? If he did drive again, could we get him a modified car? What modifications would he need? The have-to list racing through my mind seemed endless, full tasks that didn't exist weeks ago. How did anyone overcome such colossal life-altering events? Once again, I felt I was falling into a black hole of despair, all brought on by some posters of fruit and a few hanging tables.

In the middle of my catastrophizing, a familiar face approached and brought me back to the present moment. It was Dr. Hays. I liked him. He always wore casual work clothes instead of a white coat. I was tired of hearing medical jargon from people in white coats. As I was shaking Dr. Hays' hand and saying hello, a beeper went off and Stephanie said, "I have to go, Don, but don't forget what I told you. Take little moments out of each hour of your day to pay attention to the small things. Don't brush past life's experiences. Appreciate the wonderful texture of your life and make some time for yourself."

"Thank you, Stephanie. I will. I hope I'll be seeing you later."

As Stephanie left us, Dr. Hays said, "If you have a few minutes, I would like to chat in my office about Ry's medical history and maybe get some other details about his personality and activities?"

I'd become accustomed to having "conversations about Ry". I nodded and said, "Yes, that would be fine. I'd like to sit down for a little while."

"How are you holding up?" he asked as we headed toward his office. "I understand from some of the nursing staff and Dr. Benoit that you have practically lived in Ry's room since his accident?"

"I hope that's okay," I said, prepared for him to tell me that I was a nuisance and needed to leave. He just smiled and gave me a nod, assuring me all was well. There was something very comforting about Dr. Hays. Maybe it felt like talking to a friend, not a person I was pinning my hopes on to save my son. I found myself saying the one thing I had been holding in. "I'm frustrated with Ry's temper tantrums." Saying it out loud, I felt both relief and the familiar wave of guilt.

As a father, I had never had to apologize for my son. Now, I was constantly on pins and needles, waiting for the next outburst. The next "God damn it. Get out of my room." It made my brain tired, making me want to nap at all hours of the day. When I did sleep, I had dreams of hiding in a barn, trying to save the chickens from my grandmother's ax. I never could. Every time, the dream would end the same, with me jolting awake just as she lifted the ax to swing.

"I understand about the behavioral issues. It's typical of TBI patients, and unfortunately it could get worse. I believe showing unconditional love, even during a great tragedy and sadness, is all-powerful. There's a mound of scientific evidence that the brain and body are remarkably linked biologically and psychologically."

I nodded. "I remember that someone, maybe Dr. Benoit told

me too?"

"There's evidence that just the simple act of gentle touch can enhance the immune system and lower blood pressure. We promote relaxation and meditative conditioning here. There are daily sessions for our patients and parents too. The yoga and Transcendental Meditation times are posted every morning at the front lobby desk. You and your wife can join Ry at one of them."

"When can we get Ry to one of these sessions?" Once again, I found myself wanting to rush to the next step. All my life I had been a problem solver. With my work, there was a series of steps that needed to be taken, and if one did the steps correctly, in the end you'd hold a completed, bound book in your hand. It made sense to me. Go through the process step by step and the goal would be met. I didn't know how to live in a world filled with maybes, could-bes, and wait-and-sees.

"I think Ry will be ready soon. PT needs to get him more mobile, and I think that is going to happen in the next couple of days. We have a pool here too, and I want to consult with Dr. Zasler and Dr. Benoit about creating a swimming program for him."

"That would be great, but good luck. Ry gets so irritated when the PT or OT people try to get him to do something."

"I plan on spending some additional time today with him doing more cognitive testing. I might let him know that getting in the pool is contingent upon his good behavior."

I sighed, not having much faith in the process.

As Dr. Hays and I walked down the hall, we passed two young women restrained in their chairs by a posey belt. Another white rope tethered their chairs to a railing on the wall. An older woman with an exhausted expression sat in a chair next to them. The look in her eyes told me she must be a parent. There's a specific look that only parents worried about children can achieve. This woman had it in abundance.

As we approached, Dr. Hays said to her, "How are things going with Chelsea and Robyn?" He held out his hand and the lady sitting in the chair stood and greeted us.

"Mrs. Sutton, this is Don. His son was admitted a few days ago due to a car accident."

Mrs. Sutton nodded with a look of understanding. "Hello, Don. Nice to meet you. I hope everything works out with your son. These are my twins, Chelsea and Robyn." She brushed the hair out of the face of one of the girls and added, "I'm here visiting most days. If you're here and feel like company, please come by. We can get some lunch and chat. I know how it feels in the beginning."

"Thank you, I will. That's very nice of you."

After we left Mrs. Sutton and her girls, Dr. Hays filled me in on their story. They were nineteen-year-old twins who had been at Sheltering Arms for a few months. The teens had been injured in a car accident during their first semester at college. Neither had been wearing a seatbelt. Chelsea sustained the worst of the brain injuries, resulting in a coma for almost a month.

Dr. Hays went on to explain, "Chelsea had such violent seizures when she came out of the coma that she had an experimental operation at a neurosurgical clinic in Pennsylvania. The operation was to sever certain nerves in her brain in the hopes that the seizures would stop."

"Was it successful?" I asked.

"No. It's a very sad story. When the craniotomy was performed, the surgeon decided not to replace the portion of the skull that was removed. An infection set in and her brain became inflamed. She almost died of a blood infection. I guess you noticed the large crater on her skull?"

"Yes, I did. It's so sad."

"She has few memories of childhood and her language center has been compromised. If you tell her that today is Monday and then ask her what day it is a minute later, she will not know. There are always short-term memory issues with TBI."

As if that weren't enough, Dr. Hays went on to add, "Her sister, Robin, only sustained a concussion in the car accident. She seemed to have recovered but fell on the sidewalk a few months later at Virginia Commonwealth University and was unconscious for several days. She has been slow to recover. She lives at home but her mother brings her here three days a week for therapy."

"So much sadness and loss. I don't know how parents deal with it," I said, looking down at the white linoleum floor. "My son will be a college freshman who can't find his classroom or remember to do his homework. That's if he doesn't trip and end up in a coma."

My heart started pounding and I took a deep breath to calm down. I wanted to ban all teenage drivers and wrap them in bubble wrap until they turned twenty. I wanted to run out into the streets and scream for parents to never let their children out of the house during a thunderstorm. Mostly though, I wanted to go back to that night and beg Ry to cancel his date and stay home with his parents. I wanted the three of us to cuddle up on the couch, eat popcorn and watch a silly movie. I wanted to protect him from all the horrible things lurking out in the world.

As if reading my thoughts, or perhaps seeing the panic in my eyes, Dr. Hays said, "Don, it is too early to know yet what physical or mental assets have been permanently compromised. His brain is still healing. Let's wait until we do more cognitive testing." Placing a reassuring hand on my shoulder, he stressed,

"Dr. Zasler is one of the best clinicians in the state, and the staff here is talented in getting patients back to a normal sustainable life."

What is normal, I thought.

I wanted to go home, curl up on the couch and not make a single decision about anything. I used to welcome the sun on my face but that felt so long ago. Instead, I hungered for a dark room without noise and clocks that didn't tick. I wore an invisible name tag that identified me as a depressed person. Tears welled up in the corners of my eyes and I looked away. I never thought that the drizzle of depression would have the quality of physical pain.

I had become good at impersonating my former self, trying to put on my happy face every day, but it was getting harder to pretend that things were okay. There were fleeting moments that would come crashing into my thoughts, giving me a glimpse of the mystery of the afterlife. My Catholic upbringing kept nudging me to ask for salvation through prayer. Mourning can lead us back to life. It felt so hard still, to speak about God. Throwing pennies in a wishing well might be more effective. I had given up on wishing and fairy dust. But was it time to trust in what I had heard for decades, sitting in that church pew?

Dr. Hays put his hand on my back and said, "Let's go to my office and chat. I have some coffee and soft drinks. Plus," he said, with a kind smile, "I'm a good listener."

Inside Dr. Hay's office, I sank down in a leather chair. I wondered if it were harder to be the patient or the parent sitting in his office. Patients needed his guidance, but now I saw that loved ones did too. I wasn't ready to dive right into my feelings. It's never been a comfortable place for me to set up camp. So, I said nothing. I didn't have it in me for small talk and I was too tired to dig into the depths of my soul, so I sat. I sat and looked around his office until he spoke first.

"Don, I have been counseling patients and parents for the last twenty years, and I tell people that there is courage in acceptance. It frees our soul. Peace comes from accepting that some things were meant to be. This is going to be a journey, a new territory to explore. Your family's life can still be full of rich experiences."

I stumblingly tried to find the right words. "I just miss my son," I said, cradling my head in my hand. "I am missing him now, even though he is just down the hall. I don't know who that person is. We had such a wonderful summer. It just all feels so far away now. I'm homesick for that life to come back."

"Don, go live your life and Ry will follow. That's the best advice I can give you. You have to be healthy too, to help your son recover. I'll give you a list of things you can do with Ry daily that will help. But I want you to take some breaks from being here eighteen hours a day. Whatever joys you loved before the accident, go rediscover those things. You're going to be okay. Whatever Ry's outcome, he's going to be okay. What I do here every day is to help patients figure out what it means to become a person again. Take your lovely wife out to dinner."

"I want Ry to be the person he was two weeks ago."

"He is not that person any more, Don, but over time, when he does discover the person inside of him, it will be a fabulous individual."

"That is what I am most afraid of. Who will that person be and what will his needs be? Will he ever be mentally ready to go to a school as challenging as Notre Dame? I guess the swimming is going to be a long shot, as Dr. Zasler said? So many of my activities as a parent have shaped my sense of self for the last eighteen years."

"Don, I know that there can be a struggle in finding meaning in suffering, but this event can be a gift, even if this is an unwanted and uncertain gift. This can give your life and Ry's life a new meaning. Accept the new person Ry will become, because that is the only option. Right now, you're stuck on all the negative things you are seeing Ry exhibit. Don't give these events a magical label. Over time, Ry will evolve into a different but still beautiful person."

The words "new person" trickled slowly into my brain as I closed my eyes and felt as if I were falling. Dizzy with grief. I wasn't ready to accept a new Ry. I loved my son just as he was. I knew every part of him. I knew the difference between when he was nervous or just excited. He had at least a dozen different laughs and I knew what each one meant. I'd spent eighteen years learning every aspect of this human, and I wasn't ready to let him go. I wasn't ready to accept a new person in his place. All this talk of yoga, breathing and acceptance was shaking me to my core. How could I live in the moment when all I wanted to do was go back in time to a simpler life, sitting next to my grandmother on a one-legged stool as the line of milk from the cow filled the bucket between her legs? Start my life over.

When I stood to leave, Dr. Hays handed me a new publication from the National Association of Neurology. Another pamphlet full of jargon, I thought. I thanked him and stuck it in my back pocket.

Later, as I sat in the cafeteria sipping my mid-day cup of coffee, I read through the booklet on the *Managing of Patients with Traumatic Brain Injury.* There was nothing new that I hadn't already read about "outcomes," "behavioral issues," and "factors affecting brain injury." I realized it didn't matter how many pamphlets I read; none of them had an answer for me.

Everything from this point forward was uncertain. Maybe it always had been, and I'd been kidding myself with all my plans and schedules.

Each moment was going to unfold the way it was going to unfold, and there was nothing I could do to control it. I could no more control Ry's swearing and tray-throwing tantrums any more than I could control the storm that had raged the night of the accident. No pamphlet was going to give me the solutions I sought.

I closed my eyes and did something I hadn't done in years. *Lord Jesus, if you exist, and I am not sure of it, please take me to a life less messy, a simple one. Please show me how to see beauty in my life, even when I face destruction and loss. I don't want my son to go through life full of rage and where there is no gate to keep his temper at bay. Give me faith in you, Lord. Not doubt.*

Chapter 13

The Faces of Rehabilitation

I had spent a few hours in my office delegating what I could and making phone calls to clients to apologize for my absence. They were understanding and all asked what they could do to help. I didn't have a single thought about what they could do, but after a few calls, I began to say, "His name is Ry. Here is his address. Send him a card with a note. I will enjoy reading them to him."

There was a stack of messages from new clients who wanted book-printing quotes, and some who needed editorial work on their manuscripts. It was a reminder that no matter what was happening in our personal lives, the world continued spinning, factories churned out products, the stock market went up and down, and books needed to be published. Many times, while standing in line at the grocery store, I felt a deep urge to tap the person in front of me and say, "Did you know my son is fighting for his life? Did you know I have eleven book quotes to produce?"

Standing at my desk, I noticed on my calendar an awards banquet scheduled for the following Saturday night. It was being held at the Virginia Historical Society to honor me for the production of a book about Pocahontas. Usually, I would be happy to accept an acknowledgment for the hard work my entire team put into our books. I took great pride in the work we did. It's a cliché to say it's a team effort, but in publishing that's really true. The book designers and editors are the ones that win me awards.

The trouble was, I just didn't feel like going. I couldn't bring myself to care. Between the hours spent sitting at the hospital, dealing with Ry's increasingly angry outbursts and fighting off my own cloud of depression, I couldn't imagine putting on a suit and dragging myself and Lynn to an awards ceremony. But I had to, because that's how new clients are found. Organizations and museums see the awards, which leads to new clients. This was just another reminder that the world keeps turning regardless of our personal tragedies.

Later in the afternoon, I returned to Sheltering Arms and headed to Dr. Hays' office. We had scheduled a brief meeting before his session with Ry. I tried to remember what day it was. Tuesday? Maybe. Thursday? Time does not exist inside a hospital. There are markers of time: shift changes, doctor's visits, food deliveries, etcetera, but none of it means anything in terms of a day or a week or a month. It's like riding a merry-go-round.

One can count the number of times they reach out to pull a brass ring, but it doesn't change the ride itself. Round and round and round we went, all of us together: twelve-hour shifts for nurses and doctors, temporary homes for loved ones, and the slow progress of damaged brains fighting their way back to normal, only to discover that "normal" may have never been what anyone thought. Sheltering Arms had become a second home to me now—but one I couldn't wait to get away from. I had lost my freedom. My perfected running body was gone, and that thought knocked my mind flat to the floor. I needed to run.

Dr. Hays handed me a small notebook with instructions inside that he said would help with Ry's recovery. "Dr. Benoit and I put this together a few years ago as a guide for parents," he said, "It's based on the research we've done in working with over a thousand brain-injured people." The book contained little things I could do to reinforce what the occupational therapist was working on twice a day. I would be part of the cycle of people who would keep Ry on track for attaining the next level of goals.

I looked over the bullet points as we walked towards Ry's room.

Be positive and never criticize.

Remind him every few minutes that he is improving.

Stick with multiple-choice questions. What color socks do you want—red or brown?

If he doesn't immediately respond, go to the next question.

Bring puzzles and ask for his help in putting them together.

Encourage the swim team to visit with photos of anything to discuss.

Swim team and friends should be encouraging toward stated goals.

Allow for ninety-minute sleep cycles for every three hours of awake time.

Ask him how he feels physiologically: bad leg jiggling? Hungry?

Protect his brain from too much sensory stimulation, such as TV.

I looked up from the list with apprehension. "This seems terribly simplistic," I said to Dr. Hays. It was still hard for me to get used to the idea that my over-achieving son, who graduated top five in his class in the Honor Society and who I'd just completed a Japanese garden with, would now have to be encouraged each morning to pick a color of socks. I hated this. I hated every part of this. But life doesn't care how we feel about a situation. Life wants us to keep living through it.

Dr. Hays had become good at picking up on my frustration and impatience. He always spoke calmly to me. "Just think of it as a voyage in a boat," he said. "All those things you and his friends are doing are the oars navigating the boat forward. There are going to be times when he gets irritated. These little exercises will help Ry's brain rediscover how things are flowing around him. His brain will tend to move toward negative thoughts. That is why you have to be nonjudgmental. It may take some practice on your part, but try to help his brain loop back into positive patterns of thought."

"Is there anything else I can do?"

"Yes, if your schedule allows, go with him to physical therapy and his meals. Read to him. Keep his mind active, but don't forget he needs those intervals of sleep in between activities. Spend time with your wife too. Intimacy is important for couples during these stressful times. Sadness and depression are pernicious in times of grief."

I wished Dr. Hays a good day and hurried down the corridor, almost running, hoping to catch Dr. Benoit on her daily visit with Ry. Outside of Ry's door was a male patient in a wheelchair. His wheel was buckled by a posey belt to the railing along the wall. I looked over at the young man roped to the wall. "Hello, how are you?" I asked. He did not look at me but pointed his finger at the nurses' station. His legs were doing a little shuffle as he struggled to propel himself toward an unknown destination. I wondered where he would go if I untied him. Even if he didn't know where he wanted to go, I had a deep urge to set him free.

I knew what it felt like to want to be anywhere rather than where you were. After Audrey died, I couldn't stand to be anywhere. If I was in a crowd, I wanted to be alone. If I was alone, I wanted to get lost in a crowd. If I was in, I wanted to be out, and if I was out, I wanted in. The truth was, I couldn't stand being in my own skin. It felt like there would never be a place that brought me comfort. I needed to go, just go. Far. Fast. Away.

Audrey had been gone a week when I packed a small bag with her jewelry and diary. I tucked them in the side case behind the saddle of my Triumph motorcycle and left, heading west. I had no idea where I was going or what my future held. When I lost Audrey, it was the worst time in my life, yet it seemed in many ways less complicated. My wife was dead and I was alone. No mortgage. No obligations. No commitments. I was grieving, so I fled that world.

It was so simple to just pick up and leave. I left behind who I was supposed to be—the heart broken widower, lost youth—and just rode. Leaving Richmond, I pointed the bike northwest and headed to the Dakotas, Montana, and Idaho, often exceeding 100 mph. Did I have a death wish? Maybe. I never stopped long enough to think that deeply about it. My brain was under siege from pain and dislocation. A toxic tide blocking any pleasure. I was doing everything I could just to release the pain, and screaming down a mountain road at one hundred miles an hour on a motorcycle did just that. It was reckless. Dangerous. But certainly, it made me stop thinking about my dead wife for a few minutes.

I slept outdoors, drank cheap whiskey in bars and slept with countless women I didn't know. The only thing they had in common was that they weren't Audrey. I worked on a dude ranch, shoveling horse shit for three dollars an hour plus supper. I slept on a cot in a bunkhouse with a bunch of other smelly drifters running from the law, bad marriages, financial obligations or broken hearts. I did all that because I could, because I needed it, and mostly because I didn't know what else to do. When my wife died, she took my give-a-fuck with her. I didn't know if I would ever get it back, or if I even wanted to. Maybe loving people just wasn't worth the pain when they leave. Rational thought was absent.

Now, life was different. I could not just run away. I had to think about the bigger picture and what my absence would leave behind. Who would care for my aging parents? And what about Lynn? How could I take off and saddle her to clean up the mess I left behind? No, fleeing was no longer an option. I drank and fucked and raced at a high rate of speed through my grief with Audrey, but now my son was lying in a bed, his brain fighting to get back to normal, and I owed it to him to stay by his side. I had a mortgage, bills, a wife whom I loved dearly and employees who counted on me to show up and give them direction. When Audrey died, life gave me a pass to live recklessly, but I couldn't do that this time around. I had to stay here and face life. I had to look at it and say, *Okay, I'm here. I'm not running away. What do you want me to do?*

I stood beside the young man in the hall, resisting the urge to untie him. "Everything is going to be okay," I said, pointing to the door next to me. "My son is here in this room. I wish I could get him in one of those chariots, like you have." I went on, even though the man didn't acknowledge me. "You know, man carries the whole world in his head. Ralph Waldo Emerson said that. I am not sure what is in my son's head today."

If the man could hear me, he made no indication. His state did not permit the luxury of speech. Maybe in his mind he was already halfway where he needed to be.

A door opened down the hall and Dr. Benoit exited the room and began walking toward me. I leaned in a little closer to the young man in the wheelchair and quietly said, "I hope one day you reach your destination." I gently patted his shoulder again as his feet continued to shuffle.

I looked up at Dr. Benoit, and my face immediately began to flush. "How are you, Sister Angeline?" I really needed to stop blushing like a school kid every time I ran into her. It was embarrassing. I was a happily married man concerned with the health of my child, and she was a nun, for God's sake. It was ridiculous. I just wished someone would tell that to my bright red face. If Dr. Benoit noticed my teenage reaction to seeing her, she was too professional to let on. For that I was immensely grateful.

"I'm fine," she answered. "I was just coming down to see Ry. I've heard he's been a little uncooperative this morning." She gave me a sympathetic smile.

I nodded, once again feeling embarrassed by my son's behavior. Every parent knows the feeling when a child is screaming in a grocery store over a desired sweet or toy and there's nothing to do but to smile apologies to the surrounding angry glares. The difference was that my son was not a toddler, and frighteningly there was no magic pill he could take that would allow him a quick rescue. Psychologically I remained mortified as gloom began to crowd in on me.

Reading my expression, Dr. Benoit said, "This behavior is not atypical."

I had to hand it to the doctors, nurses, even the orderlies and janitors at Sheltering Arms. They were all experts at reading and diverting shame. Ry screamed curse words and the nurse smiled and rolled him over. Ry threw a tray of food and the orderly made a joke. Ry refused to go to physical therapy and Dr. Benoit simply made a note of it and continued talking about positive outcomes.

"He's scheduled for some skills testing today with the physical therapy team," she said. "Shall we go in and check on him?"

I nodded, and Dr. Benoit slowly opened the door. It was dark except for a minute stream of light seeping through the drawn curtains. Today, there was a new male patient in the room. Sitting next to the bed was a woman who appeared to be in her seventies. I figured she was his wife.

"Hello," Dr. Benoit said while reaching out her hand to the woman, who was now rising to greet us.

"Good morning. I'm Nancy. My husband, Phillip, had a stroke last week. St. Mary's transferred him here this morning. Are you one of his doctors?" she asked, taking Dr. Benoit's hand.

"No, I'm Dr. Benoit; I work mostly with adolescents," she said with a gentle smile, "but I also happen to be a nun, so I'll pray for you and Phillip."

"You're so kind to do that," Nancy said, still holding Dr. Benoit's hand. "This has been such a difficult time for our family. Phillip was always in such good health, and then a stroke came out of nowhere. I can't make sense of any of it."

"Sometimes, the lessons of life take time to reveal themselves. We must sit in silent meditation and allow God's answers to come on His time." Dr. Benoit patted Nancy's hand as she spoke. Nancy nodded and used a wadded-up tissue to dab her eyes. She went on to explain what felt like her and Phillip's entire medical history. *And then in 1979, Phillip's gallbladder flared up. And in 1983, I had surgery for my lady troubles. I stubbed my toe on Christmas morning in 1989, and Phillip had the most awful headache three weeks ago on Tuesday, or maybe that was me...* On and on she went until I wanted to scream, "Shut up, Nancy! Shut up, shut up, shut up! No one cares about your stupid headache or Phillip's gallbladder!"

But that would have been rude. And I was conditioned to

never be rude, so I waited patiently, only occasionally sighing or glancing at my watch. I wanted Dr. Benoit's attention to myself. I wanted her to focus on Ry and his recovery, not on Phillip and Nancy. Yes, it was petty, but I didn't care. Dr. Benoit was our doctor, and I was feeling territorial. If Nancy kept going on, I thought I might become the toddler in the candy aisle and throw myself on the floor.

Finally, Nancy wrapped up the history of her family saga and said, "I was just going down to the coffee shop. Would you like some coffee?"

"No, thank you. I don't need any more coffee in my system today," Dr. Benoit answered.

I don't even know if Nancy was asking me, but still I blurted out, "No," anxious for her to leave so I could have Dr. Benoit's full attention.

With Nancy gone, Dr. Benoit sat down next to Ry's bed. His back was turned to her as she said, "Ry, this is Dr. Benoit. Do you think you can turn over and talk with me just for a few minutes?"

His body moved slightly, the sheets rippling as if caressed by a puff of wind. "I want to sleep," Ry said in a monotone voice.

Dr. Benoit wasn't about to give up so easily. "I'd like to try an experiment, but I need your help. I'm going to pull the sheets back and raise your leg a few inches off the bed. I want you to help me, okay?"

There was no reply. She reached over and slowly pulled the sheets back, exposing a tanned, muscular body. He looked vulnerable. With a sudden sense of déjà vu, I realized I had witnessed him in the same pose hundreds of times before when lying in his crib as an infant. He needed protecting then and now. A part of me, that parental instinct, wanted to shout, *No, leave him alone! He said he wants to sleep. Leave him be.* But I trusted the doctor and knew I was having an emotional reaction and not reacting to what was best in the long term for my son.

"Ry, here we go, I'm lifting your foot off the bed. Tell me if you can feel anything." She placed a hand under the bridge of his right foot and pulled it up gently. As soon as she touched his left foot, Ry pulled it out of her hands.

"There's nothing wrong with that foot," he said, his voice cracking with anger.

"Yes, I know, Ry. I just wanted to see if you were still alive," she said, her tone light-hearted. When she received no reply, Dr. Benoit grew more serious. "You've got to work with me, Ry, on trying to move your right leg. I know how angry you are that this has happened to you, but it's only a small setback. If we're going to repair those damaged neurons in your brain, we have to get them firing again. Today is a good day to start that. I want you to remember something for me, Ry: neurons that fire together wire together. That's how we are going to rewire your brain. I can't whisk away your malaise without your help and concentration."

For the next fifteen minutes, I watched Dr. Benoit poke and massage Ry's paralyzed leg. He lay silent. She moved her thumb down six inches and pushed deep into the muscle.

"Tell me when you can feel something touching your leg."

"Please leave me alone. You're beginning to bug me," Ry said.

Dr. Benoit looked over at me and said in a whisper, "It's okay. This is a long journey."

She pulled her pen out of her coat pocket and ran it down the bottom of Ry's right foot. "Ry, we are not done yet." She said with a little more forcefulness in her voice.

"I want to stop taking steroids."

"Why?"

"It makes me feel crazy."

"Steroids are an important treatment, and I know that can make you confused. A few more days and I will end your cycle."

She knew I was disappointed. I felt like a sailor on a ship pulling out to sea, watching as the lights on the shore grew dim and then vanished. Hope for my son's recovery receded like the shoreline. I stared at him. It was like he had aged fifty years in less than two weeks. I leaned up against the wall and wept quietly. Thoughts of the past summer and how much time Ry and I had spent together were now a blur. I thought I'd be able to deal with whatever physical limitations he might have, but the angry emotional outbursts were more troubling. How long would it take to "rewire his brain?"

When she was done, Dr. Benoit and I retreated to a conference room down the hall.

"I spoke with Dr. Zasler this morning," she said. "He wants Ry back in the pool soon. We are going to meet with his PT team today to request an update on his physical progress."

Hearing that they wanted Ry back in the pool piqued my interest. Finally, it felt like a huge step forward. "What do you need me to do?" I eagerly asked.

"Spend time with him. Talk to him. Read to him. Call his friends and ask them to visit. Push him around in the wheelchair, but don't go outside yet. Anything you can do to stimulate the electrical activity in his brain will help with creating new cells. We need to make his environment exciting. Like a newborn, he needs to start interacting with it." Her steady gaze had a way of shaking me to my core, as though she were seeing all of me, the good, the bad, the past, the future, all of it. "How are you doing?" she asked, and I knew she really meant it.

I liked keeping things private, close to the chest, but with Dr. Benoit, it all came pouring out. "I'm feeling lost at the moment. Lonely. I'm missing my son and wife. I don't know who that person is down the hall. Sometimes I dread coming here, and then I hate myself for feeling that way." I could feel my throat tighten. "I wish you could meet the real Ry." Words failed me as I drifted off, afraid that if I spoke any more, the tears would come and I wouldn't be able to stop them.

"Don, the fact that you are here spending so much time with Ry shows me how much you love him. I've prayed to God for you and Ry. I've asked him to bring you both comforts, no matter how things progress in the next weeks and months. You must have faith that He hears our prayers. Loneliness is not the absence of someone's face in front of you but the absence of closeness with that person." Dr. Benoit placed a comforting hand on my shoulder as I stared at the floor. "You're missing your best friend. He's lost too, but by showing him that you love him, you both will find peace."

Then she said the thing I was dreading. "No matter the outcome of Ry's recovery, you need to find peace in your heart."

No matter the outcome. I thought back to the young man in the hallway, who had reached out for some unknown destination, his feet moving in place but getting nowhere. No matter the outcome. How could I ever make peace with that? I could still see Ry's muscular back and arms lifting large rocks to build our Japanese garden. I could see his lean muscles diving into the water after the sound of the starter gun, barely making a splash as he glided into the water. Visions of Ry laughing and teasing Alexis over dinner.

If I accepted "No matter the outcome," these current activities would shift into memories. I wasn't ready for that. If

Ry's brain was building new neurons, then mine was slowly being destroyed by active anguish. My mind drifted back to the years I worked in a psychiatric hospital, building 19, a locked-down unit where dozens of severely depressed people walked the dark hallways. I had been blind to feeling empathy for those lost souls as I sat with them, writing down their feelings in a daily log. Now, a sense of guilt rushed over me as I understood their despair.

My depression began to suffocate me.

"Don, why don't you go home early today? Go buy a book. Call Ry's friends and tell them to visit. I know you run marathons. Go run a few miles. I'll be here early tomorrow to see Ry."

She was right. I needed a break. Maybe see some friends and go for a long run. I went back to Ry's room to say good-bye. "I love you, Ry. I'm going home to get some sleep. I'll be back tomorrow."

"Okay, Dad," he mumbled from under a lump of covers.

I stood there in stunned silence. It was the first time my son had called me Dad since the accident.

Chapter 14

The Poster That Caused a War

Ry's hospital room had been transformed into a college dorm room. His swim team friends had come out in force early that morning. When I stepped inside, I found them sitting on the floor, resting on his bed, taping posters on the wall. Most of them would be moving into their own dorm rooms in a matter of days, but today they were here, and the sound of young women's perky laughter filled the room. I strained to find my son in the middle of the party. He was lying safe in the center, encircled by an aura of energy and affection. Two girls sat on either side of his bed, rubbing his legs while another combed his hair. All that was missing was a girl to feed him grapes. The guys joked about wanting to get sick too so they could have some hands-on healing.

Taped to the wall was a nine-foot poster that, from a distance, looked like a teenage girl in a skimpy thong-style bikini with ample breasts. When I moved closer, I realized it was a realistic sketch made with color pencils.

"Very nice," I said. "A Picasso. Who was the model?" I asked Ry's girlfriend, Alexis.

"Oh, I think it was twelve people's imaginations," she answered with a broad smile as she pointed to some of the members on the swim team.

"I like the shoulders and hips," said Dudley, Ry's swim

coach. "Definitely a swimmer's body. An Olympic swimmer."

The sight of the spontaneity and gaiety, together with his friends talking to him, slightly changed my vision of defeat. I was cautious, but it felt wonderful to see so many smiling faces and positive energy. I was not the lone caregiver any more.

"Can you feel that, Ry?" Alexis said. "I'm tying bows around your toes." Everyone broke into a loud laugh. It sounded amazing. To simply hear the sound of joy warmed my heart. Teenagers have an infectious way of bringing boundless energy and light to even the darkest of times. I loved each and every one of those kids for making the day a little brighter.

The door to Ry's room opened and a nurse entered, pushing Phillip in a wheelchair. His wife, Nancy, was in tow, chattering to the nurse the whole way. I could have sworn a slight smile came to Phillip's lips when he saw the giant swimsuit girl hanging on the wall. Unfortunately, Nancy didn't seem to appreciate the fine art as much as her husband. Her jaw dropped, as if the thong woman in the poster had reached out and punched her.

The nurse immediately began shooing the teens out of the room. "All of you have to leave, now. Immediately," she barked. "There are two visitors allowed at any given time," she said as her voice slowly turned into an angry scolding. "There is another patient in this room, and you must show some respect."

One by one, each person took their turn kissing Ry on the head, even the guys on the team. I waited for my turn and added my kiss. "Ry, I need to go to my office and get some work done. I'll be back later today. I love you." Throughout the impromptu party he had said very little except to acknowledge his friends and teammates with an occasional grunt or moan. A few smiles had interrupted the typical frown on his face. It had been a good morning, despite the abrupt entrance of the party crashers.

I walked down the hall with the group. Every person gave me a big hug before getting on the elevator. "You guys don't know how much this meant to Ry and me," I told them. "I think he likes the poster. That was the first smile I've seen on his face. Please, please come back and visit again. All of you. Today was like a scene from a wonderful opera."

Dr. Benoit appeared behind me as I was holding the elevator door open. I introduced her to Ry's friends. "Ry is lucky to have all of you supporting him," Dr. Benoit said to the group. "You should all come back tomorrow and sing to him, read to him, poke him," she said with a smile. "It will increase his vigor and help his brain heal."

"The nurse said Ry was only allowed two visitors at a time," Alexis said with a slight frown.

"Ah, yes," Dr. Benoit said, "she is a stickler for the rules." And then she added with a wink, "But a little bird tells me she is always off on Saturdays. In case anyone happened to be in the neighborhood and wanted to pop by."

As Dr. Benoit walked away, one of Ry's guy friends blurted out, "She's cool."

I couldn't have agreed more.

***

The next several days blended into each other, without much change. Sometimes a visitor would come by, a couple of Ry's friends or one of his teachers or coaches, and that would break up the routine, but mostly time stood still. I arrived at the rehab center around the same time every day, and the first thing I would do, was grab a cup of coffee. I don't know why I insisted on torturing myself in this way. There was a perfectly fine coffee shop between my house and Sheltering Arms. Hell, I even had a coffee pot at home. I could have brewed an entire pot, but instead I chose to get a cup of the most God-awful coffee I've ever tasted. Maybe I was a glutton for punishment, or maybe I subconsciously wanted to remind myself that I was in a jail cell.

Today, Dr. Zasler sat next to Ry, his expression difficult to read.

"Ry, this is Christa," he said, motioning towards the young blonde woman next to him. "Do you remember looking at some cards with her yesterday?"

Christa, the speech pathologist, had worked with Ry for the last few days. So far, he hadn't recognized her from one day to the next.

Ry looked up but did not respond immediately. He had a blank expression, like a deer in headlights. TBI affects facial muscles, Christa had told me, but with time, she expected Ry's facial expressions to return. Until then, they would work with him daily.

"Hi, Ry," Christa said, "You did really well yesterday."

"Hi," Ry answered as he moved his eyes toward Christa's face. "Hi, Dr. Zasler," Ry said slowly. He struggled for a moment to find his next words and then asked, "Home today?" Every day it was the same. My son asked to go home, and it broke my heart. All I wanted to say, *yes, Ry, today I will take you home*, but that wasn't going to happen for a long while. Frankly, I had no idea when he might be discharged which made for my unsettling pessimism. My life had become enigmatic. Oh God, grant me a new life.

Dr. Zasler sat on the edge of Ry's bed and said, "Ry, we are going to work together to help you get your strength back and go home. I want to get postcards when you're back at Notre Dame."

Dr. Zasler placed his hand on Ry's foot and asked, "Ry, can you feel my hand on your toe?"

Ry looked down at his foot and then back up to Dr. Zasler. "Okay," he answered.

"Is that a yes or a no?" Dr. Zasler said as he grinned at Ry.

"Yes," Ry replied.

"Then that is a big okay," Dr. Zasler said. "Christa is going to work with you every day. You are one of the brightest patients I have ever treated, so I know you will understand that when a person has a brain injury, like you have, your surroundings can be a blend of noise and confusion. We understand it can be overwhelming, and Christa knows how to help you reconnect with the world you knew three weeks ago. Please work with her, and you will be back in the water soon."

"Been here three weeks?"

"Yes, Ry a little over three weeks."

"I want to swim."

"Soon, Ry. Real soon," Dr. Zasler replied as he got up to leave the room, shaking my hand before he left.

Christa pulled a chair next to Ry's bed and opened a folder to assemble note cards across her lap. I sat in a chair across the room, giving them some space. It was exciting to see Ry getting so much attention.

"Ry, we are going to work on word recall," Christa said. "It seems like you are having some trouble finding the words that you would like to say. Would you like for me to help you? And, Ry, if you can, please look at my lips when I speak. Okay?"

"You are new?"

"No I worked with you just yesterday. You did well."

"Will you go away?"

"No, I am afraid you are stuck with me. I have some pictures to show you." Christa picked up the first card, which was showing a comb. "Ry what is this object?"

"You want me to tell you?" Ry's face went blank as he stared at the card with empty eyes. He thought for half a minute as Christa sat patiently, smiling at Ry as if there were nothing but time. Ry seemed relaxed, and I realized how good Christa was at her job. It wasn't just about flashing cards with pictures. It was about making the patient feel comfortable and not get frustrated. TBI patients know what they want to say, she'd told me, but they have trouble sequencing the words and sentences. I couldn't imagine how frustrating it must have been for my son to struggle over simple words. It was heartbreaking, but still I felt tremendous hope that this was a temporary situation. Small sparks in my son's eyes assured me that the boy he'd been before was still there. We just had to slowly coax him back.

"Cooomb," Ry said slowly.

"Yes, Ry." Christa nodded with enthusiasm. "That is great. Ry, can you tell me what this object is?" she asked as she held a card with a bag of potato chips on it.

"Ah, ah, a bag." Ry answered.

Christa tilted her head and gave him a quizzical look. "Are you sure, Ry? Look again."

Ry starred at the picture. "Chips."

She held up more cards. Some Ry got on the first try, and others took a couple of guesses.

"Good," Christa said. "I want you to stick out your tongue as far as you can."

He opened his mouth and his tongue slowly moved outward.

"Yes, Ry. That is perfect. Let's do it a few more times."

Ry seemed to respond well to Christa's requests, making eye

contact and turning his head toward her.

"You're doing really well. Let's move on to the next task, and then I'll let you rest for a few minutes." Christa smiled and asked him, "Do cows fly?"

Ry looked over at me and tried to smile but said nothing.

"Ry, do cows fly?" Christa pressed.

He looked straight at her and shook his head. "No," he said and smiled in a way that said he understood the question was silly.

"Do turtles crawl?" she asked.

He quickly responded, "Yes."

Ry continued to answer the questions correctly for the next ten minutes. He understood content but had difficulty with pronunciation and word finding. He had trouble speaking in full sentences and would often start to speak and then stop, as if lost.

Christa told him good-bye and promised to come back and see him tomorrow. He seemed pleased to hear that and gave a little wave as she and I left the room to chat in the hall.

Once outside, Christa said, "Don, I am encouraged that he is motived to make the attempt to follow my directions and commands to speak. He makes eye contact, which is hard for some TBI patents."

"Christa, I am so grateful that you are here," I said and meant it. Watching her work with my son had filled me with cautious hope. "I know the body and brain are resilient, but it seems like full recovery is so far from the finish line."

"I know, Don, but I am already seeing changes in Ry that are encouraging. He has good sessions with me, and then average ones. We push for seeing more good ones."

There could be relapses, she said. There would likely be days when Ry didn't want to cooperate and days filled with angry outbursts. It was part of the process, she said. Every brain injury was different, she was quick to point out.

As I turned to go back into Ry's room, I allowed myself a moment of optimism. Maybe everything was going to be okay. I reminded myself of the orb spider. A new day. A new web. We could do this. Little by little, we would rebuild.

Chapter 15

Love from Notre Dame

I spent the next two days trying to catch up on work. It was a much-needed break. My mind had to focus on something other than, *Did Ry sit up today? Did Ry smile today? Did Ry shout at the nurses today?* But as soon as I got settled at my desk, my coworkers popped in, asking if there was anything, they could do for me. I appreciated their concern. They looked at me as if one wrong look or one wrong word might make me explode before their eyes—or worse, crumble into a broken heap of sorrow. It's an impossible situation when dealing with someone who is grieving. Act as if all is normal and you seem cold and unfeeling, but showing sorrow and compassion all day every day can drive a grieving person to madness. Grief is a constant drizzle of despair. Stay in one place for too long and you are bound to get soaked.

As I sat at my desk, looking at the parade of sad faces with sympathy in their eyes, I understood that this was part of the healing process. This was how people expressed that they cared, and I needed to accept it. It caused me to feel uncomfortable emotions I was used to pushing aside, but I forced myself to stay and accept the love they were giving. Many of my coworkers wondered why I was even there. The Chairman, Wally Stettinius, came in and spent some time with me then quickly told me to go home.

"You look like hell," he said, not unkindly. "Take some time off. You trained your staff well. Let them run with the ball for a few weeks."

I had the highest respect for Wally. He had hired me and mentored me. His father was the Secretary of State under President Franklin Roosevelt during World War Two. Wally was a captain in the Marine Corps. I'm sure he had seen hundreds of tired men under his command on long marches who needed some time off.

I took his advice and went home to face the mess that had been growing for almost a month. The dining room table was covered in work papers and photographs for books that were in progress. A blanket of dust lay everywhere, because Lynn and I had spent so little time at home during the day. Looking through the window in the kitchen, I wondered what the Japanese garden looked like. Was it still the peaceful haven Ry and I had created during the summer or had weeds choked off the life of the bamboo we had planted? I looked out of the kitchen window toward the path that led through the dense trees. The Japanese garden was fifty yards into the woods.

Our cat, Nigel, wandered in and sat on the overflowing pile of mail. He stared at me momentarily and then began licking his legs. *Oh, Nigel*, I sighed, *what is next in my life?* I reached over to pick up some of the mail and Nigel jumped down. He wandered off, waving his tail at me as if I were a stranger. Nikki, our greyhound laid across my feet. I opened the first piece of mail. It was a brief note from Father King, the priest of Ry's dorm.

Don,

We will pray for Ry's quick recovery. This Sunday, we will dedicate the mass to him and to you and your family. Two thousand people will pray for him during the service, and we pray very well and frequently here at Notre Dame.

I picked up a three-foot-long tube from the stack of mail. The label read "Notre Dame." Inside was a poster of the famous golden Notre Dame Dome, which had been signed by all of the resident students in Zahm Hall, Ry's dorm. How did Father King arrange to get over a hundred signatures?

Another note read:

Dear Ryan: Just a short note to let you know that you continue to be in the thoughts and prayers of the Notre Dame community. May the Lord be with you to bring you a full and speedy recovery.

We look forward to your arrival on the campus.

With all the best,

Rev. E. William Beauchamp, C.S.C. Executive Vice-President

As I dug deeper into the pile of letters, I found notes from Notre Dame alumni who lived all over the U.S. and worldwide. They'd heard about Ry's accident and were sending well wishes, including their phone numbers in case I needed to talk. One letter with an Arizona address was from Haley Scott's family. Charlotte and Steve's daughter, Haley, had been a nationally ranked swimmer. During her freshman year at Notre Dame, the women's swim team was returning on a night to South Bend on the Indiana Toll Pike during a snowstorm. Just a few miles from the campus, the bus began to skid. The driver lost control and the bus overturned into a ditch. Two swimmers, nineteen-year-old freshmen Megan Beeler and Colleen Hipp, were thrown from a window and died of asphyxiation under the bus.

Other swimmers lay amid luggage inside the bus. Haley had suffered a broken back. Another swimmer helped to get Haley out of the bus, telling her to ignore the pain. Witnesses said they saw Haley pull herself up the side of the embankment, even though she had multiple crushed vertebrae. In the following weeks, doctors operated several times, trying to provide support for the damaged vertebrae. Due to the position of her injured spine, the surgical team entered Haley's body from the front. For months she wore a full-body cast. A letter from Haley's mother described the pain, the feeling of loss and the helplessness she as a parent had experienced.

Dear Don,

Tim Welsh, the swim coach, has called me to tell me of Ry's terrible accident. I am sure that many people are telling you, "I know how you feel." They don't. A good friend of mine said, "There are no such words."

I do not know you or Ry, nor how you feel. But I do know the feelings of helplessness, the need to have people care and continue to care long after the crisis is over and the long-term haul begins, and continues. I do know the feelings of loss. Much to my shame I know the related self-pity: that I need a rest, a break, a change of pace. Everyone tells me I deserve it and when I take it, I feel the guilt. Who am I to complain?

Haley's back is scarred, her days and nights are often long and painful, and she has so many losses to live with. It's not easy.

I don't know how you feel but I am willing to share because I do believe that sorrow shared is halved. I'm sure that many people are telling you, "God only gives this to people who are strong." Wrong. God did not give this to the Beville/Scott family.

If what those people say is true then I'm going to fold up on the floor and die. You have two choices, to quit or to go on. It's your child, you have no choice but to go on. You take each minute, each card, each phone call, each prayer as a gift.

You work hard and trust that God will give you what you need for the next minute. I'm sure that many people are telling you, "Something good will come of this." It's not something good, it's all the little good things.

A card from a long-lost friend, a new friend, a relationship with your child which is only forged in this kind of fire, the chance to reach out to another, to pass on all the love and care that was showered on you. We have been blessed with so many good things.

The Scotts were strangers, but they had suffered the same pain, the same loss, the unknown future, as I was feeling now. Loss and grief can sabotage one's life, but caring people can be the protective cloak, the Holy Grail of survival. There is no psychological gloss. I did have thoughts of giving up, but Charlotte Scott is right, this is my child and there is no giving up. The problem was, the end game continued to elude me. While only slightly, I was still feeling guilt and self-condemnation for letting my son out of the house on the night of the great thunderstorm.

Reading the heartfelt letter, I thought back to the days when Ry and I built the dam, planted bamboo and talked about his future plans. What kind of relationship would we have now, forged in this kind of fire? Would we re-examine the many passions in our lives? Would swimming still be Ry's elixir of life? Would running marathons continue to fill my cup with much-needed endorphins? Beneath the layers of masks, addictions are what they are. Addictions.

***

The next few days felt like weeks. It was now September, and all hope of Ry going to Notre Dame was only passing thoughts to me. I called the hospital two and three times a day.

"Has Ry gotten up today? What time is PT?"

"We're going to do some assessments today," the head nurse would say. I was beginning to hate those words. Ry was refusing to go to PT. He would sit in a chair in the corner and stare into the wall. Most days, he would refuse to eat or talk. The steroids he was taking had changed his face into a giant round balloon. For any teenager, regardless of what is happening in life, looks still matter. I was thankful there were no mirrors in Ry's room, or hallways. But this hospital routine reminded me of *The Myth of Sisyphus* by Camus. Poor suffering Sisyphus pushing the rock up the hillside, only to have it roll back down. Day after day, he pushed it up and then watched it roll down. But to me, the overriding theme of Sisyphus was in the absence of hope we still must struggle to survive, and isn't that we do, every day, even when we have to painfully crawl across the finish line.

I called and left a message for Dr. Zasler to ask if I could take Ry out of the hospital in his wheelchair. A change of scenery could do him good, I thought. A nurse called me back and said, "No, we want to get him into a more aggressive kind of physical therapy this week."

My mood was not lightened by hearing the word "no." I could only imagine Ry was sick of it too. That is if he cared at all. It was impossible to get a read on what he cared about any more. Most days, he barely talked to me and would simply stare off into space. The "deer in headlights" look that Christa described was still there.

The doctors had drilled into me that I had to continue to live

190

my life. Even if Ry couldn't go outside, I had to get some fresh air. It was incredibly difficult to focus on self-care when my son couldn't feel a cool breeze on his face, but I longed to feel one on my own. I knew I had to get out of the house and put some miles on my legs. Being physically inactive for weeks was making my moods lurch about. The ferocity of my temper spiked.

I became the king of sarcasm, swept up in throwing digs at Lynn. "Your flower gardens need weeding. Did you know there is no more milk for coffee? You were off for three days, but the clothes basket is full of dirty sheets. That's odd." There were moments when I would make her cry, but I did not feel any remorse. I just didn't care. I needed to run—it was amazing how much conditioning my body had lost. Ry's conditioning must have been gone too, since he'd been lying in a bed for over three weeks now. I felt like a slug with six-pound shoes but being outside might help my mood. Could it help Ry's too?

As stressed out as I was, I needed to keep my mind engaged. I was the father of Ry Beville, and he had become my project.

Chapter 16

Kentucky Fried Chicken

The phone call came early. It was the charge nurse on Ry's floor, asking if I could come to the hospital to meet with the director. Her curt tone immediately made me question if Ry's condition had changed. I could feel my pulse pounding through my temple as I held the phone to my ear and waited for her to drop more bad news. In a matter of seconds, every worst-case scenario flew through my mind. *Ry fell out of bed and hit his head. Ry had a seizure. Ry lashed out for the last time and was being kicked out of the rehabilitation center. Ry strangled the patient in the next bed.*

Luckily, before my head exploded, she quickly said, "No, his condition is unchanged." As I loudly exhaled my relief, she added, "but…"

Huh oh. In my experience, "but" with such a weighty undertone never led anywhere pleasant. "You were up for the promotion, but… I understand you love your chair, Honey, but… I really like you, but…" No, in my experience, "buts" were never welcome visitors.

Now it was her time to sigh heavily. Although my sigh had been filled with relief, hers was loaded with disapproval. "… But we need to have a conversation about Ry's visitors. How soon can you be here?"

"Right away," I said and then hung up the phone and took

my sweet time, procrastinating as long as I could, getting myself prepared. I knew what this was. This was a summons to the principal's office. I was a highly respected managing editor at a prestigious publishing house. I was a Boston marathon runner. My book titles had been reviewed in major newspapers, including an art book in the *New York Times Book Review*. I'd had more than my allotted fifteen minutes of fame. I was the father of a nationally ranked elite athlete and yet I was terrified of being scolded by the mean principal.

When I finally strode into her office, she didn't disappoint. She was tall and thin, maybe in her mid-fifties. She glared at me over the rims of her glasses, bright red hair curled over her ears. Women with red hair can be dangerous. I still remember the beating Jimmy Steel got in fifth grade by Helen, a redhead.

"Have you seen the poster in Ry's room?" she snapped. I'd barely had time to sit in the chair across from her. She remained standing behind her desk, which made me feel even more like a punished child. I felt I was in need of medication. A big glass of wine. My stress level had, once again, escalated into a higher zone.

"Yes." The question caught me off-guard. "I thought the poster was a piece of art." I wanted to show my indifference to her concern. Perhaps that would gain me some power in what I figured would be a heated negotiation.

"It needs to come down immediately. It's a *nude* swimmer." She gave me a stern look, as if we'd plastered the walls with *Playboy* centerfolds. Irritated, I really wished I hadn't sat down. This power dynamic made me uncomfortable, but if I stood, it might be perceived as too aggressive.

Taking the diplomatic approach, I explained, "It was drawn by Ry's swimming teammates. When his friends taped it on the wall, he laughed for the first time in weeks." I'd hoped to appeal to her compassionate side.

She was having none of it. Tossing the folder down on the desk, she placed both hands on her hips. "The wife of the other patient complained, and I agree."

I knew it! *Nancy*. I knew that Nancy was trouble from the first day she commandeered Dr. Benoit's attention by prattling on about Phillip's cholesterol levels. "Complained about what?" I asked, already knowing the answer.

"She found it vulgar. Please go to Ry's room and remove it."

More likely, Nancy was so offended because it set off a spark of excitement in Phillip's eyes each time he gazed at the drawing. I stood up, shaking my head. "Do you have another room Ry can be moved to?" There was no way I was going to sit back and let a woman like Nancy have any stake in my son's recovery. My sharp-edge tongue wanted to tell her go fuck off, but I knew I would lose that battle.

"I'll check with the admissions office and get back to you." With that, she motioned for me to leave.

By the time, I walked to Ry's room, my irritation had turned to hostility. It wasn't the poster. It was what the poster represented. It had been the one thing in weeks that had given my son a glimmer of joy. He deserved that. We raise our kids hoping for the best—that they become decent people—and with Ry, we'd succeeded. I felt like I had won the lottery with my kid.

With so many tragic tales and pitfalls for teenagers to navigate—unwanted pregnancies, drugs, runaways, crime, school shootings, suicide, and abusive homes—my son had made it. All the kid wanted was a poster of a swimmer that his high school friends had drawn. Was that so horrible in the grand scheme of things? What gave the Nancys of the world the right to take away the one little thing that made my son happy?

I stayed in the hall for a moment and took deep breaths until my heart stopped pounding. I couldn't enter his space with the anger I'd worked up in my mind. What was Dr. Benoit always saying? I needed to meet Ry with calm reassurance. I had to slow my angry mind from continuing its insidious meltdown.

Inside the room, Ry was sleeping. There was no sign of Nancy. Phillip lay in his bed, staring blankly at the ceiling. It would have served no purpose to give Nancy a piece of my mind, no matter how good it might have felt to get the feelings off my chest. I would have felt better, but this wasn't about me; this was about Ry. It was important for Ry to maintain a peaceful, stress-free environment, and having his father go ballistic on the wife of his roommate hardly qualified as peaceful. I had to take the poster down to avoid making waves with the administration, but at the same time, I feared what my son's reaction would be. For a few days now, he'd had no significant outbursts, and I wanted to keep it that way. What I wanted to do was wait for Nancy and then tell her, "You want it gone so badly, you take it down. Then you can deal with his anger."

But of course, I couldn't do that. I had to solve this problem myself. Could I get the poster down without Ry knowing? Maybe if I removed it before he awoke, he'd never even notice it was gone. His short-term memory was still very fuzzy, and the poster hung behind his head. Out of sight, out of mind. It could be like the poster never existed. I walked over to the head of the bed and pulled up a chair. With one foot on the bed frame and one on the chair, I strained to reach the top of the poster. I pushed my fingernail under the tape.

"Dad, what the hell are you doing?" Ry shouted, glaring up at me.

So much for plan A. I was busted in the act. Poster thievery. Caught red-handed.

I blamed Nancy.

"Ry, there's a problem with the poster," I said with the most amount of dignity, a man could muster while perched on top of a bedpost.

"What problem? Why is there a problem? Leave the poster alone." Each word that rolled out of Ry's mouth picked up additional velocity. He was irritated. What logical reason could I give him? The patient whose wife had complained lay in the bed five feet away. I was not sure how much Phillip could understand but I didn't want to upset him. It wasn't his fault his wife was humorless. Besides, if Phillip could raise his hand, he'd probably vote to keep the poster up.

"It's a policy, Ry. Nothing can be put on the walls." I hoped the lie would satisfy him.

"Bullshit. Leave the poster alone. I want it up." Even with his neurons struggling to reconnect, Ry could still sniff out a lie.

My mind raced. I wanted to appease my son instead of angering him. The only solution I thought of was to get him out of the room. "How about this, Ry? I'll leave the poster up if you get out of the bed and go with me to the cafeteria for some early lunch."

I looked down on him from the top of the bed. He had not talked much for the last week, but he had at least become human again. An arrogant, nasty human but human nonetheless. It was a step up from being a rock. "When is lunch?" he asked.

"In a few minutes." I dragged the wheelchair over to the bed and pulled back the sheets. "Let's go. I'll take you down to the dining hall and eat with you." I was excited about getting him up. For the moment, I had avoided a war over the poster and could worry about it later. I would deal with one challenge at a time. Helping Ry with his pajamas, I got him in the chair quickly before he could change his mind. Once in the hallway, I broke into a slow jog. A light wind blew Ry's hair back as we raced down the hall. I laughed as we went faster, and the hallway became a blur of closed doors, gurneys, and nurses with their clipboards and medicine trays. I must have looked like I'd gone mad, racing down the hall.

In the cafeteria, I parked Ry's chair under one of the flying saucer tables. Ry glared at me, silent.

"Ry, this is great having lunch together. It's good to see you up." His only reply was daggers shooting from his eyes. I didn't want to sit around and wait for what else might come, so I left Ry and hurried over to look at the buffet offerings. The line was short, and I knew why. It was a smorgasbord of mushy, nasty, food-like substances: flat, dry burgers, stewed tomatoes, boiled carrots, and green peas. It was impossible to discern what the dessert was. This was awful, but at least we could have lunch together. I fixed him two burgers with some chips and quickly walked back to the table.

Across from us, at the same table, sat a young man struggling to eat his peas. His name was Larry. I had seen him around the halls and one of the nurses had told me his name. If you stay in a place like this long enough, eventually you know everyone and everyone knows you. He was mashing his peas into the plate before scooping them into his mouth. Larry the Pea Smasher. His shaking hand slowly scooped up some pea mush into an oversized spoon and then moved it to his mouth. Sometimes he would miss the goal by a few inches and the spoon would crash into his face.

I slid my chair over to him and put my hand on his. "Here,

Larry, let me help you." I guided another load of peas into his spoon and said, "Okay, watch, they come up to your mouth. That's good. Open your mouth." I pushed the spoon into his mouth and turned it so the contents would spill onto his tongue.

"Good. That was perfect." He chewed on the soft peas, occasionally stopping to smile at me.

That's how it was in a place like this. We're in this together—even Nancy—and in some small way, we were a family. We were saddened for each other's setbacks and cheered on the successes. Maybe it was just eating peas, but sometimes that meant everything. I was genuinely happy for Larry, because we had to hope for each other. Larry was doing something he may not have done the day before. That meant new things were possible. It gave hope to us all that those things could still change. If Larry could eat peas today, maybe one day my son could attend Notre Dame or even swim again. We had to be each other's cheerleaders, because if not us, then who?

"I can't eat this crap!" Ry shouted, throwing his burger on the table. "It's dry and tasteless. I'll puke. Let's go home. I don't want to be here. I'm not like these people. I don't need to be spoon-fed mashed peas." His voice boomed through the cafeteria. Patients turned their heads towards us. Apparently, my son didn't share my kumbaya feelings about being in this together and cheering each other on.

I looked around the room in a panic, unsure of what to do. Larry had given up on eating peas and stared at us, mouth agape. Ry's face grew redder with anger as he demanded, "Dad, take me home!"

For a moment, I considered it. But what might happen if he had a seizure at home and I was not there? Or he fell out of the chair and hit his head? Fell down the steps? Tripped on a rug? I'd always loved our home, but now it felt like a series of catastrophic traps. There was no possibility of taking him home yet, but, I didn't want to take Ry back to his room either. This was the first time in a month that he had shined any exhilarating behavior other than just wanting to lay in bed. I did not want him to descend once again in a silent cocoon.

I pulled his wheelchair away from the table and steered him back toward his room. I'd nearly convinced myself to leave the hospital and get him some food when I opened his door and saw that the wall was bare. The hand-drawn girl in a swimsuit with the dozens of signatures was gone. A small piece of tape was dangling on the green wall.

I left Ry in the hallway so he wouldn't notice the missing poster while I stepped inside and got his slippers. As I picked up his feet and put them on, I said, "We're ready to travel now."

What swam across my vision was that I was determined to sneak him out of the hospital regardless of his severe affliction. My son may not have had a motorcycle to ride off on, but the realization was he had a wheelchair that made him mobile. Nancy may have gotten his poster torn down but she was not going to tear down our spirit. My son needed a breakaway—he needed to break free—and I was daring enough to help him do it. I knew a thing or two about making a run for it—and I knew how it felt to be reminded that you were human after feeling for so long that you weren't. A siege of doom blew through my mind as to the dangers of this planed escape.

I grinned, thinking of the first time I helped a patient escape a hospital.

It was the height of the war on drugs, and I had a job working at a psychiatric hospital while attending college. Nixon despised "hippies." and the general thought among politicians was that marijuana was a "gateway" drug to the harder stuff, like heroin.

Andrew, a young man around Ry's age, with long hair over his shoulders, was brought to Building 19, the maximum-security unit where I worked. I completed the intake form, sitting with him in a locked-down room. He did not seem afraid or nervous.

"Andrew," I said, "I'm here to help you. Do you know why you're here?"

"Yes, my father caught me smoking marijuana on the deck."

"I see here that you live in Arlington, Virginia, and your dad works at the Pentagon. What does he do there?" I asked.

"He's a two-star general," Andrew answered while staring down at the floor with his shoulders slumped.

I folded back his admittance pages to see if there was any information from an admitting doctor. As I read more, I was shocked but tried not to show it. Andrew's family doctor had signed legal forms committing him to my facility for "addiction to marijuana." I couldn't believe it. He was just a kid who smoked weed. It seemed a dire consequence.

"Andrew, let me be candid. Do you think you have an addiction? Do you take any other drugs?"

"I like to smoke weed. I was supposed to start Virginia Commonwealth University this semester but my father put me in here."

"What's your major?"

"Art. I want to be an illustrator, like, doing covers for magazines."

"What's your medium?" I asked. He looked surprised that I knew that term.

"I like colored pencils. It's easier to correct your mistakes," he said with a shy smile.

Andrew and I continued talking for about an hour, and I

couldn't see any reason why he was in a psychiatric hospital, especially Building 19. It was the maximum-security wing of the hospital, reserved for patients with schizophrenia, not for seventeen-year-old kids who liked to smoke a joint in their backyards. He was bright and articulate and I felt bad for him. He just had the misfortune of being an artistic type born to a military man. I said goodnight to Andrew with the intention that by the next day we would probably be able to clear this up and have him released.

The next night, when I reported for my shift, I pulled out Andrew's chart to see what, if any, remarks had been made by the assigned psychiatrist. As I read the doctor's instructions, I became absolutely petrified with terror. Andrew was scheduled for electro-shock therapy the following morning. Shock treatments were reserved for psychotic patients or extremely depressed individuals.

I took his chart down the hall and shared it with my friend, Harry Almond, another psych-aid. Harry was finishing his MS in Social Work and worked weekends at the drug treatment center. He was as shocked as I was, and together we knew we had to do something.

After the lights out curfew, Harry and I went to Andrew's room and explained the situation. Huddled together in whispered secrets, we hatched our plan.

"Andrew, do you have anyone you can trust in the Richmond area?" I asked.

"Yes, I have an aunt on Monument Avenue."

"See that window with the bars on it? We're going to open that window, let you out with some money, and you are going to go visit your aunt. We're then going to close the window and make some marks near the keyhole lock to look as if you had some tool to pry it open. You'll have a twelve-hour head-start before anyone realizes you're gone."

Andrew thanked us. We handed him all the cash we had, and he disappeared out of the window. The next morning, a nurse discovered his empty room and called the police. Harry and I were interviewed, but nothing ever came of it. We never saw Andrew again, although he crossed my mind numerous times over the years and I always had a wish that he made it to college and had a good life.

I had no clear revelation on how I was going to pull this escape off? But it was clear that my body was beginning to exhibit a pattern of distress. I began to sweat profusely.

Ry had a security band on his wrist that would set off alarms if we used the patients 'elevator, so I turned the chair around and headed for the other end of the hospital. Plenty of times over the past weeks, I'd seen the kitchen personnel bring up food on a service elevator. My heart was beating so fast, I thought for sure anyone could see what we were doing. But I kept my eyes straight ahead and walked with purpose. As I passed nurses and hospital personnel, I smiled with a quick nod. "How is everyone today?"

One of the nurses we passed called out, "Going for a ride, Ry?"

I thought I'd have a stroke and end up in a hospital bed, bunked up with my son.

At the end of the hallway, there were no elevators. Were we in the wrong part of the hospital?

"Excuse me," I said to a man with an ID card on his shirt. "Where are the elevators to the kitchen?"

"Right behind you. Those two doors lead to a hallway and the service elevator is just down the hall there." The man looked at Ry, slumped in his chair. "Is there something I can help you with?" he asked, no doubt suspicious.

I spit out the first thought that came to my mind. "I was going to see if there was more orange juice. My son loves orange juice, don't you, Ry? Don't you love orange juice?" I patted Ry on the shoulder as he glared at the wall.

"Orange juice." Ry said.

What wonderful timing I thought, that Ry would choose to say something that might aid us in our central pursuit of dangerous behavior.

"I'm sure there is plenty more in the cafeteria," the man offered. "Let me help you with those doors. They're heavy."

"Thank you," I said with a smile. As soon as we entered the elevator, kitchen smells filled the air. In a few seconds, the door opened and we were staring at the steam rising from pots, people cutting vegetables, and big bowls of fruit being placed on rolling carts—more green peas. I quickly whipped my head around, searching for a back door. I spotted it and saw a food truck backing up to a ramp. This was our chance. I pushed Ry quickly toward the outdoor ramp.

"Sir, are you lost?" a woman shouted from behind me.

Damn. We have failed before we got to the escape hatch. I skidded to a stop and spun the wheelchair around to see a woman in a stiff white uniform. She looked like Nurse Ratched from *One Flew Over the Cuckoo's Nest*. Her name-tag read Nancy Powell, RD. What was it with women named Nancy inserting themselves into my life? This Nancy crossed her arms and tilted her head, as if waiting for an answer.

I drew a blank and began to panic. "I, um… well," I mumbled while quietly thanking the Good Lord that Ry had decided to go into one of his silent modes. "Well, you see… I just uh… wanted to take my son to get some fresh air and sunshine."

She stared at me for a few seconds and then shook her head. "You need to go back upstairs to get a pass and then go out the front doors. Isn't that a security wrist ban he wearing? I don't think you are going to get a medical pass to take him out."

"Okay," I said. I began to turn the wheelchair around as I watched Nancy walk back to her office and sit down at her desk. Then I spun the wheelchair into a one hundred and eighty-degree turn and, like a missile hunting for its target, ran for daylight. Ry's body swung back and forth in the wheelchair. I wondered what he thought we were doing. His face was still devoid of much expressions. When we got to the door, there were two young staff members leaning against the dock railing, smoking. *Now what?* I thought. It dawned on me that I really hadn't thought this plan through.

I turned to one of the men. "Excuse me, how do I get to the front parking lot?"

"Take the sidewalk to the left, around the building," replied the taller, leaner one. "But you can't take the wheelchair. There's no ramp."

Shit, I thought. I'd gotten this far; I was not turning back. "Uh, would you mind watching my son for a second while I go get my car?"

"Not a problem, man," the shorter, chubbier worker said.

"Thank you. I'll be right back." I hopped over the railing and sprinted around the corner. My stomach was on fire from nerves. I was violating a bunch of rules, and Ry could be injured. What would I say if I got caught? What would Lynn think if she found out? As a charge nurse, she was a stickler for rules. I pushed those thoughts aside. I just needed to run as fast as I could. My marathon stride needed to kick in. I'd just left my incapacitated son with two total strangers on a loading dock.

As I ran at full speed through the massive parking lot, I recalled the letter from the Notre Dame alum: *A relationship with your child is only forged in this kind of fire.* Robert Frost said the three most important words to live by were *life goes on.* That's what I was trying to do at that moment.

Move on. Move forward.

Dr. Benoit had told me just a few days before to go live my life, and Ry would follow. At that moment, I felt pretty alive, with sweat pouring out of my skin.

Getting into my car, I jammed the key into the ignition and then drove toward the back of the hospital. I prayed Ry would still be there and that he hadn't tried to get out of his wheelchair. When I pulled up to the dock, I breathed a sigh of relief. He was in the same spot and the workers protecting our plan.

When I got out, it dawned on me: how would I get Ry into the car?

"You need some help, man?" the tall worker asked.

"Sure, thank you."

They each took a side of Ry, lifting him out of the chair and down off the loading dock to my open arms.

"Ry, I need for you to grab hold of the door frame and pull yourself into the front seat," I said. A disturbing thought flashed through my mind: *What if I had to do this for the rest of my life? Damn, damn, damn.*

I shut the door and walked around to get in the car.

"Hey, man, what are you gonna do with the chair?" one of the workers said.

"Will you hand it to me, please?"

One of the men picked it up and eased it down to me. I rolled it over to some bushes near the wall of the hospital. They knew what I was doing. They smiled and rolled their eyes, as if this wasn't the first time, they'd seen this kind of breakout.

"You guys won't turn me in to the authorities, will you? We are just going down the street to get some fast food."

"Shoot, man, I wish I could go with you. How long you gonna take to get back in this place? These doors are locked at two."

"I'll be back before then. Thanks for your help and for not reporting us."

I got in the car and buckled Ry in. Within minutes, we were in sight of fast-food heaven along Chamberlayne and Brook Road, just north of Richmond. "You want McDonald's, Wendy's, Kentucky Fried Chicken?" Another disturbing thought flashed: *God, what would I do if he had to go to the bathroom?*

"Chicken," Ry mumbled.

"Are you sure you wouldn't rather have…?"

"Chicken," he grunted with his face pointed toward the window.

I pulled up to the window at Kentucky Fried Chicken. "Ry, what parts do you want?"

"Chicken," he repeated

"May I help you?" a female voice asked, crackling over the speaker.

"Yes, I would like the ten-piece box of chicken."

"You want fries with that?" she said, sounding bored. Didn't she understand we were fugitives, making a great escape for fried chicken? Where was her enthusiasm for our adventure?

"No, thanks, but I would like two large Cokes and lots of napkins." I wasn't overly confident this was going to go well. Thinking of the numerous occasions when food had flown across the room if Ry was unhappy, I called out to the woman inside the speaker in slowed vocal equivalent of a shuffle, "Seriously, extra,

extra napkins."

"Please pay at the second window. $6.50," she answered with the same bored tone.

The aroma of fried chicken filled the car. I pulled across the street and into a Sears parking lot. I took Ry's seatbelt off and placed three layers of napkins across his lap. He was going to have to eat with one hand since he still could not fully raise his right arm. I pulled a leg out of the box, figuring it would be the easiest to hold.

"Here's a leg." The success of this operation may still falter.

"Breast."

"How are you going to hold onto a breast with one hand?"

"Breast," Ry repeated, looking straight ahead. Lord knows I loved my son more than life itself, but my God, what a pain in the ass he was being. I sat there for a moment staring at my son, the honor student, the nationally ranked swimmer, scholarship to Notre Dame, so handsome he could be the leading man in a movie, thinking this is not right. Progress is way beyond a reasonable doubt.

"Maybe a wing would…"

"Breast." Well, at least he'd moved on from "chicken".

I handed him the largest breast I could find in the box. It had a nice thick, crunchy coating. He held out his hand, palm up, and I carefully lowered the chicken into it. Ry studied the meat for a few seconds, like a cat watching a bird. With one quick motion, he became Larry the Pea Smasher. The flat part of the breast came to rest on his open mouth, lips, chin, and nose. Crumbs rained down into his lap. Attacking the chicken like a caveman, he managed to rip off a large chunk of white meat. The crunching sound of the extra crispy skin penetrated the car. The images I captured of this moment would make for an exquisite movie scene. For a few brief seconds, I broke into a fierce laugh. Happy tears made their way down my cheeks. My life, not long ago in a freefall, had for now been abated. My acute sense of loss had stopped.

It was the first real meal he had eaten in the last four weeks. I watched as he labored to get the meat off the bone. I would clean the seat later. We sat there in that Sears parking lot for almost an hour, eating the entire box of chicken. For the first time since his accident, I started to think things might be okay. It wasn't a motorcycle ride across the country, and it wasn't a Japanese garden, but my son and I had had an adventure. We'd made a memory together.

I thought back to what Stephanie had told me about trying to remain in the moment. She was right, joy could still be found if I focused on the simple aspects of life instead of getting swallowed up by the big picture. I didn't know if my son would ever attend Notre Dame. I didn't know if he would ever swim competitively again, but in this moment, this small moment of eating chicken together in a parking lot, there could be a sense of serenity.

Back at the hospital, the two men at the loading dock smiled as we returned. They helped again to get Ry safely back in his chair for the quick ride back through the kitchen and up to his room. I fully knew he may forget this day, but I wouldn't, and that meant something. It meant we were still participating in this thing called life. Also, there was joy in gleefully tricking the hospital critics.

Chapter 17

A Voyage to the Past and Back to the Future

It was ultimately the changing of the seasons that brought me back from the brink after Audrey's death.

I was camping on a logging road somewhere in Idaho when I woke to a cold sensation on my face. I had lost track of how long I'd been wandering the country on my trusty old Triumph motorcycle. Six months? Eight months? It was all a blur. But on that particular morning, a light dusting of snowflakes covered my sleeping bag and the canteen of water next to me. The sun was fighting to break through puffy clouds that surely meant more snow.

At that time, Idaho felt like the right place for me to be. I thought I'd outsmarted my trauma. Snuck away in the night where it could never track me down. I'd hopped on a motorcycle and sped away as fast as I could, so sure of myself that I would never have to answer to my wife's death. It had come like a thief and taken her while my back was turned, but I would never give it the satisfaction of seeing my grief. I was young and foolish enough to think I had won. With thirty dollars in my pocket for ten hours of labor the previous day, I felt the way a snail might feel in its shell. Safe but alone. Exactly how I wanted it.

Resting on the ground, wrapped inside my protective nylon cocoon, I felt it was my home, my hiding place. Priests have their churches. This was my cathedral. I'd abandoned the empty nest back in Virginia and made a new one that felt like a safe haven. Since coming out here, my melancholy moods had become less noticeable. I was becoming a man of the fields, thickets, and streams, feeling like that farm boy again, helping his grandmother with chores. Each day, I walked more softly than the day before as I learned to steer my sad memories in a different direction. The trade-off was, I felt emotionally unavailable. I'd denied death the pleasure of witnessing my grief and, by doing so, had taken refuge behind a wall of my own making.

Audrey and I had been two against the world. We were each other's muse, conscience, and protector. We'd fallen in love and into a bubble where others weren't allowed. Our love was selfish and exclusive. We were our own VIP section, and no one was allowed behind the velvet rope. Perhaps if we'd had more time, we would have expanded our circle and let others in, but there was no way to know in hindsight. Now I was all alone and I was still trying figure out how to live without her. Some days it was difficult to accommodate the sting of her death. I had become brilliant actor and remained mostly stoic.

Still, regardless of what I knew or didn't, what I could handle or what I couldn't, it was time to move forward. A man can only hide from his own life for so long. As much as I wanted nothing more than to hide in my sleeping bag, atop the pile of soft moss, it was time to move forward by going home. Virginia would always be my home and I could never stay away from her for too long.

I rolled up my bag then folded the plastic sheet underneath, neatly pushing them down in my hard case saddlebag. I was careful not to damage the clear baggie of neatly rolled joints I had brought along for those times when I wanted a dreamy night's sleep. Opening the gas cap, I looked down into the dark tank and figured there was about a gallon left. Enough for fifty miles.

My stomach growled. I didn't have to be at the dude ranch until eleven, so I decided to go to Hudson's Café, six miles down the road in Coeur d' Alene. It was famous for both its hamburgers and its breakfast.

It felt good when my butt touched the leather seat. I kicked the center stand up, started the motor, and a white plume floated out of the pipes. I loved to sit and just listen to the comforting hum on slow idle. I breathed in the clean, crisp air and placed my foot on the foot peg. After one more check of the hard-shell luggage bags, I clicked the shifter into first gear. I throttled her up and was off, smiling up at the big, blue sky.

It was easy for me to daydream on my bike, with the wind pushing my hair back and tickling my ears. My hair had grown almost long enough to pull back into a ponytail since my sojourn across the country. I loved this landscape with its birds, highways, flowers, and various animals. In my daydreams, I assumed different roles, adapting to my chosen personality for the moment. I was still searching for the real me and at times felt in need of protection. I was a man rising from dreams that lay in ashes back in Virginia. Which ghostly ideals I wanted to hold on to, I still could not say.

After a short drive, I pulled into a filling station just north of town to top off my tank. Two gallons in, I counted out seventy-two cents from the change in my pocket and walked into the station to pay.

Behind the counter stood a man wearing a white Stetson hat. I handed him the change and said, "Hey, I've heard that Hudson's Café has a good breakfast."

The old man, his face creased with hundreds of deep wrinkles, replied, "You from the northeast?"

"No," I replied. "Virginia."

"Virginia is pretty, I hear. What brought you this far west?" He deposited my seventy-two cents in the cash drawer.

"Trying to find some peace in my life, I guess."

The old man looked me over. His eyes softened, as if he recognized a younger version of himself. "There are a lot of folks who've come through here looking for the same thing. Lonely faces, broken hearts, running from their pasts."

I gazed out at my Triumph through the dirty garage window. Was I really just like all the others, running away from my problems? Did this old man watch dozens of broken and displaced drifters speed across the country, seeking answers from an indifferent land? What must he think, watching us parade through like an army of disenchanted souls? I turned to look at him and mumbled, "I don't know what I'm doing."

"Well, son, you take care of yourself, and I hope you find some peace. Idaho has a lot to give. I always say you can drive the wheels off all the way until the road ends, but you will still find the past right behind you."

"What's your name?" I asked.

"You can call me Ernie. Ernie Mooney."

"Thank you for the advice," I said and shook his hand. When I got to the door I said, "You take care, Ernie Mooney. I'm going to have to get me one of those hats."

He nodded and I gave him a big smile.

Hudson's Café was just a block away. Since there was no traffic, I decided to just push my motorcycle to the front door and let her rest on the kickstand. Opening the door, I was immediately hit by the aroma of frying eggs, burgers, and fresh homemade bread. The place was small, with only seventeen seats at a counter and no tables. It was fairly crowded but still I wondered how they made any money serving so few customers.

Sitting down at one of the few empty stools, I picked up a menu. There wasn't much of a selection, but that didn't matter. I wasn't a fussy eater and anything would beat the slop they served at the bunkhouse.

A waiter, perhaps a descendant of the original Hudson himself, approached me. In his late thirties, he had longer hair than the other locals and a goatee. "Hey, partner, what can I get you today?" he asked.

"How about coffee, a glass of buttermilk, and one of your burgers with cheese, onions, and mustard."

"Great. You want pickles on the side or on the burger?" he asked with a big smile.

"Pickles everywhere," I said. "I love pickles."

"Be right up."

Although I was surrounded by people hungrily eating their burgers or scrambled eggs on a biscuit, my mind glided back to memories of Audrey. Many nights we sat on our deck, looking down on Harrison Street and Park Avenue and across the way to Virginia Commonwealth University. We ran speakers out to the deck so we could listen to Frank Zappa and our favorite Led Zeppelin song, "Stairway to Heaven." On some nights, students would stop on the sidewalk, looking up at us on the deck. "Hey, man, love that song," they'd say, often followed by, "You got any weed?" If the wind blew in the right direction, the smell of onion rings frying at the Village Café would drift our way. Our love was lazy and slow, just how we wanted it. We answered to no one and made the rules as we went along. The first rule: we had no rules.

Audrey admired how evenly and tightly I could roll a joint.

There were times when we would have a pound of weed on hand, selling ounces to close friends to make a little extra cash. Our buyers weren't hippie types but clean-cut folks, like an attorney we had met in a jazz bar near campus, then some of his friends. Even our dentist would call once a month. Almost every night we would light up, passing the joint back and forth until we smoked it down so small, we needed tweezers.

Audrey would giggle when I painted her toes with bright red toe-nail polish. It was those small details that stuck with me, and I found myself longing to hold those sweet little toes just once more. The truth was, I felt terrified I would one day forget what they looked like. How long could I remember their shape or how they felt in the palm of my hand as I dabbed the polish on each nail?

"Here you go. Enjoy." The waiter slid the plate towards me. I looked up quickly, jolted from the past. "I know most of my customers," he said. "Are you a new student or visiting a relative?"

"Just taking a break from school in Virginia." I didn't feel like sharing the details of my life with any more strangers. The old man at the gas station had left me feeling exposed and vulnerable. The waiter seemed to sense my need to be left alone and thankfully dropped the conversation to take another customer's order.

As I took a bite of my burger, I opened the journal I'd religiously written in each day of my trip. I read a few entries from the previous day: *Lonely, lonely, lonely, my personality will never adapt to wearing a mask every day.* Was I ever going to feel normal again? Audrey was everywhere. Maybe what the old man had said was true: no matter how far I rode, the past was always right behind me. I couldn't imagine spending the rest of my life living with her constant memory. Still, an even more painful thought was that one day I might forget all the little details of her face, her hands, or the curve of her back. Who would I be if I could no longer recall the intimate details of my wife?

"Hey, buddy, what's your name?" the waiter asked as he refilled my coffee cup.

"Don," I replied. My own name caught in my throat and brought a tear to my eye. It was a simple question, one we are asked all the time, but I no longer knew what that meant. I no longer knew who I was supposed to be in this world. My wife was dead and I was thousands of miles from home. My name might as well have been "Lost." I quickly brushed the tear away. The sixties had just ended, and crying men were seen as lacking character. *Stuff it down and eat the poison* was the mantra of the day.

I expected the waiter to shuffle off at the sight of my humanness. Perhaps he would drop the check and recoil at the sight of my perceived weakness, but he didn't. Instead, he said, "I'm Tom, but people call me TM. We have some freshly baked apple pie. You want a slice?" There wasn't a hint of judgment in his voice.

"Well." I paused, knowing I needed to save money. "I probably shouldn't. I've got limited funds right now." I wasn't sure if I was more embarrassed over being emotional or being poor.

"No problem," he said and went to help another customer. A little while later, TM returned with a slice of warm apple pie and a scoop of vanilla ice cream. He set it in front of me and said, "You look like you can use some kindness in your life." He pulled a clean fork out of his apron pocket and pushed it toward me.

"It's on the house." With that, he walked away.

I lingered over my coffee and pie until the crowd had thinned to none. When I was the only customer left in the joint, TM poured himself a cup of coffee, refilled mine for the umpteenth time then came around to the other side of the counter. He sat on a stool, leaving an empty one between us as he spun around the opposite way and leaned against the counter. Now that he was on my side of the counter, I could see how tall he was. His long legs stretched out in front of him, tucked away in a pair of pointed cowboy boots. I would have thought a waiter would choose a more comfortable pair of shoes, but TM seemed quite at home in the shit kickers.

Pulling a pack of cigarettes out of his shirt pocket, he offered one to me. I was never a heavy smoker but took it. He lit my cigarette with a match from a matchbook on the counter before lighting his own.

I was hungry for some kindness. "Thank you for the pie," I said.

He took a deep drag on his cigarette and flicked the ash to the floor. Rubbing it out with the toe of his boot, he replied, "No problem."

I stared into my coffee and sang quietly to myself, *I get by with a little help from my friends.*

TM looked over with a knowing grin and added a soprano version of, "*I get hiiigh with a little help from my friends.*"

There I sat in a burger joint, two thousand miles from home, singing a Beatles song with a big-hearted stranger. Suddenly I felt like I was in an LSD dream. I could see everything that had happened in my life up to this point, every moment all at once—hitting home runs in Little League, my first ever date with Pat Spain, reciting poetry for Ms. Abrams in Honors English, sipping coffee and sharing a biscuit with Audrey and telling her what I wanted to do with her when we got home—I saw it all right up to this very moment, where there was the lingering smell of warm apple pie.

TM lit another cigarette and glanced in my direction. He seemed to understand that sorrow was weighing heavy on my heart. "What brought you here, Don?" he asked. I knew when he said it, he wasn't looking for a tale of adventure and sightseeing. TM was looking for the truth. This waiter of a hamburger joint in a podunk town in the middle of Idaho was looking to a traveling stranger to be genuine with him.

I don't know if it was the four cups of coffee or the cigarette that was making me lightheaded, but something in me wanted to open up. I was tired. I was lonely. And I was ready for honesty. I sipped on my now cold coffee and answered him the best I could. "I've been outrunning death. I don't know if it's on purpose or if I'm just reckless, but it seems lately the only time I feel alive is when death is breathing down my neck."

TM nodded toward the large picture window to my Triumph parked outside. "Is that your method?" he asked.

I nodded. "I have no rhythm left in my life. I've been crisscrossing this state at a hundred miles per hour on winding mountain roads. Jumping from one job to the next, from one bed to the next, when all I really want to do is lie down in the tall grass and never get up. Death is not something I dread or welcome. My brain has absorbed pain beyond what I can speak to find word to explain.

TM looked over at me for a long while. He looked about twenty years older than me and I got the feeling he was looking through me and into his past. Maybe he too had woken up one morning and taken off, leaving his life behind. Maybe this diner was where he'd run out of steam, and here was where he stayed. Maybe he wished he'd gone back home. I had no way of knowing unless I asked, and I didn't want to. I wanted TM to remain a mystery to me.

When he finally spoke again, his voice was slow and deliberate. I wondered if he was speaking to his past self or to me when he said, "You have to be careful, Don, what thoughts you carry around in your head. You have to look for a less messy life. Hunt for the soft parts inside of you."

I blew a smoke ring into the air before stubbing out my cigarette into the ashtray. "Every day I look around at the landscape and try to figure out my place in it. All I see is loneliness and solitude." I almost told TM about Audrey and her sudden passing but then held back. I wanted to keep her to myself for just a bit longer. Instead, I smiled and added, "My grandmother used to tell me that the east is always the beginning of things. It's where the sun rises first. But it's also where my feet belong. I miss my family. I miss knowing where I belong."

"Don, you need love in your life. Without it, you're going to live life on a knife's edge. Out back is my Harley 900 Sportster. I've never given much thought to how I might die. But like you, I've been down those same roads at one hundred miles an hour." TM stood up and rapped his knuckles on the counter, signaling he was done with his break. "Go home. Go east and listen to your grandma. Start fresh."

He left me alone as he went into the kitchen behind a swinging door. I wanted to tell him thank you for the kindness and advice. I wanted to tell him so much more. Instead, I left enough money on the counter for the bill and a tip and wrote on a napkin – *If you're ever in Virginia, you have a friend.* Then I added my parent's phone number.

Outside, I could see the clouds rolling in. If I wanted to get ahead of the next snowstorm I needed to move. I throttled up and got back on the highway, heading farther away from the ranch and feeling the ashes of despair flake off as the machine built up speed. It was time to head back east.

It was time to prepare for a new life. The body has a big capacity for healing itself.

Chapter 18

Where the Buffalo Roam

The window of Ry's room had a small ledge outside. I brought birdseed and would spread it out so birds would come to sit by the window. I thought the sight of colorful birds would bring Ry some joy. Sometimes, he would break his silence to ask me what kind of bird it was. A few moments would pass and he would ask again. I didn't mind repeating the same answer over and over; I was just happy he was talking at all.

Being in nature, marveling at the beauty of this incredible earth, has always been something that bonded me with my son. We both had an appreciation for the great outdoors. My fondest memories from Ry's childhood were times when we went camping together with the Boy Scouts. I had raised him to respect the planet and to understand the organic rhythms of the seasons.

Finally, the day came when I was going to legally take Ry out of the hospital on an official trip to Maymont Park. His physical therapists had been working with him twice a day in preparation for this outing. He was close to being able to stand up on his own, and to say I was excited was an understatement. The beautiful outdoors, wide-open spaces, and fresh air were calling to my soul and I knew it was just the thing Ry needed to feel energized. I just hoped my enthusiasm was enough to motivate him to comply.

When I got to Ry's room, I found him sitting up in bed and

eating breakfast. It was a good sign.

I had already decided that Ry was going on the trip, even if I had to pull him out of bed with his paralyzed leg dragging on the floor. So, it was a relief to see he was already up. Now I had about thirty minutes to get him dressed and make it downstairs in time to catch the Sheltering Arms bus to the park. I leaned over him, pulling down the sheets. "It's time to get dressed, Ry. Now."

As I stared at him, I realized he was a grown man now. It had happened so quickly. For most of his life, I had been able to protect him. But I hadn't been able to protect him from a thunderstorm that had altered both our lives. What did the word "dad" mean to him on this day?

"We have less than thirty minutes before the bus leaves for Maymont Park, Ry. You promised you would go."

He turned his head toward me. It was a good sign. Movement. Progress. He pushed himself up a little higher in the bed and pulled the Poseidon Swim Team shirt he'd been sleeping in over his head. He then tossed it toward the trash can, mumbling, "Why wear the shirt of a swim team? I'll never be able to swim again."

"Nice shot," I said as the shirt landed in the trash. "Now get your ass out of bed." I chose to ignore his no swimming again statement. Opening the dresser drawer, I grabbed a pair of jeans and a blue Notre Dame t-shirt. I raised his limp arm over his head and pulled the t-shirt down. He sat still as a stone, making no move to help me. While yanking and tugging to get his jeans up, I pleaded with my rather large son. "Ry, I can't do this by myself," I said.

He grumbled as I helped him stand. Then he tugged his pants up with his good arm. Not wanting him to get back in the bed, I reached for the wheelchair while spinning him around to sit down. I was feeling like a caretaker ninja, and my respect for people who did this as a profession continued to grow. Taking care of my only son had exhausted me, and I was with him for just part of each day. I couldn't imagine how the nurses and physical therapists with multiple patients felt at the end of the day.

With Ry dressed and in his chair, out the door we went. I hoped this adventure was not going to be some pious folly. I knew we needed a pass to leave, but I'd forgotten to get one the night before. Worried we wouldn't make it to the bus in time, I ran down the hall as fast as my legs would allow. When I got to the nurses' station, I locked the wheels on Ry's chair and leaned over the station counter. "Excuse me, I think today is the Maymont Park day, and I'd like to get a pass for Ry to leave the hospital."

The young nurse reached over and pulled up Ry's chart. "I'm sorry, but there is no authorization for a trip outside the hospital."

"Can't you page Dr. Zasler? Ry would really like to go to the park. Wouldn't you, Ry?"

He sat silent. I loved my son, but he had become a terrible accomplice.

"I'll try to get him, but he usually doesn't come in until nine thirty," she said, picking up the phone.

The nurse paged Dr. Zasler three times but he didn't return the page. "Sorry, I tried, but there is no one else who can authorize the pass," she said. "You do know that Ry has refused to go to physical therapy today, right? I'm not sure if Dr. Zasler would even give him a pass."

I sighed but didn't argue. My heart rate and blood pressure were high enough these days. I was disappointed but figured we could go to the park another day. I looked down at Ry. If he was disappointed, I couldn't tell. I rolled him down the hallway back towards his room and cringed, thinking of another long day of sitting in silence. Maybe we'd get lucky and a bird would land on the window.

When I opened the door to his room, I was hit with a sharp, repugnant smell. Two hospital aids were changing the soiled sheets on Phillip's bed as he sat in a chair facing the window. Something in me snapped. I couldn't do it. I refused to spend one more moment in that stuffy, smelly, claustrophobic room. I backed out into the hall, turned the chair around and briskly rolled Ry toward the elevator. My antic style personality decided that we were going outside. It felt exhilarating to break the rules. I perceived the decision as anarchic individualism.

We'd just go downstairs and take a chance the van driver would let us on the bus. I pounded the elevator call button, hoping it would arrive quickly. A sign next to the door read, "All patients on this floor must not get on the elevator without first deactivating their safety wristbands. ALARM WILL SOUND." Shit, damn.

I was about to give up on going to Maymont Park when I thought, *why not use the kitchen exit again? There is no alarm system governing that freight elevator.* It had worked once; why not try it again? We had ten minutes before the bus left. I started to sprint.

Desperate to get us outside, I didn't even consider I could be putting Ry in danger by running down the hallway. Something kept hitting my knee as I jogged along. Looking down, I realized it was his seatbelt. Shit. He wasn't buckled in. Could I have put my son in any more danger? Letting go of one of the chair handles, I grabbed the back of his shirt and clenched my fist around his collar. Clutching him as if my life depended on it, I said a prayer and ran faster as my hand tightened its grip on his collar.

"Hold the door," I shouted. A kitchen worker looked up at me as she pushed an empty breakfast cart into the freight elevator. A few seconds later, we were a blur racing through the kitchen, past pots boiling, dishwashers washing, and about ten pairs of eyes watching a crazed man and a stone-faced boy fly toward the exit. I pushed the back door open and rolled Ry onto the loading dock. Unlike last time, there was no one there to help me get him down.

"Dammit, double damn!" I said, as beads of sweat started dripping off my chin. "Having fun yet, Ry?" As usual, he responded with silence.

For most of his life we had enjoyed deep conversations. We talked all morning while sipping coffee on our deck. We talked while riding in the car after school or on the way to swim meets. We discussed what colleges he wanted to attend and the application process. We went over his swim times and where he felt he could do better. But my favorite conversations were when we talked about words. Ry's love for the written and spoken word inspired me. He could analyze and critique a poem or a passage in a novel with great beauty and depth. I could listen to him all day and never get tired. More than anything since the accident, I missed the sound of my son's voice. His silence had left me with a particular emptiness. This event, the accident, the brain injury, the rehab hospital, the lost opportunity of going to Notre Dame, the angry outbursts, had been given a further dimension of poignancy, by what I must begin to regard as my final predictable reaction. Acceptance. I could no longer disclaim the truth, that I could have somehow prevented the accident, if I or my son had behaved differently. I cannot alter the past, but accept the jagged contours of my son's future existence.

As I tried to figure out our next move, I saw a van coming from the end of the building. As it got closer, I could see "Sheltering Arms Hospital" on the side door. It was the van to Maymont Park. "Well, I'll be dammed," I said.

This was not the time for a fit of dark despondency. Jumping down from the dock, I flailed my arms and hurried into the alley, forcing the driver to stop. He opened the doors, letting me step in. The cheerful elderly man, unfazed by the events of the last twenty seconds, greeted me with, "Good morning."

"I'm really sorry, but can you help me get my son on the bus? We really want to go to the park," I said as I pointed over to Ry, who sat several yards away on the vast cement dock. A small stigma of guilt began to creep in to me. I felt a tiny self-inflicted shame of having to tell a lie. Not a little lie either.

The driver looked at Ry and back at me. I could only imagine from his point of view how suspicious this looked. "Where's his pass, and what are you guys doing out here on the kitchen loading dock?" he asked.

I looked down at his nametag. "Well, Brad. My son got up a little late, so the nurse said we could come down to the kitchen and order a plate of eggs and bacon. Then, once we got down here, I remembered today was the day we go to the park. It was too late to go back up to get the pass to catch your beautiful van. I have a pass but it's back in my son's room. I'll be happy to go get it. It will only take a few minutes." In the last month, I had acquired a basic knowledge of how to negotiate around the huge chunks of hospital rules and demands place on poor patients who just want to eat Kentucky Fried Chicken or catch a bus to a serene park. In other words, I had learned to erase road blocks at all costs.

Brad pushed down on the safety brake and shut the bus's engine off.

"All right, let's get him on the bus. There's no time for you to go back to get the pass. Don't forget it next time. I need to position the van closer so the ramp will be level and sit on the dock."

Brad positioned the van next to the dock, pushed a large red button next to his seat and the hydraulic ramp came out toward the dock. I opened a swing gate and pushed Ry along the extended ramp into the van. The van was already filled with wheelchairs locked into place by safety clamps.

I looked into the faces of the other occupants. They all had the same blank faces as Ry. It must have been over a hundred degrees inside the van. Sweat turned my light-blue shirt into deep-sea blue. My mood quickly began to fluctuate. I could sense depression creeping into my brain once again. I had such high hopes and expectations for Ry, but the scene in front of me was shattering those dreams. My heart sank, thinking of how this might be Ry's future: a constant blank stare, a feeling of despair. Being pushed in a wheelchair for the rest of his life. Never swimming again. I tried to think of my garden, its earthy smells of lavender and mint. Anything to break the despair I was feeling the danger signs once again of depression.

When we arrived at the park, it took twenty minutes to get all the passengers unlocked from the steel floor of the van and out on the sidewalk. I unhooked Ry and rolled him out and across the street to a concession stand. We both needed a cold drink. It was barely September and the sun had pushed the temperature to over ninety degrees. The sweat poured through Ry's shirt.

"Anything you want to see, Ry? Maybe go down to the pond and see the Japanese carp?"

Silence.

"There is a food truck here. Any type of drink you want?"

Silence.

"They have donuts too."

Silence.

My annoyance with this scene was becoming intense. How do I exorcise the demons in him?

Across the way was the pond where Ry and I had dug the bamboo that we'd planted in our garden. We split off from the group and I pushed him along a paved walkway toward the bison pasture. The air was not moving, but still it was better than being inside the hospital "I've always liked seeing the bison," I said. "These shaggy beasts once roamed this country in herds of thousands. Native Americans treated the bison with respect, only killing them to obtain food and hides for their clothing. We come along and slaughter them for sport." I knew my son was already well aware of the history of the bison but I needed to fill the silence. How much longer must I endure this pain?

By the time we arrived at the bison pens, sweat had soaked my shirt and was running down the back of my shorts. I pushed Ry's chair as close as I could get him to the fence. Three bison stood just a few feet away, chewing on the grass, taking time out every few seconds to let out a loud burp. They didn't look our way. I stood behind Ry's chair, looking down at the back of his head and neck. It was so still here, so peaceful.

Ry sat still as an oak. What was he thinking? I was truly mystified.

Who is this kid? I thought. What did he remember about his childhood? About me? His mother? About anything? Were all the beautiful memories we'd created over his lifetime gone forever? I remembered every precious moment of all his birthdays, vacation trips to the ocean, but what did that, matter if my son's mind had gone blank? We'd shared so much together, and now I had a son with no memories. An overwhelming feeling of sadness washed over me. I loved him so much. If a lion had him in its jaw, I would attack it. It felt as if chains were binding both our souls. What was I doing? Dragging him around, putting him in dangerous situations... for what? A bite of crispy chicken? A walk in the park? I didn't know which way was up any more. Every instinct I had, in hindsight, felt reckless. And yet, in that moment, it felt right.

I couldn't get on solid ground. For most of my life, I'd trusted my intuition, but now it was failing me. Why was I so determined to drag my son out into the relentless heat to stare at a couple of bison? Had my character begun to crumble? Was I demonstrating a frailty?

I wiped a tear from my cheek and placed it on the granite rock next to his chair. I flicked a small fleck of mica from the weatherworn rock into my palm and looked at it. It was still part of the granite. Even something as durable as granite can be worn down by natural forces. Wind and rain beat down on it day after day. Slowly it wears away. I knelt down to look into the rock's grooves. Lichen sprouted like barely visible stars. Even on this hard rock, signs of life and renewal were everywhere. Staring at that tiny ecosystem, I realized that every day would be a battle to keep looking for the positive—but every day was a chance for rebuilding. For a moment, I felt a flicker of hope: this was our new normal, endlessly bouncing between "Why bother?" and "Never give up."

We may get worn down, but we could survive.

We could rebuild.

Lost in my thoughts, I was startled by a deep grunt coming

from one of the bison. I looked up just in time to see what looked like gallons of acrid-smelling urine flow onto the ground from the beast's elongated male organ. It felt like it went on for several minutes. When the deluge stopped, the big fellow dropped to the ground and rolled over as if he had been shot by Custer himself.

Wallowing in his own stench, he pointed all four hooves straight up toward the blue sky. They were like rods holding up the clouds. He gazed at us with his huge brown eyes and, like a whale spouting water, he blew yellow snot from both nostrils. This bison had to be the most disgusting creature I'd ever laid eyes on, yet I had never witnessed such a moment of freedom. This beautiful beast had absolutely zero shame. He was entirely in the present moment, pissing and blowing snot and rolling around without a care. It was both vile and poetic.

But mostly it was hysterical. Spontaneous.

I started laughing for what felt like the first time in months. Then from Ry, came a soft chuckle. There has never been a song written that could come close to touching my soul the way that little giggle did. The sound grew and grew, becoming a burst of uncontrollable laughter as my son nearly fell out of his wheelchair. For a month, he had sat motionless in his bed or wheelchair for hours, his misery lightened only by the ill-fated, brazen poster of a near-naked swimmer above his bed. Had the fog finally been broken by the unsightly, hilarious vision of a beast wallowing in his own urine and snot?

Ry stopped laughing and said, "Dad, it's hot as shit out here. Let's go back to the hospital. I want to get in the pool."

It was the most complete thought he'd spoken since the accident. Had our trip inadvertently helped unlock a closet in which souls of brain injured people were eager to escape? This was momentum. I said nothing. I put my hands on the back of the wheelchair and rolled him as fast as I could up the long hill to the park entrance.

Back at the hospital, I went straight to the head nurse's office and asked her to get Dr. Zasler's or Dr. Benoit's permission to get him into the pool. I wasn't going to take no for an answer. I didn't care if Ry refused PT or if Ry was being difficult with the staff. It was time for my son to return to his peaceful place, the water. Swimming represented his life, and it manifests unvarying characteristics within him. His happiness.

Chapter 19

Sink or Swim

Today was going to be an exercise in faith or failure. For the first time since the accident, Ry was going to feel the chlorinated water on his skin. Dr Zasler and his team had agreed on faith that this was going to be an experiment in evaluating Ry's physical assets. The PT team knew he did not lack enthusiasm, since he had requested permission to get in the pool several times a day to anyone who entered his room. If the attempt turned out to be a complete failure, then it was time for self-reflection by the staff, Dr. Zasler, and me.

The morning of the big day, I was awake at four thirty a.m., my mind buzzing with excitement and worry. My heart was holding high hopes. As an athlete, I knew success came with ceaseless struggle and sometimes agony by fiery trial in an attempt to win glory crossing the finish line. Would Ry's battered body respond? How would his suffering, bruised brain instruct his limbs? Arms and legs that once possessed vast energy and power were now functioning at a fraction of their capabilities. Failure would take a toll, and I was concerned for his mental and emotional state. At the same time, there was a part of me locked into a version of wishful thinking. I played the fantasy over in my mind of Ry getting into the pool and a miraculous change coming over him, with the holy water instantly returning him to his former self.

We were in the kitchen, and Lynn was pouring us coffee. "You know, Sweetie, today is not going to determine the course of Ry's life," she said with a calm voice as she handed me my cup. "There is tomorrow and the next day. Each day he improves a little."

"I know, but I am aching with fear. I think today is more important to Ry than you realize. He is going to examine, measure, and calculate every movement of his body. How do we respond if he just sinks?"

"We will be happy with the outcome. He will learn what his body can do, and what it cannot, and he will improve on that," Lynn responded in a stoic voice.

I set my steaming cup of coffee on the counter and reached out my hand to her. "Give me your hand," I said, with a crooked smile.

"What do you mean?"

"Let me have your hand."

Lynn reached over the counter and laid her hand in mine. I looked at her perfectly groomed pink nails as I placed my fingers on her wrist.

"What are you doing?" she asked.

"I want to see if you have a pulse," I answered with a slight edge in my voice. "You just don't seem to have any exuberance for the spark a successful swim could have on him."

"Look," Lynn snapped as she yanked her hand away, "I carried that swimmer in my belly for nine months. I am enormously excited about today, but I am also trying to be realistic so we can support our son even if he fails.

"I'm sorry. Maybe I just misread your body language. I am ready to accept what comes today. I am excited for even the opportunity to watch him get in the pool, even if he can't do any strokes. I just pray we have some clarity today that illuminates our path going forward. He has worked so hard in PT."

Lynn took a couple of slices of bread from a bag on the counter and popped them into the toaster. "You need to accept some imperfection in your son. I think we both know that he is not going to have any swimming form," she replied.

"I know. By the way, I forgot to tell you that I called my parents yesterday and invited them to come to the hospital. We can go out for lunch later."

"That's good you called them. I have been thinking about them. Your mom has left several messages for me to call her but with back-to-back twelve-hour shifts, I have been exhausted."

The great lens of family support would cheer him on. My invisible grief remained, but perhaps there would be a burst of happiness due to my belief in the power of presence. I believed in the healing power we create just by being there for another person. We not only give to them; we are also changed. Six weeks I had been present for my son. I knew some days he was indifferent to my daily sojourns to his bedside, but my compassion and commitment to his full recovery are what was expected of a parent.

When we arrived at the hospital an hour later, I noticed my parents' car already parked near the front entrance. We would be the audience to an event that stoked enthusiasm and hopefully ignited the possibility of nudging our way to a normal family life. We would endeavor to experience a perfect day together, my family and many of the hospital staff. The outcome would test the aggressive recovery plan developed by Dr. Zasler and his team.

My exhilaration increased as we were escorted to the pool area by one of Ry's physical therapists. I could smell the chlorine permeating the air as we got closer. I could only imagine the emotions flowing like waves through Ry. His recovery had been filled with zigzags, wrong turns, setbacks, and a hard struggle to find the finish line. Glory had become a long shot, but daily doses of Dr. Zasler's almost delirious exuberance for hard work, would bring us one step closer.

We sat in a small bleacher section, looking down on the calm water. Sunlight coming through skylights appeared to be stars bobbing like water lights on the pool deck. My mind shifted away to what my grandmother had told me when I was small. "The sun rises and it is where flowers, wheat and corn orient themselves, so they can flourish." Maybe the spirit of my son would bloom as the sun played on his skin.

Lynn and I hugged my parents. My dad had tears in his eyes. Maybe he was sad to be sitting in a rehabilitative hospital that was treating his grandson. It was hard to tell. My relationship with faith steadfastly remained in doubt. I wished my grandmother were there. She always had an answer for new problems. There were dozens of ghosts in my head of conversations with her. Whatever heartbreak I might have had, she had gone through it before and survived. Raising fourteen kids, there was never any elusiveness of reality. Throughout her life, she faced down illness, death and chaos. I gathered my strength from her and decided I would accept whatever the outcome may be today.

Ry was rolled through the doors in his wheelchair, and a cheer erupted from his four biggest fans. He looked up at us and smiled. A brief wave of one hand. To me, it was the most important swim meet of his life. No medals or ribbons would be handed out. Carl Jung said that the morning of our lives is totally different from when we step into the afternoon of our lives. For what was great in the mornings had little to do with the values and truth in the evenings. Had my life's experiences prepared me for this moment? Had I not had enough clicks of sadness and loss to sustain me? John Updike and my father believed that we needed God. Their belief was different from mine.

Two physical therapists lowered Ry into the pool. It was strange to see a life vest strapped around a nationally ranked swimmer. I smiled when I saw the vest on him. It reminded me of the first time Ry had bobbed in the water at the YMCA at age four. The vest had been almost as big as he was as the swim coach released the little minnow, his arms thrashing in the water. I'd yelled, "Swim, swim, swim. That's beautiful. That's wonderful, Ry." For the next fifteen years, as Ry's exuberance for winning exploded, I stood poolside, hurling words of encouragement, "That's beautiful, Ry." I knew one day he would break records as his body unzipped the water.

Now we sat in the first row, just like in a church pew, eyes fixed on the most important person in the room. Would today be a milestone in the Beville family? A breakthrough in neurological treatments of brain-injured patients? Having a type-A personality, I wanted them to get on with it. It was going to be impossible for me to sit still much longer. My foot was already tapping out a steady beat until Lynn placed her hand on my knee to stop it.

Finally, the calm, clear water rippled as the chair attached to posey belts slowly lowered Ry into the pool. I nervously clasped Lynn's hand while keeping my heart on a short lead. I had to water down my expectations, but this was the new reality. The physical therapists positioned Ry's body straight out on the surface of the water then gently pushed him forward. He began to move through the water like an elderly tortoise. I yelled, "That's beautiful, Ry! Swim."

His right-arm range of motion was ugly and incomplete. His left leg paddled the water, while the right leg was a drag, barely moving. I could not see Ry's eyes through his swim goggles, but I knew there would be no bowing to fear. There would be no unzipping the water today, no graceful form, but the experiment opened the door to the imagination of possibilities.

He managed to swim two lengths of the twenty-five-meter pool. Afterwards, they let him sit in the shallow end for a few minutes to relax. The physical exertion had been a lot for his body to take, and he was out of breath. Still, I detected a small smile on his face. I couldn't have been prouder as I gave him a thumbs up and yelled, "Wonderful!"

My mother and father were both crying. Lynn's grip on my hand was like a python's, squeezing off the blood flow. Our excitement was at full throttle. I walked over to where Ry was being lifted out of the water and hugged his wet head. "You won that race, Number One Son."

Dr. Zasler walked over and patted Ry on the back. "That was good. Really good. You have struggled through an immense setback in your life. A howling storm in your brain. I am proud of you."

Over the next few days, I began to see a shift in Ry. In the past month, we had gotten into a habit of having daily pep talks every morning before he started his day, which meant I spoke, trying to encourage him, while he stared off into the distance in stony silence. But now things were slightly different. Ever since the trip to Maymont Park and the pool experiment, there was a noticeable change in him. He still exhibited dark moods, but he also realized there was a path to recovery. Now when we spoke, he engaged.

"Ry, you've got to be receptive to the reality that your

recovery is multi-layered events over time," I said as I helped him put on a t-shirt.

"I am pleased with my pool day, but going to Notre Dame is fucked," Ry said with no noticeable emotion in his voice.

"If you keep repeating that and believing it, then you will be fucked. We'll be fucked. The Sheltering Arms staff and Dr. Zasler will be fucked because we all have failed to prepare you to accept what your new life is destined to be."

"You don't get it, do you, Dad?" He looked me in the eye as the shirt was pulled over his head.

I smoothed his messy hair and answered, "I am here to do whatever I can to help you recover, get back in the water, to come home, and to help you prepare to go to Notre Dame."

"Dad, a month ago I had swim times that put me in the top ten in the country. Now, I'm living in… in…" He struggled to find the right words. I wanted to help him but knew it was best to let him find his own words, so I waited patiently. Finally, he blurted out, "… black hole!" Covering his face with his hands, Ry leaned back in the chair, talking to the ceiling. "I put myself here."

"Ry, the car accident was not your fault. You didn't create the thunderstorm that night. If I could take all the words in a dictionary and string them together, it would not adequately describe how much I love you."

"I need to get out of this place." He brought his hands down and looked into my eyes. "Help me," Ry pleaded.

It broke my heart to see him that way. The hardest part of being a parent was always saying no for their own good, especially when the denial caused great pain. "No, son," I said. "I can't take you home." Watching the disappointment and pain in his eyes nearly killed me. "This is the best place for you now.

237

How are you going to climb steps at home?"

"Leave my room," Ry shouted.

"Ry, you really need to figure out how to overcome those self-defeating thoughts and habits. Let the staff help you. They're the experts."

"Leave my room," he repeated.

I stood up and paced the room out of frustration. *Where do I hang my anger? Do I have a right to have anger? How do I separate the old Ry from the new Ry?* So many thoughts ran through my mind. The best parts of my son had disappeared and I didn't know where to look for them. Although I tried to be hopeful, there were just too many bad days where he seemed too weak to move, too despondent to ever get better. I felt like an emotional pinball game, bouncing off rubber bumpers, trying to find an escape, only to be smacked back down by cruel flippers controlled by someone I couldn't see.

On the day Ry had been transferred from Saint Mary's to the rehab center, Dr. Zasler had told me that "good things happen slowly." We seemed to be moving at a glacial pace. It was one or two good days, just enough to get our hopes up, followed by a bad day, which would bring us all crashing back to reality.

I sat with Ry until early afternoon, even though he had stopped speaking to me. He was so angry at me, and I didn't know how to deal with it. My son and I had never been combative with each other. As parents, we'd been spared the teenage years filled with anger and angst. Other parents complained of slamming doors and rolling eyes, while we'd been blessed with a happy child. Ry had always been too busy and focused to stomp through the house shouting and being defiant. It seemed now he was making up for all those peaceful years.

When I could no longer stand one more moment of the silent

treatment, I kissed him on the forehead and left with an excuse I had to get to the office only three miles away. As I drove away, I thought about Ry's begging to go home. I wanted to fix this for him. I wanted to love him back to his former self. I wanted to give him his every desire.

But coming home was incomprehensible.

Chapter 20

The Great Escape

I had barely sat down when my assistant rushed into my office and said, "Don, there's an urgent call from Sheltering Arms."

Because of the way I'd left things with Ry, I had an awful feeling as I picked up the phone. My voice shook as I said, "Hello, this is Don Beville."

"Mr. Beville, this is Margaret Spicer." The woman on the other end of the phone sounded desperate. "I'm so sorry, but Ry figured out how to escape from our lock-down unit. We've looked everywhere and can't find him."

"Good God," I said. "Have you notified the police?"

"Yes, and they agreed to send several units to check the neighborhoods around the hospital." She tried to reassure me, saying, "I'm sure they'll find him soon."

I stood up and grabbed my keys. "I'm on my way."

I ran to my car and sped the short distance back to the hospital, all the while imagining the many horrible things that could go wrong. Ry could fall out of his wheelchair and hit his head. Worse, he could get hit by a car or forget his way back to the hospital. He could, at this moment, be wandering the streets, lost.

When I rushed into Margaret's office, she wasted no time. "This is terrible," she said. "We don't know how Ry got the security wristband off, but one of the nurses found it under his bed. The police dispatcher said they have three officers scouring the neighborhood. They'll find him. I guess the inevitable question is why he did it?"

I sat in the chair, feeling like I might faint. How could he have gotten out of here? Ry's imagination and intuitive intellect had at times in his life created drama and fireworks. I had encouraged him to create his own universe of ideas. He'd been excitingly different from other kids, in problem solving, and articulating his quest for learning new things. Today, his imagination was again creating drama and fireworks. What was I witnessing? An escape, or a new person with vigor rising in his veins?

Margaret took a seat next to me. "The puzzling part is, no one saw him near the elevators. We can't figure out how he got out of the building."

My mind immediately went to the kitchen loading dock. He wouldn't have tried that route, would he? The two times I took him out that way, he barely seemed to be paying attention. I couldn't imagine he had the ability to retrace our steps. He must have gone down the regular elevator and the staff just didn't notice. Either way, I kept my mouth shut. The last thing I needed was the hospital finding out I had taught my son the escape route. The Beville men were already skating on thin ice. I said a prayer in my head. *Oh Lord, please send an Angel to protect my boy.* I wanted to believe it was possible, but there was no science or logic to prove those things ever happened. Well, maybe in movies, like *A Wonderful Life* with James Stewart, and of course, the Angel, Clarence.

Just then, the telephone rang, interrupting my solemn promise never to do anything wrong ever again for as long as I lived and to faithfully attend Sunday Mass every week without fail. Margaret answered and quickly put the phone on speaker.

"Mrs. Spicer, this is Officer Pollard. Can you give me a description of the young man we're looking for?"

I stood up and leaned closer to the phone. "Hello, Officer, this is Don Beville, the patient's father. He has strawberry blond hair and huge shoulders from swimming. I can't remember what clothes he's wearing but he's in a wheelchair."

At that point Margaret added, "I saw him at lunch today and I remember he was wearing a white t-shirt with big blue-green letters that spelled Notre Dame."

We listened intently as the officer said, "Okay, I think I see your son. I'm currently on Westwood Avenue. It appears he's trying to get his wheelchair over the curb." Officer Pollard gave a little chuckle before saying, "He sure is working hard, but the wheels keep slamming against the side of the curb. I'll approach him now."

We waited for what felt like forever but was maybe ninety seconds. I could hear two voices speaking but couldn't make out what they were saying. There was no doubt the other voice was Ry. I'd never felt such relief as I did at that moment.

After a while, Officer Pollard's voice came over the line. "Okay, it's him, but he's refusing assistance. Is he seventeen or younger?"

"No," I answered. "He just turned eighteen."

"Okay, then I don't have the authority to bring him in. He isn't breaking any laws, just struggling to get out of his wheelchair."

Margaret jumped in. "Officer, we can arrange to send a staff member there immediately. Just let us know exactly where he is."

Officer Pollard gave us an address and then added, "He really wants out of this wheelchair. In fact, he's standing, pulling his right leg up over the curb."

I felt like I was about to have a heart attack. "Officer, please watch him. I don't want him falling and doing more damage to his head."

As scared as I was, there was a part of me that was also amazed at my son's perseverance. This was the first time since the accident he'd put weight on his legs. Did he have any feeling in his right leg? Just a few weeks ago, two neurologists told me that walking normally would be impossible within six months. But Dr. Zasler and Dr. Benoit also said no two brain injuries are the same. Dr. Benoit had told Ry to think about pushing any sensation he felt down his leg. Was he doing that now?

Despite my intense worry, I smiled. Was this the beginning of a miracle recovery? Could he stand now due to Dr. Benoit's touch, her commands to him that he was in charge of his recovery? According to sports psychologists, no two comebacks' stories were ever alike. A frequent common thread is that, once the healing begins, injured athletes seem to attack rehabilitation with the energy of ocean waves. Cathy, his primary therapist, had told me recently that Ry had asked them to work with him longer. I knew Ry. He was ready for his comeback.

I heard the officer say, "Hello, Son, I'm Officer Pollard. How is it going?"

Ry mumbled, "I have to piss."

"You need some help?" Officer Pollard asked.

"No, thanks. I'm coming right back," Ry replied.

Officer Pollard spoke into the phone again. "He's walking over to an insurance building just on the other side of the sidewalk. He seems to be determined to do this without help. He's dragging his leg a little but managing to get up the steps to get in the building."

"Officer Pollard, let him try," I said. A feeling of peace washed over me and I was no longer alarmed. They didn't know Ry like I did. They didn't know how determined he could be, how much he'd fight to rearrange his world. I heard Margaret tell the officer that Dr. Hays was on his way and would be there shortly. I imagined Ry even telling Dr. Hays he wanted to walk back to the hospital. I smiled, thinking that as scary as this was, it was progress. This was the same kid who tied his bully to the bus seat. That was the spark I had been hoping would return. Ry had always been a doer. The hospital staff may not have liked what was happening, but I was starting to see the return of my son.

Twenty minutes later, Dr. Hays was pushing Ry up the hospital sidewalk. I greeted Ry at the front door. The entire hospital was buzzing with the news of his escape. "Ry, where did you think you were going?" I asked. "You know, if you fall, your recovery starts over." I was proud of him but could not show it. Though it was a good sign that he wanted to take charge of his life, this could have ended in disaster. Dr. Hays' stern expression told me he was not amused by Ry's escape.

"Kids fall off their tricycles every day," Ry said flatly.

"That is true," Dr. Hays said, "but small children on tricycles wear helmets when they go outside. You want me to lend you a helmet next time you want to escape?"

"Sure," Ry said, without looking at Dr. Hays. I smiled inside, but what Dr. Hays had said was true. I did not want Ry to have another accident. He didn't need a setback, but I was conflicted in how I felt. Part of me wanted to protect him in bubble wrap and the other part wanted to cheer on this rebellious streak, because it meant he was ready to some degree stagger on down the road.

***

For the next week, Ry continued to rebel against the hospital staff. He demanded crutches and wanted to get in the pool. He'd had a taste of the water, so now that was what mattered to him, but the staff was limiting his time in the pool until he could walk without the aid of crutches. Rehabilitation became his only goal. His muscles were weak and his face still puffy from the steroids. Although bloodied and bowed by accident the day-to-day business of recovery ran relentlessly through his veins.

Each day, PT rolled him down to the exercise room, where twenty different weight machines awaited him. I watched him go through all the machines, get to the end then go back to the first machine. It was like catnip. But like Sisyphus, each time Ry thought he was making progress he was told, "Pool time is limited to fifteen minutes." The boulder rolled back on him. He told me that every day when he woke up, he could smell the chlorine. It fueled his drive.

He would pull himself into his wheelchair and propel himself toward PT, passing the same mute faces in the hall. Ry felt chaffed by life's razor but he never gave up. Instead, he became a rebel, unaware of his ugliness and incendiary behavior. His daily conversations with the staff were mere pissing contests. "I've had enough of this shit," he would sometimes shout at his therapist daily. "Take me to the pool."

For the most part, they ignored his behavior, but some days I would get the calls. "Don, Ry tried to leave the floor again." After the fourth or fifth call, my response was the same.

"Let him swim," I told them. "If he drowns, he'll die happy and smelling like chlorine." I knew it sounded callous, but I was tired of fighting with Ry. I wanted him to just listen to his

245

therapists and do the tasks they gave him. The old Ry would have understood the importance of training, doing things in the right order, but this was not the same Ry.

Finally, Ry triumphed by exhausting everyone around him. Dr. Zasler sent a note to Cathy, the head of the PT department, and told her, "Please make daily arrangements to let him swim for thirty minutes."

A week after the executive order to allow him to swim, Dr. Zasler requested a meeting of the PT department and wanted me present. When I arrived at the meeting, all of Ry's PT, OT, and other staff members were there. This couldn't be good. It felt like I was walking into a meeting with all the mob bosses of the surrounding boroughs. I took a seat looking around the table with lots of faces lacking smiles. I wondered which one was going to pick up the bat first and pull an Al Capone to the back of my head.

"Don, he's not coping well emotionally," one of the staff members said. Another jumped in, adding, "Ry presents a clear danger to himself. He does not realize the risks. If he falls, he could be paralyzed forever. Have you explained that to him?"

I sat quietly, calmly, listening to what they had to say. One after another, each story was the same. Ry refused to go to group therapy. Ry refused to go to group dinner. Ry left his room, and they could not find him. I understood it was disruptive to the staff, but to me he was trying to restore his emotional intelligence, and to find the exuberance that had engulfed his life since childhood. Was he pushing to change his environment. Yes, he was. He was thinking and making decisions—albeit not the safest decisions—but they were decisions all the same. Wasn't that the point? Wasn't that what all of this rehab was about?

"You are all experts at what you do," I said. "I can't be here twenty-four-seven to attend to him or be the hospital police.

Would you like me to take him home?" For a moment, my words shocked me and I instantly regretted my offer. What the hell was I going to do with him at home, especially when dishes and trays flew across the room?

I was trying to figure out a way to back pedal out of my offer before someone said yes when the sound of someone playing the piano broke the silence. We all looked around, wondering where it was coming from. The music grew louder. Mozart, I thought? There was a certain beauty in the choppy presentation. It was certainly more passion than technique. The emotional music was coming from the other side of a partition splitting the large room into two smaller ones.

"Please go tell whoever that is that there is a meeting in this room," Dr. Zasler said. One of the staff members rose and pulled the partition back. We were shocked to see Ry sitting at a piano, fingers spread out on the keys, poking out his tune. I smiled. The PT folks smiled. Dr. Zasler smiled.

"Ry, where did you learn to play?" I asked.

No answer from Ry.

Then I remembered that Alexis had taken lessons all of her life. Did she teach Ry? A spark of joy surged through me. I had not seen Ry on fast idle in such a long time. To see him engaging in a new passion, embracing the magic of life once again, was beautiful. I didn't need him to answer with words. His actions were singing his needs loud and clear.

Dr. Zasler said, "I would like to suggest something. Sheltering Arms has an outpatient rehabilitation center at Stony Point, which is not far from where you live. Don, if you take him there every morning, there is a bus that can bring him back to your home. I will approve his discharge."

"What's he going to do there all day?" I asked.

"Activities that will help him with mental acuity, memory, and building physical strength," Cathy said. "I'm in charge of that facility. I'll work with him daily. I know his strengths and I definitely know how much he wants to be a competitive swimmer again." Cathy had been working with Ry every day, through his good moments and his difficult ones. "I have gotten him to this point in his recovery. I would like to continue."

"The Riverside swim club is just two miles away," Dr. Zasler said. "I'll clear him to swim on his own soon but under the supervision of the pool lifeguard." He looked around the room at the other staff members and then went on. "Don, you need to be diligent in creating a safe home environment, motivating and challenging him every day to make improvements in his mental and physical state."

Ry stopped playing the piano and looked at me as he turned his body in the chair. "Today is a good day to go home."

It was time for a change. I knew there would be some risks with Ry coming home, but I was confident that the family could make it work. I had to let him prove he could handle the physical stress or let him fail and learn how to move forward. Was I making a dangerous miscalculation? Only time would tell. But as a father, I had to step back and let my son take the reins. I believe that within every person there lies an inalienable right to live a life free of coercion. Our life in this troubling malaise had to end.

"Okay," I told him, placing my hand on his shoulder. He smiled for the first time in weeks, and I prayed that I was making the right decision. Life to Ry had always been an adventure. The harder the problem, the more he dug in. We were ready to make an investment in a new adventure.

Chapter 21

A Child Comes Home

I got up early, with a dream still floating in my head, as if my shoulder was scraping crisscrossing clouds in the sky. I've had to stop drinking. *To sing the blues you've got to live the dues and carry on.* The lyrics from Carry On by Crosby, Stills, Nash, and Young, played continuously in my head like a tape looping around spindles in my brain. Today or tomorrow I would be on the way to pick up Ry from the rehab hospital. Not everyone was on board with his discharge. Although Dr. Zasler was okay with it, his staff wasn't thrilled. During my last meeting with Ry's rehabilitative team, one of the OT team members cited Ry's continuance of angry outbursts toward people in her department. "How are you going to handle him at home, Mr. Beville?" she asked.

"I'm his father. I think I can figure it out after raising him for eighteen years." The truth was, I was putting on a brave face even though I was incredibly nervous. But in the end, I trusted Dr. Zasler's clinical decisions. I could have spent months waffling back and forth but sometimes you just have to dive in and go with your gut. My gut said trust the doctor.

A few years ago, I started doing triathlons. Before one of them, I stood at the water's edge, looking west of the James River. I was going to have to swim six hundred yards in the middle of the river. Laurie Householder, the race director, who was also my endurance swim coach, approached me and asked how I was doing. "I don't want to drown," I said nervously. I was considering dropping out of the race and going home. I had done the distance in a pool but not in the river. If you get too tired to continue, there are no walls to grab hold of in a river.

Laurie looked at me while patting my shoulder and said, "It's amazing what the mind can do when faced with death." I knew she meant her words to be encouraging, but for me, drowning was feeling like a distinct possibility. I'd only ever felt that same sweeping fear once before. It was the moment I was told my beautiful Audrey had left the earth. The thought of bringing Ry home rekindled the same fear.

For more than a decade, I was the production editor for the *Guide Book for the Marines*. It was a book that was given to recruits when they arrived at Marine Corps Base Camp Lejeune for their basic training. It was their Bible that served to teach them the tenets of becoming a Marine. One of the chapters on leadership cited George Washington's philosophy *First you listen, then you learn, then you help.* That was going to be my mantra in searching for some common ground with my son. Would it be with an embrace, or would his return home become a burden?

For the last month, I felt I had been suffering from some form of incurable neurosis. Would Ry's daily behavior sock me in the jaw? Dr. Benoit told me that our unhappiness is caused by the view we take. "Don," she said, "We desire happiness and peace but suffering is unavoidable. Everyone experiences a low tide in life. But the experience of suffering can connect us to others who also suffer. That is how we come to know empathy. Acceptance of Ry's fate will be the path of self-healing for both of you. Continue to pray for his recovery. Live every day of your life as close to normal as possible. Always look outward and forward, for looking inward can scar you."

I had heard the same message from Dr. Zasler, "Move on with your life and Ry will follow."

A few days before, I met briefly with Dr. Hays, the hospital's psychiatric counselor. He handed me a folder with several brochures published by the Brain Injury Association of America. "Don, there are wonderful pamphlets that will help you understand the healing process for TBI patients. There are pages of coping strategies."

"Thank you, Dr. Hays." I opened one of the brochures, fixating on a page that listed symptoms of TBI:

Self-centered in actions

Verbal responses may lack logic

No short-term memory

Poor ability to organize

Difficulty in thinking abstractly

75% possibility of seizures for one-year post-trauma.

The only positive was the reference to anger. "Anger" usually meant that the patient was improving. Well, then Ry must be getting better.

The anticipation of Ry's homecoming was in high gear. But Lynn and I were worried. Was it going to be a time to experience the contentment of having our boy back under our roof, or would we be suffering the frustrations of dealing with a brain-injured child with all of the negative symptoms we were warned about? Competitive swimming was Ry's divine drug. Maybe that would be the key.

"Lynn, we need to feed his addiction," I said, one night before going to bed.

She looked at me with a raised brow, while continuing to put lotion on her elbows. "What do you mean?"

I pulled back the corner of the cover and climbed in while explaining, "Dr. Zasler's plan from the first day he met Ry, was to get him back in the pool, with some limitations, and safety first. Ry's addiction to exercise began at age six when we registered him for his first swim lesson. Whatever I can do for him to have all the pool times he needs will be a priority."

"I never thought of Ry's swimming as an addiction," Lynn answered. She turned to face me and added, "But we need to make sure that we follow Dr. Zasler's guidelines. Ry has to go to physical therapy. That is the ticket for swimming."

"Okay, I agree with the PT," I said. "Do you think we should have a homecoming celebration? Balloons maybe. Buddies from his swim team, and coach Duncan? Should we make a list?" I reached into the nightstand drawer and pulled out my notebook for my middle of the night ideas. "I am a make-a-list guy. You know that."

Lynn climbed into bed beside me and snuggled up to my shoulder, so she could see the list. "Sweetie, there is no guidebook for this, but, we only have half a day to plan." She pointed to the paper for me to write, "Why don't you make the calls to his swim team, and I will go get some balloons." She thought for a moment, as I scribbled down all the names I could remember. After a moment she asked, "What should we do about food?"

I started laughing. The answer was so simple. "Kentucky Fried Chicken?"

Lynn chuckled and nodded her head. "I remember the chicken story," she tapped the notebook for me to write it down and added, "Chicken works for me."

It was the first time in a long while my wife and I had shared a laugh over a silly joke. It felt good. No, it felt amazing. My family was coming back together.

As I steered the car on my way to pick up Ry, a familiar feeling crept in. My hands squeezed the steering wheel a bit too tight as images came to my mind—Ry throwing dinner across the room, Ry screaming at me and his mother, Ry refusing my help up and down the stairs. With each paranoid fantasy slapping my brain with a dueling glove, my fear grew. What had I gotten us into? The OT member asked the right question. What was I going to do?

When I stepped through the doors of Sheltering Arms Hospital, the antiseptic smell reminded me of where I was. I breathed it in, smiling because I knew this would be the last day my son would be a resident here. No more sitting on a chair, watching him sleep and feeling obligated to do so. For weeks, I'd discussed Ry's condition with doctors, nurses, physical therapists, occupational therapists, psychologists, and dietitians. There would be no more ticking off the succession of items on my daily to-do list at the hospital. Finally, the day had come where the only thing on my schedule was to be a father and safely chauffer my son home. Home. Just thinking of the word, I released some of the tension in my shoulders.

I pushed the scary, yelling, and throwing food thoughts out of my mind and replaced them with memories of Lynn and me laughing and planning the big party. What was there to be afraid of? I was being silly. This was my son, and he was coming home. What could be more joyous than that?

I smiled as I saw Dr. Zasler next to Ry slowly walking toward me. They smiled too, even though Ry had a noticeable limp. I was pleased Dr. Zasler was with him. He was a daily sign of hope and guidance in Ry's recovery. His devout professionalism and genius provided memorable and positive outcomes for brain injured individuals.

"It's my beautiful smiling number one son," I said as I hugged him. "You ready to go home or do you want to stay a few more days in this hotel?"

"I am ready dad," Ry said, seeming to have to push the words out with little help from his tired lungs.

"Thank you Dr. Zasler. We will be in touch," I said as Ry and I turned to leave."

Dr. Zasler left us with the parting words, "Ry, remember the chat we had this morning. Nothing great happens without PT. You agreed. I look forward to seeing you next week in our outpatient therapy sessions."

Ry was quiet during the trip home, only mumbling about being hungry and wanting to sleep. I was hoping he would show some sign of his old positive identity once he was at home. With his current introverted mood, I started wondering if the balloons and swim team visitors was a good idea? In our excitement Lynn and I may have jumped the gun. I would still view this day as a gift no matter how the next few hours went.

As we rounded the corner on our street, I looked over at Ry. His chin rested on his chest. He was napping I thought. I wondered what senses would be alive today? He sat, like a big piece of stone. Michelangelo said "Every block of stone or marble has a statue inside of it and it is the task of the sculptor to discover it." Could I find my boy inside that stone.

My heart sped up as I saw our house. Wow. It seemed like Ry's entire swim team was standing on the porch and lining the driveway. Balloons flying from all the trees in the yard. It resembled the pageantry that the Roman citizens gave to their victorious returning armies.

"Look, Ry, I think you know these people," I said in an excited high-pitched voice. I was so proud of my wife for organizing this homecoming. The poetics of our space. Our home. Our family.

Ry raised his head and a big smile appeared. A little chuckle floated through his lips. Oh, what person would he become in the coming months, years? He would have to write the poetry of self-invention. The cheering and clapping of his friends and neighbors as we turned into the driveway almost drowned the beating of my heart.

Ry raised his hands from his lap to salute them. He stuck his hand out of the window, each swim team member shouting, "Ry, Ry, Ry." As they smacked his open palm, Ry's eyes sparkled and he laughed wholeheartedly with the playfulness of the moment. The dance of energy was slowly returning to my little butterfly. What statue would rise from Michelangelo's stone block?

For the next hour, Ry answered questions about what he remembered of his stay at Sheltering Arms. I could tell his short-term memory prevented most of his stories from revealing accurate facts, but who cared. His friends laughed when he talked about escaping from the hospital through the kitchen to go get Kentucky Fried Chicken. He didn't mention that the floorboard and car seat were covered in a layer of crumbs from his vigorously gnawing on the chicken breast that had become a prisoner in his hands.

I reached out to grasp Lynn's hand "This has been a pilgrimage for us. When I saw Ry laugh, I wanted to run over and kiss him on the head."

"I am glad you didn't. He would be embarrassed. But you can kiss me."

"What now?" I asked as I leaned over to kiss her. "What

now?" She had been my rock through this journey. Her courageously wise support of my pursuit of being there for our son had given us both insight into the realization of who we really are and to know that family is the most important gift we can have. During the night, I lost count of how many times we both got up to quietly peek in Ry's room to make sure he had not somehow thought he was back in the hospital and was planning another escape.

The account of the last three months had been one of self-discovery, growth, and resilience. At times, I questioned my purpose as a father and husband. When I reach the afternoon of my life, maybe I will look back on this journey as a guide through the passages in daily living. Every human has their own stories of a painful loss followed by a rebirth. I would have to wait a little longer to witness the new Ry. But regardless of Ry's days ahead, he will be worthy of my unconditional love. I had discovered that even when the mind goes haywire, the defects are correctable.

Chapter 22

Inhale, Exhale and Nudge a Little More

My life's experiences had taught me that prior suffering and chaos give you no protection from future chaos and pain. Life can be thorny. I'd tried in the last month to cultivate some ability to resist falling into despair over my son's condition, that is, what he had potentially lost physically and mentally from his head slamming against the steering wheel. I had wrongly, I thought, diagnosed myself as being depressed. At times, feeling that I was all but dead, except I had a pulse. My mind was no longer crisp. But sitting on my deck, with black coffee in hand, watching the sun rising over the Japanese garden gave me hope.

The feeling of being depressed was slowly dissipating, and now I had come to believe it was grief that had conspired to bring me low. I knew from working with patients in the psychiatric ward twenty years ago that depression can be and often is malignant, and it grows. Grief is a journey and over time it wears off. Freud made it clear that grief is a natural part of living: "After a lapse of time it will be overcome."

Two facts that occurred to me, as I looked out through the opening in the trees where Ry and I had planted bamboo just a month ago, were, that firstly, I was missing time usually spent with my son. There had been no more talks over coffee or walks in the newly created pond, and secondly, I was not attending to my needs as an athlete. I felt alone in this present situation, with only our past events to keep me company.

As puffy clouds pushed daylight over the treetops, there was still a pull of nerves in how I was going to create and respond to the next phase of life with a different person in the house. While he had turned the corner on the paralysis, the emotional rehabilitation was still in play. The shock and denial of the accident were behind him, but a resolution strategy needed to be interwoven in his daily routine to combat the depressive reaction.

In childhood, we learn to become masters of our bodies. As we move into middle age and old age, we reverse course and struggle to deal with disabilities associated with aging. Ry had just turned eighteen, and he was dealing with a disability. Some things that he once took for granted—going up steps, a curb, an incline, scratching his head with his right hand—were no longer automatic. He had aged ten years in the blink of a yellow stoplight swinging in the wind.

It was Ry's first day home. I was pleased to see his right leg was improving, with increased mobility. His toes moved freely and he could almost pull his knees up to his chest, but every bodily movement seemed in slow motion. I was profoundly happy, yet cautious, while constantly trying to mute my fear he would not be able to fulfill the demands of the world. I ate, slept, and worked on a teeter-totter between joy and anxiety. More so, my expectations of him as a father were that I wanted him to go to PT, and I was going to demand it. We had both lost precious days out of our lives. The illusion of immortality had vanished in my world. I had seen life-threatening and near-death experiences with my grandfather, a wife taken from me, and now my son having to rethink his life's goals in a regressed mental state due to trauma.

Just as Ry's goals had shifted, so had mine. I was even

considering seeking a practitioner for grief counseling. I had noted some alterations in my thoughts about marriage. Things that were once routine had shifted. I wanted some return to predictability. I missed my book publishing job dearly. I had to recover the sweetness of my publishing career and not dwell in the pain that life had handed me in the last months. I remember Dr. Hays telling me that with TBI, there would be parts of my son missing. That is, as his brain healed, I could take solace in knowing new skills would bud. This thought did not automatically bring predictable comfort to me since we did not know what those new skills would be. Perhaps too, new poems and writing ideas would take bud in my head?

Life is fragile, but I tried to imagine how to cultivate a new one full of positive possibilities. Joy is essential and needs to be a big part of our daily lives. Finding joy in what, though? It must be infinite and all-absorbing. But what, I kept thinking. My senses must be assaulted, elevated, and expanded. Ry needed to get back to swimming and writing poetry. I needed to get back to expanding my publishing career and pleasing my wife's heart. Lynn needed time off and getting back to her garden beds. Do we look to the heavens? We needed to be under the spell of discovery. If something was not working then we would do something different. It was time for my family to let go of regret. Time is infinite, but my family's time together was not.

I trusted Sheltering Arms and loved the staff, but I lacked the knowledge of whether Ry should be further along in developing new skill sets for walking mobility and mental acuity. There was no point of reference other than what I had read over and over in the TBI pamphlets and the advice given by Dr. Benoit and Dr. Zasler. Adversity always builds strength and wisdom for the next adversity. I had taken a leap of faith by bringing him home. I was in a new territory. Making big decisions was part of my job every day, but this was different.

I only had harsh optimism, but previous life's blows had taught me not to lower my expectations that I could make no demand that the good life can be rebuilt. Chaos and grief had taught me since childhood how to build new roads to happiness. I just had to begin with minute actions. I knew I had to modify my behavior to affect continual positive changes in Ry. I would have to work on my anger when he had outbursts. I kept reminding myself to be adaptive.

All through life, moments flow and new journeys begin. My son and I were on a new journey. We just had to inhale and exhale. We had to be a team. He was a swimmer and I was a runner. We were used to competing as individuals against our own best selves, working on conditioning, pushing our bodies to perform at their peak and shaving seconds off our fastest times. His enthusiasm to regain swimming skills was not something I would have to push. Ry's temperament and love of competition would fire up his willingness to push himself through all the painful threads of daily practices. That came naturally to Ry. Still, I worried his form would not improve and his strength would level off below his expectations. This would be a crushing blow to a competitor like Ry.

Communication boundaries had to be configured. Was his reality the same as mine? We had to share some common reality. I knew people with TBI suffered a disconnect in their nervous systems and how they now perceived reality. They internalized external information on a different spectrum. Information travels in the brain from one neuron to another neuron. With a diffuse axonal injury, the fibers of the neurons, the axons, lose some of their protective coatings. Information entering the brain is severely slowed. Which neurons were not communicating? Might it be in the speech centers? Yes, I already knew that. But what other centers were affected? Reasoning, motor skills?

He was still having difficulty with word recall. We all have a map of the world based on our priorities. What did Ry's map look like? Ry certainly could not tell me, because he did not know how he had changed. He still could not string yesterday's events into a storyline. I had to figure out a work-around. Maybe give him a small pocket notebook to write things in? At least he was home and I could control or modify the environment. I had clearly stated expectations. He would go to PT and I would register him for a class. Inhale and exhale.

I took a sip from my second cup of coffee and started making a list of the positive reasons he should be enrolled in a class. Attending a class would stimulate his brain and motivate him to get out of bed every morning. I knew this was going to be a difficult adjustment for him, but I remembered what Dr. Benoit had said about keeping his brain active, all the while trying to balance that theory against Dr. Zasler's warning about how much sleep TBI patients needed.

The class would also create an opportunity for social interaction with other students. Lying in bed at home was passive behavior, and Ry had never been a passive spectator of life. A classroom would be active and challenge Ry to assume more control of other areas of his life. Hopefully, there would be fewer negative outbursts as he interacted with more people his age. Finally, students asking him questions might help with his word recall.

I examined my list: enroll in a class, PT every day, limited laps in the pool, naps, homework. After seeing it written down, I felt more confident that we now had a tangible plan. Had his IQ changed? Should I have Dr. Hays at Sheltering Arms test him for deviations from his high school tests? Was it important even to know? I went upstairs to wake Ry, feeling positive about the journey we were to embark upon.

I knocked on Ry's door and called out, "Ry, you have to get up now. You have PT in one hour, and I'm going to the University of Richmond to see if I can register you in a beginning Japanese class."

"I don't want to go to any fucking Japanese class!" Ry shouted back from his room.

So much for my grand list and enthusiasm for team players. I went downstairs to wait, thinking maybe he just needed a few minutes to wake up. After a while, when I didn't hear any movement from upstairs, I went up to his room. This time, I knocked and opened his door without waiting for a reply. He had not moved. "Ry, I'm not joking, you need to get ready."

"Did you come to check on the prisoner?" Ry said with some rancor, "When can I go swim?"

I sat down on the edge of his bed. "That depends on you. Today you need to go to PT and OT. That was the deal for you to come home. You have to realize that all your anger and venom is emotionally destructive to all of us: you, me, your mother. I'm kind of over it."

"I don't get angry. You're angry," Ry shot back.

"Ry, you have to stop challenging everything. Stop with the "F" words. I want to help with getting you back to a normal daily routine. I see glimpses of improvement and then you slip away into vulgar rants," I snapped.

He remained quiet, staring at the far corner of his bedroom. I wished I knew what he was feeling. I'd stopped asking. Whenever I did, he went to stony silence. Maybe he was lost in some newly invented world only he could vision. Maybe he couldn't find the words to express his feelings or maybe he was completely unaware of how his behavior came across to others. Whatever it was, I was locked out of knowing, and pushing him to "talk about it" only made it worse. I wanted to peel back the layers of his skin, like bark on a birch to see if I could find him. I was not going to leave his bedroom until he got up. This was going to be my defining moment as a parent and caretaker.

"Ry, if I could combine all the words I have edited or written in the books I have published, they would not be able to describe how much I love you and how much I want you to thrive as a young man."

"This sounds like one of my psychotherapy sessions at the hospital," Ry spat out.

Swish: his statement was a perfect shot through my heart. "Yeah, this is therapy, face-to-face therapy right now at this moment," I said, staring at his static body. "I'm searching for the son I had five weeks ago, the one I almost lost in a horrible car crash. There's been a black hole where he used to be."

"That was not my fucking choice," Ry snapped.

"Well, Ry, life is filled with lots of particulars that we don't like, but we still have choices."

At that moment, I felt like Sylvia Plath walking on a tightrope, soon to fall to her death. Most days, I'd felt like I'd been stuck with Ry, in this upside-down version of our lives. I wanted us both to climb out of the abyss together, to have the life we'd had before. I was so hungry to see some change in him and I was trying not to be overly reactive to his angry outbursts. I needed him to have an epiphany and to somehow guide him to a reunion with his inner self. "Ry, here is that person who used to be positive, optimistic, and ready for a challenge?" He looked at his world as if it had no future, and that must have been terrifying.

In one of my first graduate classes in counseling, my professor pushed on us the mantra, "Compassion, compassion, compassion. Listen with compassion and nudge to get the patient to see a different view." I had spent the last five weeks down on my knees, pouring out compassion, and what had I discovered? Nothing more than an aching heart. His PT and OT therapists had compassion. The nurses had compassion. Even the orderly cleaning up his flung tray of food had compassion. Every day he'd been showered with compassion.

All of us had been a positive force in his recovery process, and on some days it seemed that it was getting us nowhere. Should I stop being overprotective, clinging to hope, and projecting my goals on him? I was beginning to question my worth in this recovery process. Maybe I needed to be the bad guy. Challenge him harder. Take the gloves off. Isn't that what coaches do, reinforce goal solutions, teach, encourage stimulating initiatives? The overall effect of his continued disrupted behavior was disturbing. It was causing heightened anxiety which contributed to my insomnia and suffocating gloom.

I asked myself, what would my mother do? She was one of fourteen children raised on a farm near Wilsons, Virginia. They had no electricity or running water. The food they ate was raised on the farm. Each brother and sister looked out for the other. She became a merchandise buyer for JCPenney, and at the age of seventy-five, began modeling clothes.

My mother's experiences and wisdom were born out of living a tough farm life, but she told me often how important the clasp of family was to survive in difficult times. "You can't back away from the world," she would tell me. "Nature is your first teacher. On a farm, you are touched daily by the seasons, unknowing if the seeds you planted are going to get rained on so they will sprout. If something doesn't work, you experiment and do something different. Your knowledge comes from the spell of nature." She did not let poverty and hard work grind her or her brothers and sisters down. My mother was pragmatic and learned life lessons from living.

On the other hand, Ry's therapists had learned all of their clinical knowledge from a textbook. I knew they meant well, but they didn't know Ry the way I did. They only knew the changed Ry. They had never witnessed his zest for life or how passionate he could be. They had not pulled back the curtains and seen the tedious recoveries from previous injuries. Today, my mother's thread of decision-making would weave my actions. My enthusiasm for what I must do next was inspired by life's discoveries of my previous generation. It would not be a blueprint in a therapist's handbook but a blueprint in line with my mother and her generation's belief system. I leaned over Ry's bed, grabbed the back of his soft cotton-blue t-shirt and yanked him out of bed.

"Dammit, what are you doing, Dad?" Ry shouted with wide, shocked eyes.

Lifting him was like pulling a weed from the ground. I steered him to the bathroom and stopped when we were in front of the mirror. His head was bent down, his upper body slumping as he gazed toward the mirror. A long scar still visible over his eye.

"Ry, half my life is over," I said as I peered directly at him in the mirror. "You have your entire life ahead of you. Tell me what you see in that mirror."

"I am sorry, Dad," Ry said with a soft, soulful voice. "I

fucked up the car, didn't I?"

"People have accidents. You had an accident. Let's get back to you. What do you see in the mirror?" I repeated with a little more force in my voice.

"Are you disappointed in me?" Ry said, tears welling up in his eyes.

"No, I am not disappointed. I am concerned. Here is what I believe. The person you see in the mirror is the same person who existed five weeks ago, minus a few thousand brain cells from hitting the steering wheel, and some scars and lumps. You are intelligent, handsome, and..." I stressed this most importantly, "You will graduate from Notre Dame."

"I'm not sure I'm the kind of student Notre Dame would want now. They wanted a butterflier, not an eighteen-year-old disabled student."

"Not true," I said with confidence. "You have some challenges ahead of you. You must attack your PT and OT, just like you attacked your two-hour, twice-a-day swim practices. Don't let your emotions overwhelm you. Slow your mind down when you feel you're close to an outburst. I think this is a critical moment in your recovery. You have to figure out the physical and psychological mechanics of making the transition to your former life. You have to reset your mindset."

For a few seconds, I looked at Ry, the kid I had raised, who was my side-kick for eighteen years. I walked away and left him to his thoughts. He was going to have to choose who he wanted to be. I hoped my son would see himself through my eyes. We could drift back or drift forward. Backward takes the air out of the room. I went downstairs to see which direction he would choose.

A short while later, he appeared in the kitchen, trying to

button his shirt. His weak right leg was still noticeable, although his mobility in the last week had been transformational.

"Can you take me to swim after PT?" he said, each word highlighted with a shadow of slowness.

I was silent. The question of swimming blew through me like a crashing wave. Was it time? Was it too soon? What were the dangers? He could slip on the pool deck and hit his head. What then? Could I handle the guilt if something happened? At Sheltering Arms, a team of people lowered him in the pool and swam next to him. My most sincere inner self maintained that the stakes were too high. I was acutely attuned to the guilt I would sustain if something dreadful happened at our club pool. Lynn was at work but I decided to call her. Having him home was one thing, signing him up for a language class was a positive thing, but taking him to the pool to swim on his own was not something I was willing to decide on my own.

When Lynn answered the phone, she sounded tired and rushed. She was on another long shift at the hospital.

"Sorry to bother you, Sweetie, but Ry wants to swim after PT. Is it time? I'm not sure what to do. I'm struggling," I said with anxiety in my voice.

"He has to rebuild his confidence. Let it be in the place he loves."

"Okay, if you think it's a good idea."

"I don't have an issue with it, but make sure you are with him or someone else is in the water to help if he falters. I love you. I have to go." Before I could respond, she had already hung up. I was used to quick calls with my wife. It was the life of a neonatal nurse, always rushing. I held the phone to my forehead and made the only decision I could. I had to bow to the love I had for my son and hope he would safely drift back to the life he had

267

once lived. I didn't want my fear to kill the rebirth of his passion for the water. I wanted to have enthusiastic confidence that I was doing the right thing, but still, I noticed my hand was shaking as I hung up the receiver.

I looked over at Ry, still struggling to get the buttons in the right holes on his shirt. I walked over and stood in front of him. "Let me help." Standing this close, I looked into Ry's eyes and said, "I still worry about your safety in the pool."

"Dad, my dream of swimming for Notre Dame is probably gone," Ry said softly, slowly pushing out each word, "but I won't know for sure unless I can get back... water... back *into* the water."

I had left my son to take an in-depth look at himself in the mirror and decide who he wanted to be, and this was his decision. As much as it scared me, I had to support him. I needed to join his team and support his decision. Ry wasn't the only one who had to adapt. I did too. So, I decided to go for a compromise. "Ry, here is the deal. I'll drop you off at PT and OT, and then I'm going to see the registrar at the University of Richmond to see if I can get you registered for the Japanese class." I took a deep breath. "When I pick you up, we can have a discussion, and if you still feel like swimming, we'll see what options are available."

"Dad, I just want tiny victories. Swimming is one."

I finished buttoning Ry's shirt and pulled him close, hugging him tightly. Tiny victories were all any of us could hope for.

Chapter 23

The Second Great Escape

I dropped Ry off at the Sheltering Arms Physical Therapy Center just two miles from our house. A few minutes later, I was standing inside the registrar's office at the University of Richmond. I explained to the lady on the other side of a huge glass window that my son wanted to attend a freshman Japanese class and it would be the only class he would take for the fall semester.

"Has he been accepted to the university?" She sounded rushed.

"No," I said. "He was going to Notre Dame this semester but was injured in a car accident. He'll be going in January," I lied. I had no idea what my son would be doing in January. Possibly he would attend Notre Dame or perhaps I would be dodging bowls of cereal he threw at the wall. One life lesson Ry's accident reminded me of was that the future is never set. You may think one thing is happening and then find out in quick order that life has other ideas. I never thought I'd be a widower at the age of twenty-two or be sleeping under the stars in Idaho a few weeks later shoveling horse shit out of a barn, but there I was. So, was my answer truthful? Maybe. Was it wishful thinking? Most likely.

I was willing to tell this woman, who couldn't have cared less about my situation, anything she needed to hear for my son to attend a Japanese class and engage with something instead of sitting in bed and staring at the wall.

"Well, he still must apply to the Department of Continuing Studies. We will need his school transcripts and SAT scores, plus teacher recommendations," she said as she handed me a stack of forms.

Good God, I thought. "All of these forms just to take one class? You have got to be kidding!" Yet another obstacle to conquer.

"Yes, all the forms must be completed before we can even consider admitting him."

The scene from *Terms of Endearment,* where Shirley MacLaine screams at the nurses, "Give my daughter the Shot!" flashed through my mind. I wanted to scream, "Give my son his fucking class!" It wasn't in my nature to cause such a scene, and for a few seconds I thought about leaving; going home and going for a long run; letting my wife handle it; letting my son figure it out. I was exhausted, and the fight had gone out of me. First, I'd had to drag Ry out of bed and now, the simple task of signing up for a class had become an ordeal. I had trained for twenty-two marathons, but this was much harder. It was just the first day of Ry being home and I was already feeling overwhelmed. I had to set up a book signing for the next day at a bookstore in Shockoe Bottom. The bookstore had taken out several days of advertising in the *Richmond Times Dispatch,* which meant hundreds of people might show up. I had to arrange for boxes of books to be delivered that afternoon and I still had to contact a caterer. I had no enthusiasm for this time suck. Why was I standing here pleading with a lady who had no clue what I'd experienced in the last month? It was once again time to put on the boxing gloves.

"Could I possibly speak to the registrar, please? I don't mean to be rude to you, but there needs to be an important decision made here today. Please let me talk with her." The woman turned and left the small room with a peeved look on her face. A minute later, a tall woman dressed in a blue business dress walked over to greet me. She was at least smiling. The landscape was looking better.

"Hello. How may I help you? I am Beth Johnson, the Assistant Registrar."

I related Ry's story: his acceptance into Notre Dame, the swimming awards, the accident, his four weeks plus two days, six hours and twenty-nine minutes in Sheltering Arms. The start of his physical and mental recovery and Dr. Zasler's suggestion that he take a class. Call Dr. Zasler if you want to. I have his number. He is one the best neuro-rehabilitative medical doctors in the state. Maybe the country. He wants Ry in the class." I'm sure it was much more than she had bargained for, and by the time I was finished I felt like I had been through a therapy session. It felt good to get it all off my chest.

"Please," I finished, "can we get him registered today? The class starts in two days, and I have no time in my life right now to get all the forms completed, teacher recommendations, and school transcripts." I thought my storytelling rose to a magnificent performance, a Pulitzer Prize for sure. I took a deep breath and hoped she would take pity on me and offer a helping hand.

"Let me see what we can do, Mr. Beville. I do want to help. I might be able to eliminate some of the paperwork. If you can fax me his acceptance letter from Notre Dame then I don't need any high school transcripts. However, since it is past the registration deadline for fall classes, you will need to get Professor Akira Suzuki's permission to let Ry in his Japanese class."

It felt like a sign from Heaven. Finally, something had turned in our favor. I might get to cross one thing off my long list of things to do. She handed me a note with Professor Suzuki's phone number and suggested I go to her office and call him immediately. When he answered the phone, I told Ry's story for the third time.

When I finished, there was silence on the other end. Then Professor Suzuki's measured voice came over the line. "You know Japanese is a complicated language to learn. Considering your son's brain injury, is he going to be able to concentrate and complete his daily assignments?"

Just as I had no idea what he would be doing in January, I didn't know if Ry could complete the assignments or not. With TBI, all dimensions of brain function can be affected, with difficulty producing speech, word recall, short-term memory issues, emotions, and motor skills. Any number of these things could affect how he performed in class, especially a Japanese class. "Ry will do great in your class. He's a smart kid," I said with total conviction. I was all for advocating for our kids, but I was becoming a wizard at information fabrication.

"Mr. Beville, if your son was accepted at Notre Dame, I agree with you. He should have no issues with my beginning Japanese class. I will enjoy having him."

I exhaled for the first time since walking through the door and replied, "Thank you, Professor Suzuki. I will make sure he gets all his assignments done."

After Professor Suzuki confirmed his approval with the assistant registrar, Ry was officially registered in Japanese 101 at the University of Richmond. I was proud of myself for having accomplished something that seemed impossible just a short time before. They were baby steps but I was willing to take what I could get.

I called Lynn to give her the news.

"That's great," she said, "but you know he's going to have to study more than any of those other students just to pass. How is he going to get to class, then to PT, and then home every day?"

"Well, I guess I'll be a taxi driver, since the state temporarily suspended his driver's license. He has to go six months without a seizure and then get a letter from Dr. Zasler." The conversation took a little wind out of my sails. I was on cloud nine after getting Ry into the class. Now the realities of what we were about to undertake started to set in. I had just added another task to our already packed schedule.

Since he'd gotten his driver's license, Ry had been so independent. I'd forgotten what it was like being on "dad duty," shuttling him and his friends from school to swim practice to someone's house for a sleepover. Our life had already slowed down a lot and had been about to slow down even more with Ry off to college. Now, we were stepping back in time.

**

In the last five weeks, I had missed dinners with my beloved wife so I could stay at the hospital to eat with my son and make sure he didn't throw food trays across the room. I was forced to put several authors on hold and missed essential deadlines for returning edited manuscripts. Mail was piled up on my desk, and my assistant was doing her best to respond to my clients and get corrected pages back to authors. This was my dream job and I was itching to get back to it.

Since high school, I had always wanted to be involved in the production of books or be an editor. Thanks to my brother, Bill, my first job out of college was as a field editor for Macmillan Publishing Company in New York. My brother worked there and alerted me to an opening. I interviewed and got a job working with college professors in developing textbooks. It was intoxicating to read the first chapter of a manuscript and two years later see the finished hardback book on a college bookstore shelf. It was intellectually stimulating because I got to read manuscripts on topics like Biology, Chemistry, Geology and Physics.

Producing a book requires putting a team of talented people together for a year or two and managing the team to make the right choices, from page design, page count, hardback versus paperback, and marketing. My job was to hammer out all the details and visit the deadlines daily. I liked all the moving parts of the process: it was like fitting a puzzle together. But what was happening with Ry was a different kind of puzzle, one that I felt like I was missing half the pieces.

With Ry's class figured out and Lynn on board, I decided to go to my office. I was long overdue for a good day's work. I loved my job and missed being away for so long. With Ry at PT and the day ahead of me, I was starting to feel normal again. Maybe I would even buy everyone lunch and we could reconnect over all the book projects currently stalled, waiting for contracts to be signed by me as the head of the publishing department. I was excited for the day, excited by the opportunity to get a full day of work in. I would unclog the jam in the system caused by my absence and get books flowing to the printer. Already I was feeling lighter and ready to push up my sleeves and get busy. Life was moving in a forward direction once again, and I felt the storm of murk I had been living in was subsiding.

I was just walking out of the University of Richmond when my phone rang.

"Hello?"

"Mr. Beville, this is Cathy at Sheltering Arms Southside Center. We met several weeks ago, when I first worked with Ry at Sheltering Arms Rehabilitative Hospital."

"Yes, I remember you, Cathy. How are you?"

"You're not going to believe this, but Ry skipped his last PT session, and I'm walking behind him on Huguenot Road." She sounded out of breath. "He's on the right side, walking with traffic, which is freaking me out. I've asked him multiple times to please turn around and come back with me."

"What?" I said, practically shouting into the phone. I couldn't believe this was happening. Less than ten minutes ago, I was convincing a well-respected professor that my son was completely capable of keeping up with his class, and now I was being told that Ry had gone on another escape venture. This was crazy. No wonder I couldn't get a handle on how I was feeling—everything changed every five minutes. "I'm leaving the University of Richmond now and will be there shortly. Please tell him to stop and I'll pick him up." I was worried he would stumble and hit his head or worse, fall in the street. "Is he walking all right?" I asked.

"I wouldn't call it walking," Cathy answered. "He's holding on to his pants pocket and kind of yanking his leg forward with a lot of determination. His swim goggles are in his hand, so I can only assume he's headed to the Poseidon Swim Club on Robious Road."

I rushed to my car, feeling an overwhelming sense of anger. My hand was shaking so hard I couldn't get the key in the ignition. My mind was swept up in the dangerous situation he had put himself in *again*! We had just talked about this at the house and agreed we would discuss swimming later.

A few minutes later, I pulled into a side street just in front of where Cathy and Ry were walking. I turned the engine off and yanked on the door handle. I wanted to scream at him for being so reckless and scream at Cathy for letting him leave the facility, but I knew that wouldn't do any good. He paused when he saw me, and Cathy approached. She'd been just a few steps behind Ry. Their clothes were soaked by late summer Virginia humidity.

"I am so sorry this happened, Mr. Beville. He went to one session but was a no-show at my session. I looked out of the window in my office and saw him walking across our campus toward Huguenot Road. Once I caught up with him, I begged him to stop. He just kept walking."

"Well, Ry! It's a hundred degrees, and I am standing on the side of the road in a goddamn suit. What the hell?" I shouted.

Cathy's eyes went wide. She'd never heard me angry before but she said nothing. I got the feeling she would have liked to shout at him too if it wasn't considered unprofessional.

"I don't want to live under a microscope, Dad. Sorry."

"Oh my God!" I threw my hands in the air, wanting to pull my hair out. "Your brain has taken a sabbatical from logical thinking." As soon as the words left my lips, I was remorseful. I knew he had little control over his behavior. Danger did not enter his mind. I took a deep breath and lowered my tone. "Get in the car." Before I could take a breath, a Chesterfield Country police officer pull up behind my car, and turn on his bright flashing red lights. Oh my God, I said to myself. This is really the fucking antithesis of happiness. My mind was near paralysis. My psychic energy had been throttled back to zero.

"Good morning everyone," Officer Chalkley said. "May I be

of some assistance? Is your car ok?

"Yes sir. This is my son Ry, and his physical therapist Cathy Armstrong. Cathy is working with my son at Sheltering Arms just down the street. Cathy is helping my son with some leg issues. They got a little hot, and Cathy called me to come give them a ride back to the rehab center." I thought my mind would go into convulsions any second. He is not going to believe my story.

"Officer Chalkely, here is my badge I.D. from Sheltering Arms. I am the senior therapist there. I know this appears to be rather dangerous to walk next to a highway, but we were just going to go down a side street then head back to the medical campus. We did not realize that it is 90 degrees. My patient was feeling a little dizzy so I called Mr Beville."

Bloody good story I thought. Lying had taken over full passion our souls. But it was a creative story.

"Well, you folks be careful. Drivers don't always pay attention to where they are going. Good day"

"Thank you, officer, for checking on us." I opened the door for Ry and he slid into the front seat. "Do you need me to buckle your seat belt for you or is that something you think you can manage to take care of?"

Ry glared up at me but said nothing. With his good arm, he reached over and yanked the seatbelt over his shoulder.

I shut his door and Cathy climbed in the back seat on my side. As I pulled on my seatbelt, I could see Ry struggling to get his into the buckle. I waited patiently for him to get it, not offering to help. Even at the height of my anger, I still knew it was important to let him do the things he could for himself. When it eventually clicked in, I turned the car around and headed back to Sheltering Arms. "Ry you know what you did was dangerous," I said as we pulled up to a red light.

He stared straight ahead in silence. Cathy leaned forward to the front and broke the silence by saying, "I am so sorry, Mr. Beville. This has never happened before. I'm going to present this to my supervisor, so it won't happen again.

Within a few minutes, I'd pulled up to Sheltering Arms and dropped Cathy off. Looking over at Ry as we left, I asked, "Where do you want to go, Son?" My blood was simmering at a slow boil but I worked hard not to show it. It would not have helped to change anything if I blew up. Calm perseverance was the way to go.

"You know the answer to that," he snapped.

It took every ounce of willpower I had to not show any reaction. My son was working my very last nerve. Maybe I had been too lucky, and this was karmic payback for having a son who never acted out as a child. I remember looking at parents with screaming toddlers and thinking, *Glad that's not my kid.* Well, now I knew what it felt like. I took a few deep, cleansing breaths and kept my eyes focused on the road while silently repeating *I love my son. I love my son. I love my son.*

When I felt my blood pressure come down, I asked, "What's balled up in your hand?"

He slowly opened his hand to reveal his swim trunks, along with his goggles. He must have planned this move since this morning when we left home and I drove him to PT. The whole time I was buttoning his shirt, thinking we were having a bonding father/son moment, he was planning his escape. I was once again beyond livid. So, I did the only thing I could think to do. I drove him over to the swim club, perfectly prepared to let him sink. Of course, I would jump in if that happened, but a tiny part of me wanted to teach him a lesson about thinking he knew better than an entire hospital staff full of specialists.

I pulled up in front of the swim club and put the car in park. Ry didn't move, so I said, "Well, go on. What are you waiting for? Go swim."

He gave me one final look to see if I was serious and then got out of the car. I was determined to sit there and not go in with him, but after watching him drag his foot across the parking lot, I couldn't bear it. I quickly jumped out of the car and ran to catch up. No matter how angry I was, I couldn't let him get in the pool without me there. I wanted to prove a point, not kill my only child. If he was calling my bluff, it had worked. My bullheaded son was getting his way. He had won.

Once inside the pool, I waited for him to come out of the dressing room with his trunks on. I did insist on one rule—no diving off the blocks. I reminded him he had a bad concussion and a brain bleed just a month ago. He agreed and climbed down into the pool using the ladder. He moved slowly, his steps a bit wobbly, and I gritted my teeth.

It was mid-morning and the pool was mostly empty. I wasn't sure if this was a good thing or a bad thing. On one hand, I'm sure Ry felt better not having a lot of eyes on him. He was quite well known at the pool and probably appreciated not being pitied by strangers whispering, "That's the kid who crashed his car. He used to be a great swimmer. Look at him now. Poor thing." But from my perspective, the place being empty meant that if something went wrong, it was going to be on me alone to save my son from drowning. That terrified me.

Thankfully, he didn't sink, but it was not pretty. There was little rhythm in his arm stroke, and one leg could not paddle very well. He was out of breath after one length of the fifty-meter pool and had to stop. He was hanging on the wall at the end of the pool, looking down at the water.

Seeing my son so defeated broke my heart. It didn't matter if he had been a pain in my ass all day. That was my kid. The same boy who had gone through so much in his eighteen years. He had endured multiple surgeries over his lifetime and never complained. The kid who loved words and was willing to spend this past summer before college hanging out with his old man when most kids would rather be out partying. Most of all he was the athlete who'd trained his whole life just to see it all taken away in an instant. My heart wasn't just broken, it was shattered, and I'm sure his was too. Six weeks before, he swam this distance in under twenty-six seconds, four seconds off the U.S. record.

Today it had taken him almost one minute.

Any anger I had felt earlier was gone, replaced only with compassion and sympathy. I walked to the end of the pool and waited until he looked up. "What was your goal today?"

"To swim," Ry said, trying to catch his breath.

"Well, then, you met that goal. I don't see any failure here. There is a lot of risk in going after something that has meant so much to you for most of your life. It's simple: you want to be majestic in the water again, then go to PT and OT. Double down on your commitment to improve and don't let disappointment take full possession of your mind.

"You don't understand, Dad. My going back to Notre Dame is contingent on being able to make the team again."

Sometimes, I had to take off the father hat and put on a coaching hat. Having a child who excels in sports, it's always a delicate balancing act. But I knew instinctively this was one of those moments. "Ry, we've both been injured before. You know how this works. After qualifying for the Boston Marathon, I injured my knee two weeks before the race. I had to have knee surgery and thought I would never run again. But the following year, I requalified for Boston by running the fastest marathon I had ever run. Chasing excellence means accepting failure."

He looked up at me with pleading eyes. "Dad, how am I going to get to PT and OT, then to class and then to swim? I don't have a car."

"Let me figure that out. I want you to focus on three things: choice, clarity, and mastery. Choose the effort you want to make in the water every day. The clarity comes when you stay focused in the moment on what you're doing to make yourself faster. Mastery comes when I get to see you swimming for the Irish. But your swimming is contingent on you going to PT and supervision while you are in the pool. Are we clear?"

Ry looked at me with little enthusiasm, but there was a slight smile. It was enough for me. He pushed off the side, paddling away from me, and I went back to my spot on the bleachers. My words might not have had any effect, and he might not even remember the conversation tomorrow, but for today, we both had met our goals.

***

Two days later, it was Ry's first day in the Japanese class at the University of Richmond. I pulled up to the Puryear Building and found a shaded parking place under a big oak tree. We were twenty minutes early, just as I'd planned. Ry was still feeling the effects of his brain injury, with fatigue, headaches, and slowed reflexes. He needed some extra time for even the simplest tasks, and I didn't want him to feel rushed.

I had come to realize there was no straight path to a full recovery from a traumatic brain injury. Even with an aggressive combination of physical therapy, occupational therapy, and cognitive stimulation, he still needed daily nudging from me to stay positive and motivated to get dressed so he could go to PT, to class, then to the pool. He was still suffering from fatigue and mental fog that continued to affect his word recall and motivation to complete tasks. My passage through this long event had been a continuous grind. My moods changed hourly, from excitement over any improvement I observed, only to end the day in cycles of darkness, because my life had been placed on hold, with no expiration date.

"You excited about the class?" I asked, hoping to get a positive response.

Ry answered my question with a question. "Do I have to go to PT today?"

"We have an agreement. I agreed to let you come home just as you wanted, and in exchange, you must continue going to PT and be enrolled in one class," I answered with a little force, hoping to let him know I was not going to back down. I gave him a moment to respond, knowing sometimes it took a while for him to find his words. When he said nothing, I continued. "It has been a rough six weeks for all of us. I wish you would be a little more positive about things, Ry. This is not the first setback you've had in your life." Again, I paused, giving him a chance to respond before I went on. "When I was in college, I took a meditation class. We were given a booklet of Buddhist phrases. I have forgotten most of them but there is one I repeat. *May my life unfold smoothly with ease.*"

He sat quietly, staring at the pen he was rolling back and forth between his fingers—still no verbal response. "Think about repeating that chant silently when you are feeling uneasy about things in your life."

I knew we had to come to some transformation, if we were

going exit this spasmodic life style. Something in my son needed to shift. I had to get it through to him that he needed to face the obstacles ahead and keep pressing on. It was time for me to come clean about my past. I needed Ry to know that I too understood what it felt like to be dealt a tough hand. I too knew what it was like to feel like the entire world had conspired against me.

I'd never told Ry about Audrey. For a long time, I barely spoke of her, because it was too painful. Lynn knew of course, but after we had Ry, I never mentioned Audrey, because he was too young to understand and I didn't want to confuse him. As he grew older, Audrey drifted further into the past and there never seemed to be an appropriate time. Maybe I was afraid to tell him or maybe I was being selfish and wanted to keep my life with Audrey all for my own. I don't know the answer as to why I let each day blend into the next until over twenty years had passed. But now it was time. If I told him, perhaps we could both heal.

"You aren't the only one to have suffered trauma, Ry. There was a time in my life, before I knew your mother, that I thought I was immortal. I thought I had it all. Nothing could touch me. My life was going as perfectly as I had planned it out, just like you. And then suddenly, one day, in the blink of an eye, I lost the most important person in my life. I went out to get a sandwich and when I got back, she had died. It was like everything went black. I stopped caring about anything. The pain was so great, I didn't want to live."

Ry turned his head to look at me as I continued telling him the story. "I dropped everything—my college classes, my job. I left my apartment with most of my belongings, stopped talking to my friends and family and got on my motorcycle. I left everything behind and ran. I didn't know where I was going or for how long. I was so lost and I was so scared, trying to fill my heart with anything that would stop the pain.

I wanted to tell him more but stopped, because I was aware of how awkward this revelation of my past life might be for him. If he wanted to know more, I would gladly have that conversation at a later date. It was a lot to dump on him before his first day of class. I didn't want to overwhelm him, but I also wanted him to know that I understood the devastation that despair can cause in one's mind. "You are alive and you can rebuild what you have lost."

No one is spared in their lifetime from loss and grief, but it can mean growth. A new beginning to live life with passion and grace. I wanted to be emotionally precise in explaining to Ry that grief does not discriminate. If we look deep into our souls, we will discover that suffering does not mean that our lives are doomed. In the battle to recover from our mourning, we will eventually arrive to open a gate of discoveries. A life that can be more beautiful than the one we lived in the past.

Ry looked at me. His eyes were wide with more expression than I'd seen in a while. "Wow," he muttered. "I had no idea. I can't imagine you like that. You've always just been..." He trailed off, not having the words.

"... Dad?" I said, finishing for him.

"Yeah," Ry replied. "I guess I never really thought about it. I just figured you lived a regular life."

"You mean boring," I said with a laugh.

Ry laughed too. "Well, yeah. Kinda. A regular, boring life. Went to college, met Mom, had me. I had no idea you had been through all that." Ry sighed and added, "Was she your girlfriend?"

"Her name was Audrey, and she was my first wife."

A look of deep sadness came over Ry, and he replied, "I'm really sorry, Dad."

"Hey," I said, grabbing hold of his shoulder. "I'm not telling you this so you'll be sad for me. It was a long time ago and now

I have you and your mother. You've both been the greatest gifts of my life. I too had to rebuild myself: my image, my body, my mind. Just like you're doing now. You've been in this place before with injuries. This time is no different. It's about finding your rhythm again. Life's rhythm. You might not realize it yet, or sense it, but you will discover that you are different today from before your accident. Your map of the world is different. Nuances of emotions are different. You might be able to do things better, have insightful distinctions about playing your guitar, or poetry writing, even how your body responds to the water."

"Water is my sanctuary, Dad. You needed a motorcycle ride across the country to find yourself. My life is in the pool," Ry said with conviction.

I sighed. "The last six weeks Ry, you and I have been islands to each other, and that is not your fault. As a family, we need to communicate better. Love will get us to the other side of anything. I love you, Ry, and I know in my heart that you will thrive, you will sparkle, and you are my hero for never giving up."

"Thank you, Dad."

"Now, Number One Son, get your ass out of the car and go to class. You are in room eleven."

As Ry got out of the car and walked across the parking lot, I realized that for the last month, I had been looking at him as if he were broken, all the while thinking it was my job to put him back together. But I was wrong. There was nothing broken in my son. Yes, his limped slightly when he walked, but as I watched him rise to this latest challenge, I saw nothing but perfection. The grey drizzle of despair was no longer immediately identifiable.

Chapter 24

A Return to Homeostasis

A couple of weeks into Ry's Japanese class, I was once again driving him to the University of Richmond. I knew he was frustrated at losing his ability to drive himself, but I enjoyed our afternoon drives and chats. Ry had always been so independent; it was tough for him to go back to being at the mercy of his parents for rides. When we arrived at the college, I pulled into a shaded parking place and cut the motor instead of just dropping him off in front. "How are you feeling about your class?" I asked as we sat in the car. He hadn't talked much about the class, and I wanted to check in to see how he was feeling. I'd hoped he'd tell me more about what was going on inside his head, but usually, it was like pulling teeth to get a few words out of him.

"Exhausted," Ry answered while picking at the corner of his Japanese textbook. "Some days, I want to sleep in class."

I reached over and rubbed his shoulder. "I am so proud of you for your hard work. You know that, right?" I lowered my head to make eye contact. He eventually glanced over and caught my eye while nodding. Satisfied that he understood, I moved on. "How are you doing with the pronunciation?"

Ry was silent for a moment. I had become accustomed to giving him a few seconds to find his words. He had improved tremendously, but there were still lingering side effects. When he was ready, he said, "Dad, I think I might have better word recall with Japanese words. I don't know why. Christa, my therapist, thinks it's because I am creating new memory cells with the Japanese words and sounds."

"Wow. That is crazy thinking, but it makes sense. Each day, I have noticed more energy in your step. Life is in front of you, son. You better head in. I will see you in two hours. Don't nap," I added with a smile.

"Thanks, Dad, but I am still having memory issues. It is hard to stay focused in class. It's a competition between taking notes and taking a nap."

Ry opened the door, but before he got out, I added, "Time is a healing thing. Believe me, Ry, your mental momentum will return."

Ry gave me a crooked smile before closing the door and walking to the building, still with a slight limp. His massive swimmer's shoulders appeared slighter than they had been before the accident, but with each day, he was coming back. What a history in life's struggles this had been for my family. The greater the struggle and doubt, the greater the awakening to the mysteries of life. I was a witness to a profound transition in a little over seven weeks.

I too had become a different person. More stoic. Calmer. Now I found comfort in the quiet of the night. I no longer enjoyed watching television, because it was hard for me to sit still, and the constant talking bothered me. Weeks of sitting in silence with Ry in his room had changed me. I think it changed Lynn too. I noticed we talked much less. When we were no longer so focused on Ry's needs, we poured our energy into developing new directions and becoming more independent. Once again, I had to rekindle my dreams. Dig out a new path to re-measure my purpose. I could no longer continue to be a fugitive from the past.

I looked at my watch and started the car. It was lunchtime, and I had no appointments back at the office. Turning the car toward Libbie Avenue, I felt pulled toward St. Mary's. The hospital was a few miles away. Things were going well with Ry and life was moving forward, but I needed to go to St. Mary's one last time.

I got off the elevator on the second floor and headed down the hall to the Department of Clinical Psychology and Neuro-Rehabilitative Services. Inside, a woman was sitting behind a counter, looking bored.

"Hi, I am Don Beville," I said to her. "I was wondering if Dr. Benoit is in?"

"Well, Mr. Beville. How are you and your son? I was here when you came the first time to see Dr. Benoit," the woman replied. At that moment, I remembered her. It seemed ages ago that I had been standing in this office for the first time and she was offering me terrible coffee.

"Yes, of course," I smiled. "I remember you."

"Would you like some coffee?" she asked, brightening.

"No, thanks!" I said quickly. Realizing I may have insulted her, I tried to cover with a joke. "I have traded coffee in for a little more wine in my diet." She looked at me with a blank expression, letting me know my joke had fallen flat. "Is Dr. Benoit here?" I asked, wanting to change the subject.

"Yes, she is." She smiled. "Let me go check if she has a minute to say hello."

As she walked down the hall, I instantly felt that this was a mistake. I had no idea what I was going to say or why I was even there. I saw a mass of curly black hair heading my way and my heart immediately began to pound faster.

"Oh my," Dr. Benoit said. "What a treat to see you, Mr.

288

Beville. Please come into my office."

Dr. Benoit followed me into her office and her assistant closed the door to give us privacy. I sat in the same chair and Dr. Benoit took her place, leaning against her desk. "I want to hear all the good news," she said. "I know Ry is in outpatient services at Sheltering Arms."

I still felt like a silly boy with a schoolyard crush, but looking up at her face, I realized it was more than that. I'd been struck by the calm on her face that night in the parking lot when she came to my rescue. She'd wrapped me in a protective cocoon that night, giving me a feeling that all would be okay. Even now, I still felt that same way in her presence. She gave me comfort, and some part of me felt like seeing Dr. Benoit would always be like coming back home. Or maybe coming into light out of the darkness.

"He is taking a Japanese course at the University of Richmond, which tires him out," I told her. "Naps are in order when he gets home, but he manages to stay up with his homework. His professor says his pronunciation is fabulous for a first-year student. But of course, he had taken two years in high school."

Dr. Benoit uncrossed her arms and clapped her hands together. "Mr. Beville, that is wonderful, and in regards to the naps, encourage them. Dr. Zasler tells me he is back swimming at his swim club. How is that going?"

"It's slow going, but at least he is swimming. His coach is working with him, with videotaping, so he can see his form in the water." I was feeling better about the visit and began to relax. Dr. Benoit was always so easy to talk to. She was cheerful and confident and just hearing the sound of her voice sent a flow of endorphins through my brain.

After a moment, I said, "May I ask you something?"

"Ask all the questions you want." Her smile brightened the room.

"Do you miss us, Ry and me?" I blurted. Immediately, my face heated and I regretted asking the question. What was I thinking, saying such a thing?

If Dr. Benoit found it odd, she didn't let on. She had the grace to take the question at face value and not read too much into it. Breaking out into a broad smile, she said, "I do. You and Ry love poetry. So, do I. I love W.H. Auden's perceptive take on medicine: *Healing is not a science, but the intuitive art of wooing nature.* The body is all-natural, Don. It gets easy when doctors understand that in the mind and body, all things are connected. Your support probably helped in his recovery, at least as much as all the therapy sessions combined. I want to invite you to speak to the parents who attend weekly psychotherapy sessions at the Richmond Brain Injury Foundation."

"I would like that very much," I said, feeling like I'd just received a gold star from my favorite teacher.

"Don, a great French psychiatrist wrote that, "Every life is a piece of art, put together with all means available.""

She called me Don. Was that significant? Maybe she always wanted to call me Don and not Mr. Beville. Maybe sitting there in her office, things were more casual. My son was not an active patient, and she could relax the professional labels. Whatever the reason, I liked hearing her say my name.

"And how are you doing?" she asked. "Are you back at work, publishing those beautiful coffee table books? Still running?"

"Yes, although at times it feels strange to be sitting in my office, or stopping at the store to pick up dinner, or going for a run. All the day-to-day aspects of life feel sometimes foreign but at the same time I no longer feel that smothering confinement of balancing my job, managing teams of people, my family life, and running competition. Life seems more natural and I don't worry about things as much. Does that make sense?"

Dr. Benoit nodded. "It makes perfect sense."

"It's almost as if the whole thing is now anti-climactic. There was so much chaos and stress for weeks and now it's just gone. I don't know how to put it in words." I sighed and thought about what I wanted to say. It had been hard to sort out everything I'd been feeling lately. "Sometimes, I look around at my life and think, what was that all about? It's like a bomb went off, followed by silence, and I'm standing there in shock asking myself, *what just happened?*" I looked down at the floor and then back up at her. "I can't say that I miss it, but maybe I miss that I knew exactly where I needed to be every day. Ry needed me. I'm thrilled he is getting stronger, and at the same time I realize how tragic and frantic events can eventually help us find a higher purpose in our daily life. Ry's accident and its affective aftermath was a serious onslaught of daily stress, doubt, dying energies, and endless woes. But, I believe what I can take from all of this is that we survive and are able to rebuild our lives through the support of a community of people. You, Dr. Zasler, the staff at Sheltering Arms, the people who cook the food, right down to the man who cleans the floors make up that community."

Dr. Benoit sat quietly for a moment, fixing her gaze upon me. I missed being at the center of something, and when it went away, I did feel unneeded.

Finally, when Dr. Benoit spoke, she did so deliberately and methodically. "Sometimes, we run the risk of allowing grief and tragedy to define us. That's not to say that we sit around feeling sorry for ourselves, sometimes it is quite the opposite: we never stop moving, we never allow ourselves a moment to feel the trauma. We may even block it from our thoughts altogether, but that doesn't mean it isn't defining us. Grief is simply running the show behind the scenes."

"So many people contributed to helping me find a little sunshine each day."

"Don, I agree with the aspects of a healing community. Being surrounded by loving caring people is as effective as medication, and I believe it can alter the course of the length of time a patient spends in the hospital. I have a question for you. Has your Audrey come to see you lately?"

The question hit me like a shot to the chest. I could see Dr. Benoit already knew the answer to her question. She looked at me, like a teacher waiting for her student to catch the meaning of a lecture. When it seemed I did, she said, "You must let go of the past, Don. Sometimes, we will never get the answers to why bad things happen. Why was Audrey taken from you? Why did this accident happen to Ry? Maybe the answers to these questions are not for us to know. It is simply our job to believe and have faith that God has a larger plan. When we accept life on life's terms, we are telling God we have trust in Him."

I let Dr. Benoit's words wash over me. It was hard to accept everything she said, especially about God's larger plan.

I was lost in my thoughts about grief and God and what it all meant when Dr. Benoit broke the silence by saying, with a laugh, "Or maybe you just miss the adventure of escaping with Ry through the hospital kitchen?"

My head immediately shot up as I looked at her in shock. Did she know about the great chicken escape? How could she? Dr. Benoit gave a hearty laugh at my expression. "So, it is true!"

She clapped her hands together. "Rumors were floating around among the staff that an escape had occurred. Most of the Doctors and nurses were laying bets it was you and Ry."

I couldn't believe we'd been found out. "Did Dr. Zasler know?"

Dr. Benoit nodded. "I believe he was quoted as saying, 'Good for them. A healthy sense of adventure never hurt anyone.'"

I filled her in on the rest of the chicken story and it felt good to share a laugh. After that, it was time for me to go. I had taken up enough of her busy day. When I stood to say good-bye, I was shocked that a lump had formed in my throat. This would likely be the last time I would see Dr. Benoit and I didn't have words to express my gratitude. And if I tried, I would probably break down into an embarrassing, blubbering mess. Instead, I quickly thanked her and said I would keep her updated on Ry's adventures. After a long handshake, I left before she could see my eyes start to well up. As I walked down the hall, she called out, "Take care of yourself, Don. I will pray for you and your family to be happy and well."

It was the last time I saw Dr. Benoit. I would speak with her on occasion over the phone to discuss Ry's progress, but they were usually very short conversations, to the point. She had multitudes of patients all needing her guiding hand and it would have been selfish to take up too much of her time. There was no doubt in my heart, I was going to miss her. Her advice during this journey had kept me from drowning, maybe even from jumping off a bridge. There is life even in the throes of devastation.

I was beginning to find my way back into life, but everything seemed new, like I had been transported into a far-off frontier. The season was changing. My life was changing. My relationship with my wife had changed. We spent more quiet moments when we were together. Not talking, not touching, not reaching across the expanse of time to ask about the welfare of each other. My heart became a roaming spirit, seeking beauty and comfort in other places. My son's life was evolving too. Progress remained a mystery. He could be cheerful one minute and defiant the next. September was ending and October had just begun.

When I finally went back to full-time work at my job, I stood in the doorway, catatonic, afraid to enter. I'd tried so many times to go in over the last month, and nearly every time I'd been pulled away by an urgent phone call regarding Ry. *Mr. Beville, Ry, is refusing to eat. Mr. Beville, Ry escaped. Mr. Beville, Ry is dragging his leg down the street, headed toward a swimming pool.* I didn't think I could take one more panicked phone call.

For once, the problem wasn't Ry—it was with me. Had I lost confidence in my ability to perform my duties as a publisher? The machinery inside my brain was working against me, amplifying a wave of fear when I tried to organize the mass of decisions that lay across my desk.

My office was full of morning light as I tried to remember my old routines. What was the first thing I did when I walked through the door? It all felt so unfamiliar. I sat down behind my desk, picked up the phone, dialed an outside line and called my mother. I knew the simple act of hearing her voice would calm my nerves. "It's been overwhelming," I told her, feeling a rush of relief to say it out loud. My mother was a good listener and was sympathetic to my cascading feelings of loneliness.

"Life is about transformation. We walk through shadows then are washed by light. Every person, Don, is a participant in a dance of birth, death, love, and suffering. Your dad and I love you."

When I hung up, some joy returned to my thinking. My heartbeat slowed. Stephanie's words came back to me. *Give one hundred percent of your concentration to being in the moment.* I began to lay out orderly rows of contracts, manuscripts, budget quotes, employee evaluations, speaking requests, and author book-signing events. Maybe in organizing, I could find some moments of peace. It was in my nature to seek perfection in my work, and that required my team to be participants in a dance of creativity. After all, no author writes alone. It takes a community.

Producing a coffee table book is not done in a vacuum. The tricky thing about being the managing editor on large book projects is that I was in charge of interviewing, hiring, and managing dozens of freelance people, like copy editors, photographers, and book designers. I also oversaw the creating of printing specs while tracking budgets and deadlines. Daily deadlines. My mother was right: in life, you have a lot of dance partners.

My current project was a coffee table book about the Marines in the Gulf War. The previous month, I'd hired a research assistant to help me organize my projects. She was doing follow-ups with clients and would meet with me to discuss them later. Approximately one hundred photographs had been sent to me from over fifty international photographers traveling with the Marines. The book's copy was written by a journalist from the *Baltimore Sun* newspaper, and now that copy had to be approved by a military team at the Pentagon, then by several Marine Corps officers at Quantico. It was a book I'd been captivated by and a project I was anxious to finish on time and on budget.

I could feel myself getting back into the rhythm of the job I loved. Eventually, the hours started to fly by as it all came back to me. I told my team that all the piles on my desk would be sorted and organized by the end of the day. My page designers could start preparing the books to go to press within the week. Later, I met with two photographers about a book I had just agreed to do for the Henrico County Department of Industrial Development. They had signed a contract with me to produce an oversized book about the county they would use to lure foreign corporations to open new headquarters in the county. They were targeting companies in Germany and Japan, and they wanted the book produced in English, German and Japanese.

That meant I had to find four translators: two for the writing of the German and Japanese and then two more to do proofing of what the first two translators had written. The best place to find such people was the Virginia Commonwealth University, or, as luck would have it, my son's Japanese professor at the University of Richmond. By the end of the day, I had contracts in place with four translators, plus another person whose services included the Japanese typesetting.

Though the day went by in a flurry of activity, it felt amazing to be back. Whatever nerves I'd had in the morning were gone by the time I left that evening. Every book I'd produced in the past fifteen years had filled my life with meaning. With every project, I learned new things. Every author and every client were a little different, and they brought their life experiences and knowledge to each book project. There is durability in love and hope, just as those two ideals sustained me during my journey learning new things about my son and his brain injury. It was not a road trip my family had reckoned on, but like each book project, I was inclined to hope that through the power of love, my actions would be transformed into something beautiful.

***

That night at dinner, I was giddy to tell Ry and Lynn about the book projects I'd signed and the completed manuscripts sitting on my desk with pages of copy reflecting the author's beautiful voice. Prose that was fluid and fearless. Photos that took my breath away. Events documented by gifted writers and editors would soon occupy the bookshelves of libraries and bookstores. With each book, I could feel the joy of knowing that my hand had touched parts of it in some way.

"Ry, how was your day?" Across the table, he ate with a slow but steady hand. A long scar had formed on his forehead. The swelling over his eyelid was gone. He was no longer on any steroids, and his facial swelling caused by them was receding. He was almost looking like his old self.

"The paralysis is still lurking. I feel weak and…" He thought for a moment to find the word. "Um…swimming was a bust, but I managed to stay afloat for twenty laps."

"PT and OT. That is the answer," I said as I dished up my plate with a hearty helping of roasted potatoes.

"I like my OT sessions with Cathy Armstrong," Ry said. "Today, she had me close my eyes and told me to visualize my last swim meet, starting with standing on the block and the sound of the gun. I could feel my body relax in the chair just as it does when my toes are extended on the edge of the blocks."

Lynn smiled and said, "You know, Ry, the body is extremely resilient."

I agreed, adding, "Sometimes we don't appreciate and understand how wonderful it is to be at the top of our athletic abilities until we crash and walk the path that you have been on."

"I want my driver's license back," Ry said, making a face.

"Can't be done until you meet with Dr. Zasler and he writes

a letter to the DMV. We don't go back to see him until the end of November. And you might be required to take a driver's test too. In December, we have your court case. Don't forget you got a reckless driving ticket. You went through the red light and the other driver was hurt."

There was shock in Ry's eyes as he said, "I didn't know the other driver got hurt." He waited for me to say something and when I didn't, blurted out, "Well, are you going to tell me?"

How much should I tell him? I didn't want to lie, but I also wanted him to stay focused on his classwork. He needed to focus on the future, not the past. I took a sip of wine and decided it was best to answer him honestly, "Both cars were a total loss. The man who hit you required knee surgery. He's eighty-two and suing our insurance company."

"Wow," Ry said. He put his fork down on his plate, looking forlorn. "Why didn't you tell me?"

"You'll get to see him when we go to court, make a statement to the judge and get a chance to listen to a police officer give the accident report. It won't be fun, but we'll get through it."

Lynn gave me a cautious look, no doubt wanting to diffuse the building anxiety around the topic. Placing her hand on my knee under the table, she squeezed it. This was her way of telling me to change the subject. I squeezed her hand back, as my way of saying, it's okay, I can handle this. Being married for so long, we could have an entire conversation with looks and hand squeezes.

"I don't know what to say in court, Dad. I don't remember anything."

I pictured Ry in that courtroom, dressed in a nice suit, fumbling for his words. Would he have an angry outburst? Would he be overcome with tears? I decided that whatever was to come, we would walk through it like everything else we'd been through, concentrating on each moment as life's continuous transfigurations appeared before us. Ry had never been in trouble, never broken any laws. I was sure any judge would see this for what it was: an accident in a thunderstorm.

"That's why we have a lawyer," I said, to reassure both my wife and son. "Let him worry about everything. The other driver is suing us and will probably win. There isn't much we can do about that. But if he's awarded more money than the amount of our car insurance limit, we're responsible for the additional money."

"What a fucking nightmare," Ry blurted out while shaking his head.

My back and shoulders stiffened. It was a nightmare, but we had come so far; I wasn't about to slide back to the past. Also, I was so done hearing F-bombs from my son. Spearing a carrot with my fork, I said, "Yeah, but it's not *fucking* cancer, and you don't have to go to *fucking* chemotherapy."

Both Lynn and Ry looked shocked, neither used to hearing me swear. There was a tense moment of silence and then Lynn turned to me and asked, "Can you pass the *fucking* salt?"

"Of course, sweetie, any other *fucking* thing on this *fucking* table you need?"

That was all it took for Ry to burst out laughing. I'd missed seeing his big smile, his perfect teeth. I'd missed hearing Lynn's contagious laughter, seeing the tiny wrinkles at the corners of her eyes that appeared when she laughed. Things had been so hard for so long, and it felt like finally there was a crack in this darkness, a way for light to come in. It felt good to laugh together as a family, and I allowed myself a moment of pure optimism that everything might just be okay for the Beville family.

When Lynn stopped laughing, she wiped a tear from her eye. Her tone more serious, she said, "Ry, your dad is right. You don't have cancer, and you've come a long way physically and mentally in just the last two weeks." She sipped her wine and leveled her eyes on his. "Some of the babies I help in the NICU are so small, I have to hook IV lines into the veins of their heads, because their arms are too tiny. I'm constantly checking the oxygen flow in their incubators and ventilators. Some of the babies never leave the hospital for months, and when they do go home, I have to train their parents to operate all the machines just to keep their newborn child alive." Lynn stabbed a carrot onto her fork and waved it at Ry. "Your life is not nearly as bad as you think."

My wife was a positive force when dealing in a landscape of intense emotions and circumstances. Every day, she witnessed the despair on parents' faces as they were briefly allowed to hold their premature babies, some hooked to life-sustaining machines that helped them breathe. She told me many times how she could sense hopelessness. "It's not always easy to swing the parents back to a joyful scene when there is such an undertow of sadness. But I speak to them in encouraging words, saying that they will, one day, hear the laughter of their child."

In our twenty years of marriage, I looked to her as a life-enhancer. She was a creature of laughter and a delightful companion. One look at Ry told me that her words were sinking in. The way he chewed his lip, the way he furrowed his brow— he was thinking hard about what she'd said. For a moment, it felt like having the old Ry back, the contemplative, thoughtful Ry. I reached over and kissed Lynn on the cheek. My son wasn't the only one who should be feeling grateful.

She looked at me and smiled, and I smiled back. In the

moment of hearing Lynn's demure giggle, a memory of Audrey's all-consuming whoops of laughter surfaced. The tacks I had put on those memories were not holding. I had loved only two women in my life. One lay in darkness, sleeping in the clay of the earth. The other was sitting beside me. I sat in the duality of my mood, both the sadness of loss and the fullness of joy. I could choose to lean into either side. Stay in the present moment or let a heavy heart take me back to the past. Remembering what Dr. Benoit had said about letting grief define us, I chose to lean over to my beautiful wife and whisper in her ear, "I love you. You have saved my life more than once."

***

A few weeks later, Ry and I went to court. My son looked handsome in his new charcoal suit. We had gotten his hair cut for the first time since the accident. His fingers were fidgeting at his side. He looked a lot leaner, and the puffiness in his face was completely gone. His face appeared younger than he did before the accident.

The session didn't last long. The other driver sued us for an enormous sum of money, well above what the insurance company had paid to replace his car. He claimed the accident had required him to get knee surgery, and we'd believed that to be true in the beginning—but it came out in court he'd had a long history of arthritis in his knees. The surgery he'd received was something he'd needed for years and was not due to the accident. The man was looking for an easy payout, but the judge saw through the scam and pretty quickly and dismissed his personal injury case. He did, however, get a nice sum from our insurance company to replace his car.

Ry walked alongside me to the parking lot, steadier now on his feet. The slight limp in his right leg remained but was barely noticeable. He'd been swimming every day, had not missed any of his PT sessions, and was getting As on his Japanese quizzes. Now, the court case was one more hurdle we could leave in the past, bringing us another step into a new brighter future. There were days when I saw the son I knew during the past summer, when he'd sit at his desk writing poetry or playing his guitar.

Still, Lynn and I continued to tear up when we saw him struggle with getting his shirt buttoned or when he got frustrated as he fought to remember the right words to use. Also, the intensity and success of his swim practices fluctuated from day to day. It was a sign to me and his swim coach that he had not fully recovered physically. His slow lap times created wildly disparate mood swings and gave us a continuing understanding of the underbelly of brain trauma. It made him spend more time at the pool and less time at home. The doctors had told us it could be a long recovery, and they had also prepared us for the possibility that Ry might not recover completely. He might always struggle to find his words. He might always have short-term memory loss. The hemispatial event to the left side of his brain still was affecting motor movement on his right side.

Days turned into weeks. Our tragic family dance had changed our way of thinking and I believe our personalities too. Maybe temporarily. Maybe forever. Ry was not as animated as he had been before. He was less of a social butterfly, flittering from flower to flower. He didn't see his friends like he once did, and he didn't mention interacting with students in his Japanese class. There was still an occasional angry outburst from time to time, and he still struggled with walking up or down steps. His right leg would jiggle just before the bottom of his foot touched the step. But, more and more the veil of his disabilities lifted, and I would get glimpses of the son I had pre-accident.

A few weeks after Ry's return home, it seemed to me that I had become more pensive, with a deeper sense of keenness in understanding the flux of life. My brain was getting rest and recovering from the daily hospital visits. There are limits to the ability of our brains to absorb the perpetual variations and shades of ambiguities that we must deal with in our waking hours. Children raised on farms learn early the hardships created by nature: the death of the cow that provided milk for oatmeal; the horse that you loved, sold to a neighbor; crops that curl in the summer heat and crumble for lack of rain. It is flux in the greatest sense. Somehow you get done what needs to get done.

I got Ry to PT, class, swim, worked in my office for a few hours, told my wife I loved her and kissed the back of her neck, making her heart beat softly. I got done what I needed to get done. The collapse of our world caused us to travel in and out of bouts of melancholy. We crawled back to a life dictated by familiar rules and traditions. The blanket of perceived normalcy felt comfortable, soothing, and protecting. However, homeostasis can be porous, and when we are least expecting it, memories of the past can bring us to our knees.

Often, I thought about what Dr. Benoit had said about Audrey and grief. After I met Lynn and we had Ry, I forced the memory of Audrey out of my mind, thinking that was how a person moved on: push the pain away and keep running. This is how athletes are trained to think. Ignore it and keep going. Keep moving. Move faster. The faster you go, the less it can hurt you. Go. Go. Go. It was all I had known, and I'd passed that thinking on to my son by constantly nudging him to kick the soccer ball harder, swing the bat faster, put more weights on the bar.

In the springtime of my life, maybe age six, on the hard soil in our backyard in Petersburg, Virginia, my father put a glove on my hand and told me to catch the baseball. He was driving my life toward sports and I loved it. Over the years, he taught me to accept the pain of the wounds from training. There was no magical thinking in my brain. I learned that every night, my body would forget the weight of fatigue from the bruises from football practice or a lump on the cheek from a stray baseball. Dad did not believe in hibernating. I never became a bear.

My high school legacy included the highest batting average in the state, scoring the most touchdowns for the football team, running track, and starting on my black belt in judo. There was never a veil of fog in what my father expected of me. Winning was a long progression of sorting through minefields of injuries, coming out the other side motivated to do better. My dad was my hero. His guidance and wisdom were a platform for glory. The glory of crossing the finish line first.

Chapter 25

Closing the Door on the Past

I wanted more than anything to be a hero for my son. So, in the springtime of *his* life, around the age of six, I put swim goggles in his hand and, standing on the damp floor of a swim club, I told him to jump in. There would be no hibernating. I was excited for him. Like me, he would become addicted to the adrenaline and endorphin highs of putting all of his energy into a sport. For eleven years, his body absorbed thousands of hours of bone-weary training sessions. His beautiful form in the water was schooled by coaches and admired by other swimmers. One of his coaches, Dudley Janke, who sent several of his swimmers to the Olympics, said that Ry had the smoothest butterfly stroke of all the swimmers he had coached. Dudley was also caught up in the excitement of Ry being accepted to Notre Dame and winning a spot on the swim team.

The accident had forced us both to stop. We were made to fight back the sorrow and the exhausting weight of our fears. Each day during Ry's recovery, I'd wake up in the morning and it crossed my mind, *what if I got on a motorcycle and just took off?* But that's the funny thing about pain. No matter how fast you run, it's always waiting for you when you come home. I couldn't run from this the way I'd run from Audrey. Things were different now. I had been blessed with a loving wife and an athletically gifted son. My career was flourishing, with a backlog of books to create and publish. Somewhere along the line, I had grown up, and running was no longer an option. No longer impromptu scrambles to hop on my motorcycle to see what was waiting for me in the next town. My child was in trouble and I would remain close by to love him unconditionally.

One afternoon, while Lynn was at work and Ry was still at OT, I took a walk in the Japanese garden we'd built. It was time to take Dr. Benoit's advice. I had to stop running and let Audrey go. I had turned away from her for so long, it was time to finally face her memory and say good-bye. Alone in the garden, unafraid, I allowed unvarnished memories of our short marriage to enter me. Cherished thoughts of birthday celebrations, scraped knees falling off our bikes on the beach sands, snowball fights, meandering late-night sex talk, all bound together in layers to be rediscovered. I didn't care how painful it was, I was determined to feel it all. For my son, for my marriage, for my life— it was time.

Waves of grief I'd been suppressing for over twenty years bubbled up and came to the surface. Every cell in my body yearned to go for a run, just to escape these feelings. I'd been running for so long, it was instinct—a way my body had learned to escape pain. Just lace up the shoes and run, my brain said, but I refused to tamp this sorrow down any longer. The tears came as my body shook with grief, and yet I stayed in that garden. I had to. For Audrey and for the new future I was rebuilding with my family.

Audrey would always be with me in some way, but I needed her to stop chasing me. I wiped away my tears and turned my face to the heavens. *I can't come to visit you any more, Audrey, a glass of wine in hand, bare-footed, like so many nights, whispering in your ear how much I love you. My world has changed since you left. I loved you once with all my heart and nothing will take that away, but the addiction must end. It's time to let you go. Good-bye, my love.*

I took a deep breath and looked around once again at the beautiful garden and pond Ry and I had built. The beauty of the flowers and the sound of the running water were intoxicating and swept me briefly to another world. I closed my eyes and let my thoughts wander without judgment or control. I could see images of my son touching the wall first at a Notre Dame swim meet. I saw my grandmother milking cows; Lynn blowing out birthday candles; my feet crossing the Boston Marathon finish line. I stood in the garden and allowed the entirety of my life, the sad moments and the joyous, to wash over me again and again until slowly I opened my eyes. A feeling of contentment spread throughout my body. Everything was quiet and peaceful.

I was finally in the present moment of my life, and it was beautiful.

Chapter 26

Welcome to Notre Dame

I sat staring out of the van's windshield, the engine running. Snowflakes were piling up on the driveway, making it look like we were Santa's sleigh inside a snow globe. The depth of winter and its bone-chilling cold was here. January 6th, six a.m., the journey to Notre Dame was about to commence. Next to me, Lynn had rolled the window down and was catching snowflakes in her hand. "I love snow," she said, with a happy grin on her face. "When I was a kid, I would run around the yard catching snowflakes on my tongue."

"I bet that was fun to see: your neighbors peering through their windows saying, 'Look at the crazy girl.'"

Lynn was filled with happiness as the snow began to come down harder. In a manic mood, I would say. She had been talkative, singing, humming, before we even got out of the bed. "I made a list of sites to see in South Bend," she said with excitement. I loved that she was enjoying this moment.

"Dad, what are you waiting for?" Ry asked from the backseat, a notebook open in his lap. "Let's go."

He had told me he planned to write a poem a day, saying poems are the carrier of dreams. I was silent, not yet motivated to move the gearshift from park to drive. I wanted to savor this moment. My heart was happy. Today was a gift. A hard-won chapter was culminating in our pilgrimage to Notre Dame. I looked at Lynn, reached for her hand. "I can't believe we made it to this day. It's been a crazy six months."

"You made this moment possible," Lynn said. "The daily stress of Ry's rehabilitation cut me to the bone. I don't know what I would have done without you."

"We didn't have a choice but to be there every day. You were amazing…"

"When you guys are finished giving each other credit for my recovery, I would like to see this van moving northwest," Ry said.

My son's meteoric ascent to recovery could not be explained. Most of the recovery from a TBI happens in the first year or longer, but Ry's recovery had been like turning on a light switch. Ry had come out of being partially paralyzed and brain-injured faster than any of his doctors had believed could happen. He would still have lasting effects for a while, which he would have to learn to overcome. Short-term memory issues might remain. Would he remember his class assignments? Would he remember his way around campus? His doctors warned him about the consumption of alcohol. TBI patients could develop addictions quickly. I wanted him to have an independent life on campus but with no crushing accidents or injuries.

We had one rule: don't look back. It was like the Greek myth of Orpheus. His love for his wife, Eurydice, was so deep that when she died, he traveled to the Underworld to retrieve her. He found her but lost her again when he failed to obey the one rule told to him: *Don't look back.* This had become the rule our family lived by since the accident. Ry had kissed death, blood on his face, and he had come out on the other side. He was stronger. We all were. And we would not look back.

I pulled the van out of the driveway and headed west, sensing the enormous weight it carried with three humans, ten boxes of books, five boxes of clothes, two boxes of speakers and other stereo equipment, and twenty-six gallons of fuel in the tank. My nerves crackled as my brain moved through dense layers of emotion: fear, excitement, joy. We were doing this, six months late, but it was happening. When I reached over and put my hand in Lynn's lap, she closed her hand around mine. We knew what the other was feeling, even in silence. At that moment, I felt lucky to have a partner who made my life beautiful. I loved her deeply and she helped me live fully, as our hearts still beat for one another.

By the time we reached the Pennsylvania Turnpike, closing in on Pittsburgh, the small flakes had turned to heavy show. It sounded like we were being pelted by snowballs. I turned the defroster on high and tried not to blink as cars in front of me seemed to be losing their grip on the road. I saw a snowplow up ahead and carefully sped up to get behind it. I would follow it as long as I could, since the left lane had disappeared under slush and chunks of ice. Behind me, dozens of drivers fell in behind us with the same idea. Stay behind the snowplow, I kept repeating.

Fifteen exit ramps later, the plow was forced by deep snow to reduce its speed to twenty-five miles an hour. I sighed, letting my thoughts fill with the image of Notre Dame's Golden Dome. It was put in place in 1882, with Mary standing atop, symbolizing our faith.

I needed that faith today.

"Ry, are you having fun yet?" I asked as I gripped the wheel a little harder.

"When can we stop for food? I have to piss." Ry delivered the words with a shot of irritation. His angry outbursts and mood swings were still a work in progress, but after so many months, I hardly noticed them any more. I had learned to pick my battles, but part of me wondered how this would affect his relationships at college. Not everyone would be so understanding, so compassionate. It was another moment for me to learn to let go. I had to let some faith return and understand it was time for Ry to walk his own path.

"How about you, sweetie? You ready to stop for some food?" I said, looking to Lynn, who was clutching the armrest of her seat.

"It's okay with me if we just hit a fast-food place off the turnpike. I don't want to get off and explore snow-filled side streets then get stuck." From the stern look on her face and her white knuckles holding onto the door handle, I could tell she was enjoying this ride about as much as I was.

"Good advice," I said, nodding in agreement. Although I was disappointed about leaving my comfortable place behind the snowplow, I pulled off onto a ramp with a blinking sign that read, "Food. Gas. Restrooms." Touching the brakes, I felt a staccato-like vibration in the steering wheel. It was the brakes telling me the front wheels were losing their grip and overcompensating. We stopped at the first place I saw and ordered burgers and fries. We sat at a booth by the window, watching as the snow piled up around us.

An hour later, with full bellies, we crossed over into Ohio. We still had two hundred and fifty miles to go. At least four more hours. Interstate 80 was full of snowplows, and the snow finally seemed to be tapering. Ohio knows how to do snow well. The roads were clearer, the traffic steady. We were almost going the speed limit. A little after eight, we reached the town limits of South Bend, Indiana. It was dark, but we could make out some of the towering brick buildings on campus. Peering out of the windshield at the white terrain transformed my mood to one of ecstatic happiness.

"Wow. We are on the doorsteps of Notre Dame. It's where we are meant to be. I feel like we are home," I said, reaching over and giving Lynn a closed fist pump. "Ry, look, there it is. The Golden Dome. What do you think, Number One Son?" I said, almost singing out the words.

Ry unbuckled his seatbelt so he could move closer to the front for a better view. He leaned over the back of Lynn's seat. "Wow. Magical. I can't believe I'm actually here." He paused for a moment and said, "Dad, Mom, I love you. Thank you for everything you've done for me. I know it's been a rough few months. There was no way I could have made it without you."

His words were wonderful. "Ry, I know that you're excited. We are too. But put your seatbelt back on." I quickly looked in the rearview mirror to see my son's elegant visage, wide-eyed, with the beautiful bone structure, and a happy smile. I was witnessing a miracle in my backseat. Dr. Benoit and Dr. Zasler said I'd see this one day, either driven by prayer or science. Maybe it was both.

The snow picked up again, the wind blowing it sideways. We drove by the Fifth Third Bank on Michigan Avenue. The bank signage was blinking "Twelve degrees. Good God," I said, "what's the wind chill?"

As we pulled onto campus, Lynn took out a map and looked for Zahm Hall. Ry was assigned the same dorm and the same roommates as last year, the ones who had been sending him updates on the campus events he had missed, like coed parties in the basement and group outings to nearby restaurants and movie theaters. Zahm Hall was also famous for its residents streaking across campus for the annual Bun Run that happened just before exams.

We made our way along winding streets and snow-covered

alleyways. The beauty of the campus could be on a postcard, with the gilded Golden Dome and statue of Mary atop the Main Building. We turned into a small alley behind Zahm Hall. The snow was still falling headfirst past lamplights attached to the building by rusted bolts. It had taken six months to get here. Six months of unfamiliar turns, inclines, days of wandering down hospital hallways, therapy that pushed Ry to a miraculous outcome. My fear of never seeing my son on this campus was now in twilight. I felt intensely alive.

My heart felt like it would explode with joy. I was not too proud to let go of my tears. We sat in the quiet of the night, watching the snow become our blanket—three humans with different visions of the future, carriers of new meanings. We'd overcome our pain and grief, shaped it into something new. There was only love now. It felt as if we'd reached the center of the earth. I leaned over and kissed Lynn's cheek.

"I love you so much. Thank your helping put all the broken pieces of our family back together."

She smiled at me, looking a little teary-eyed. Then she turned to Ry and said, "I want to go up and see your room."

"No way, Mom. This is a men's dorm," Ry pleaded.

The only word that came to mind was dilemma.

"Sweetie," I said, "maybe we should let Ry get settled in his room tonight, and he can meet his roommates. We can slip by tomorrow." I tried to compromise, seeing Ry shake his head in the rearview mirror.

"I want to go up and see where my son is going to live for the next five months," Lynn insisted.

In geology, rocks and diamonds are formed by pressure. I knew how this rumble would end if I didn't add something to the architecture of Lynn's request. Sometimes, it only takes a spark of kindness to create a favorable outcome.

"I have a thought. Ry and I will take a few boxes up to his room. If there are no naked guys roaming, I'll come down and you can run up for a minute. Does that work for you, Ry?"

Lynn folded her arms and set her jaw tight. "I do not see the problem with me going up to his room. I bet most mothers do that."

"Mother, do you have a shut-off button?" Ry said.

"Ry, that's enough," I said. "Lynn, just wait here, please."

When I opened the door, the cold wind sliced through me. I reached in the backseat for my LL Bean parka. I handed a box of books to Ry then grabbed the lightest box I could find. Ry's room was on the third floor and there was no elevator. I didn't see any reason to try and be a hero and lift that much weight. As Ry and I walked inside the big brick building, two male students walked by us.

"You need some help, sir?" One of the students asked. Both of them looked like they were ready for an Alaskan Iditarod Trail Sled Dog Race. Their coats were thick enough to withstand subzero winds. Their heads were covered with wool beanies.

"Yes. I'm Don, and this is Ry. He's moving in tonight. Some help would be great."

One student, a young man with a rounded face and glasses, stopped in his tracks. With his mouth dropped, he asked, "Are you Ry *Beville*? The swimmer from Virginia?"

"Yes," Ry answered, a bit surprised that the guy knew his name.

The student turned to his friend and said, "This is the guy I was telling you about. He's that fast swimmer from Virginia, the fastest time in the butterfly."

"Hello, welcome to Notre Dame. I am Kevin McBride, and

this is Brian Doyle," he said, motioning toward the shorter guy.

I looked at Ry, who was blushing more than I'd ever seen him blush. The students left for a moment and quickly returned with three others. Then there were seven of us in a little parade, marching up the stairs with all of Ry's stuff. I carried a box of clothes up the three flights of stairs, walking slowly behind Ry as he chatted with our guides. I had so many things in my life to be grateful for, but seeing Ry walk up the stairs without a limp or misstep was something of pure beauty.

I walked down to let Lynn know it was okay to come up to room 311. When we arrived back up, Ry was sitting on his bed. The other boys were gone and the place was quiet, in contrast to the rest of the dorm, which buzzed with the activities of youth. All of Ry's worldly possessions now resided in a corner next to his bed. Lynn looked around then sat next to Ry. "Nice firm bed," she said, giving it a slight bounce. There were two wooden desks in the room, each with a window looking out across the campus. A bookcase resided in between the two beds. It was small but clean and tidy.

"Ry, your roommate is an engineering major," I said as I looked over the sampling of books on the shelves. One could only conclude that this was an engineering major when the title of the books read, *Introduction to Statics and Dynamics*, *Elements of Concrete*, *Structural Engineering Reference Manual*, and *Machine Design and Materials*.

I took a seat at the desk, looking at Lynn and Ry, and found solace in the assurance that while each of us was one single strand of thread, woven together as a family, we became a beautiful cosmic fabric. What was next for us?

Lynn seemed pleased that the room was a satisfactory cocoon for our butterfly. From the window, we could see the quad below, filled with glowing light from numerous lamps on crisscrossing sidewalks. A man with a snowblower slowly walked the length of one sidewalk ending at the lake. Ry's room faced east. When the yolk of the sun rose and reflected off the lake, the room would fill with golden light. "Ry, your room faces east. Your great-grandmother always said that east is where each day and each new story begins. Our soul emerges from the point where the sun rises."

I imagined when Ry stood by this window each morning, his soul would open and blossom. It was a fresh opportunity to wake up each day and create who he wanted to be. If he possessed any self-doubt about being at the crossroads of his new journey, his voice remained quiet. As his father, I knew his mind was engaged in processing the events of the past five months, and he knew in his soul that he had survived with all his vehement passions intact.

"Ry, before your mother and I go get some dinner, let's go down and meet Father King." Father King was the dorm priest, and it was customary for parents to introduce themselves. If Ry would have started school in the fall, we would have met him along with all the other parents during orientation week.

"Dad, I just want to stretch out and rest," Ry answered, although I suspected he wanted to hang out with his new friends. We could hear them chattering down the hall, the steady thump of music coming from one of the rooms nearby.

"Ry, I just drove an entire day in the snow. I feel like I have body parts falling off but we have to do this. Let's go. Now." Teenagers are still teenagers, even if they have had a traumatic brain injury.

We headed to the first floor down a cold and empty stairway. Each level had a window looking out onto the grounds. The snow was still falling from the Indiana sky. We reached Father King's door at the end of the building. Father King and I had talked by phone soon after Ry's accident, at a time when I felt the most helpless. He'd been a witness to my suffering and had been strong with his compassion to help me. The Father's words had fed my mind with positive thoughts, as he told me to have faith that God would hear our prayers. More than once, I'd told him my faith was in question, and it was hard for me to believe how God let these things happen. One of the first times we spoke, I told him, "The loss of my first wife and now my son suffering has put a stain on my faith, Father."

He listened without judgment and didn't try to convince me I was wrong. I could only imagine being a dorm priest. He'd had thousands of conversations over the years with young people questioning their faith.

I knocked on his door just above the gold plate that read "Father Thomas King, C.S.C." The door sounded solid, maybe carved by hand from a big oak in 1932. Three breaths later, the door opened and a tall man wearing a black sweater with a bright white priest collar smiled at me, extending his hand.

"Hello, you must be the Bevilles," he said while reaching out his hand to shake mine.

"It's nice to finally meet you in person, Father King," I said, shaking his hand.

He turned to Lynn, taking her hand and opening the door wide. "Come in. Please come in. One of the students who brings me my mail said he helped to get things to Ry's room."

The room was dim except for several candles burning on a table in the corner. I looked around for spirits. I could feel them. Priests say prayers and give eulogies for the dying. The living say farewell. But maybe the spirits of the dead dwell in the community of the priests. They travel in and out of nearby homes, where people are sitting at dinner. They hear our conversations and pass over the slopes of our skin. At least I'd always hoped that was true.

There were still times, after all these years, that I would be walking along and get a whiff of Audrey's perfume, even if there was no one else around. I had to believe she was stopping by to say hello. There would also be times, years later, when I would run a marathon and feel my father's hand on my back, pushing my tired body forward. Some people I know say that when you die, that's it, you are gone, and none of your earthly energy remains. I believe spirits stay with us and I rejoice that they have continued to communicate with me.

As we looked around, Father King turned to Ry. "You are the famous swimmer Ry Beville," he said. Barely pausing long enough to let Ry nod, he went on. "You are finally here. Please sit down. Ry, I am told that you are going to be a great addition to our swim team. Coach Welsh has told me about your accomplishments in Virginia. I was saddened by the news of your terrible accident." Father King was about to sit in a large leather chair but seemed to change his mind and spun around saying, "May I fix you tea? It's excellent tea."

"Father King, we would love some of your tea," Lynn replied as she sat in the middle of a large, worn-leather Chesterfield sofa.

"Yes, tea sounds great," I added while taking a place next to Lynn. "This is the longest sofa I have ever seen," I said. "The tufted leather is soft."

"Ah yes. My predecessor brought it with him from a church in Ireland. When he retired, he donated it to me and I am so grateful. I believe he said it was made in 1832, when furniture artisans began using button tufting. That sofa bears witness to delightful and transformational stories of thousands of students and parents. Deep, honest stories of their fears and faith," Father King answered.

I was beginning to realize that Father King was never going to be short on conversation. The man seemed able to talk about anything and had an infectious enthusiasm for life. He left us for a moment and soon came back with steaming cups of tea on a small tray. The scent of cinnamon filled the room, winding in and out of an assortment of bookcases touching the twelve-foot ceilings. I felt I could have stayed in this room forever, with two of my favorite things, the smell of old books and intense spice.

As Ry took his cup of tea, he looked up to Father King. "Thank you for your letters last year. I brought them with me," he said, his voice filled with gratitude. "Last year, I felt as if I had stepped off the earth. Then your letters arrived and your words helped with my recovery. There were times when I would go to a dark place and your letters brought me out."

"That is kind of you to say. No matter how embattled we are with sickness, injury or other pains of the soul, God will provide us a portal to grace." Father King took a seat in an armless chair and leaned toward Ry and asked, "Are you comfortable talking about the accident?"

Ry was quiet for few seconds, noticeably rubbing his tongue along his gums. Finally, he said, "I have no visual memory, only sound. The sound of crushing metal and my girlfriend's screams."

Father King said nothing. He simply nodded in a quiet, assuring way. I imagined being a good priest would be like being a good therapist. I was beginning to admire Father King more for his ability to know when to speak and when to listen. Ry must have felt comfortable too, because he continued by saying, "I remember someone yelling, *cover him*, and then loud, very loud buzzing of saws grinding through something hard and thick." His voice began to tremble at what must have been a terrifying memory.

"Ry, be assured that mental imagery or a lack of is not essential for human thought," Father King said.

"I do remember periods in the hospital, when I had thoughts and emotions but could not express them. Then one day, there was this door that opened in my mind. I could see my future." Ry closed his eyes for a moment as he spoke. "Surreal. Was it real or fantasy? I'm still not sure." He opened his eyes and went on, "For days, I could open that door again and again. Even smell chlorine. I could see myself rise and stand in the threshold of that door. My hands on the hinges, leaning backwards, I fell through the door and then felt water splash over my skin."

My heart quickened, as Ry had never expressed this to me.

"You know, Ry," Father King said as he pushed himself to the edge of his chair. "The Swiss psychiatrist Carl Jung wrote, *People will do anything, no matter how absurd, in order to avoid facing their own soul... Who looks inside, awakes.* You looked inside and asked, how do I change? This was a dark time in your life, but now you have come through the other side stronger. I have heard many stories from parents and my students also about a door opening, letting the mind see into the future, especially when the stories are connected with the knowledge that one's life is slipping away at an accelerated speed.

"Yes," Ry said with a little smile, "like Victor Hugo wrote, *What makes night within us may leave stars.* I see the accident as a blessing. I am a better swimmer. I can feel every inch of water move over the hairs on my skin as I glide through the water. I can play complicated melodies on my guitar that I could not play before the accident. I am not sorry the accident happened."

"Ry, your dad told me that one of your doctors is a nun? Interesting. Unusual. One might surmise that that is the reason you are sitting on my old confessional sofa," Father King said in a serious voice.

I sat in quiet awe listening to my son talk about his experience. We had never spoken much about what had happened. I often asked him how he was feeling or what he was thinking, but it took someone else to bring out his experience.

"The more time passes, the more I am beginning to believe that someone or something other than the medical staff had a hand in my recovery. At the end of my hospital stay, Dr. Benoit, the one who is a nun, did on occasion sit with me for long periods of time, reciting her favorite scripture."

"Oh my. That is wonderful to hear." Father King looked almost giddy at hearing this. "Might you remember any of the conversation?"

"No, not much," Ry said. "I do remember she favors Psalms."

"Well then, let me tell you my favorite Psalm. The Lord will guard your coming and going, both now and forever."

Ry smiled and nodded, taking in the words. I couldn't have been prouder to be his father in that moment. That he was able to sit and have a deep, meaningful conversation about spirituality, psychology and literature. Although a somewhat different person emotionally, the TBI and all of its physical and mental manifestations had for the most part dissipated.

Father King turned his attention to Lynn. "Lynn, mother of this wonderful child, tell me, what do you do in Richmond, Virginia?"

"I am a neonatal nurse at Virginia Commonwealth University, Medical Campus. It used to be called Medical College of Virginia," Lynn answered with pride.

"Ah, you are the voice of the smallest and the sickest. God bless you."

I gazed into his eyes of quiet compassion, his face lit with kindness. Father King's voice had counseled many and I felt privileged to get an hour of his time. Over the next half hour, Ry talked of his goals and his excitement to swim for the Irish. This was the same kid who a short time before had wanted to stay in his room and stretch out on the bed. A kid who six months ago had struggled with word recall. I was witness to the creation of a new map of the world inside Ry's brain, a map that had been ripped apart the night of the accident, and now a new one was scrawled across the surface of his beautiful mind. His self-esteem had blossomed.

Eventually it was time to leave. "We must go, Father King. Thank you for letting us visit with you and for the tea." I was exhausted by the drive and needed to get some rest. I could tell by the look in Ry's eyes, he needed sleep too.

Before we left, Father King handed Ry a folder containing helpful suggestions on dorm life, a map of class buildings, and phone numbers and addresses of guidance counselors. As he walked us out, he patted Ry's shoulder and offered, "If you ever need help with anything, come knock on my door. I imagine great things happening for you, son. You are going to shine. Every day, I want you to awake with a sense of wonder."

For the first time in a long while, I too fully believed Ry was facing a future where the world of possibility had reopened that sense of wonder.

Chapter 27

Growing Love is a Continual Process

Book publishing is constant problem solving. There are countless moving parts: interviewing and hiring editors and book designers and understanding and managing clients' expectations. Some projects landed miraculously in my lap, the client articulating the exact kind of book they wanted me to produce. It was like throwing a box of puzzle pieces up into the air that fall magically back on the table in perfect order. This resulted in little suffering on my part and I was revered if not seen as a genius.

Other projects, however, provided daily doubt. Doubt about the client's ability to pay; doubt about the design approval; doubt about the resilience of my patience when things blew up— and they always blew up. In that way, book production and publishing were really no different from living life every day. We must attend to living with unflinching honesty, not be afraid to ask for help and accept the challenges of self-invention. Changing who we are into who we wish to be does not come easily.

Persistence is something you learn early. You have to learn how to approach people. You have to learn when to take your time and when to pursue something at full throttle. Once, I told Henry Kissinger I could not pay him twenty-five thousand dollars for writing the Foreword to my USTA Tennis book and then convinced him to write it for free. When I asked President Gerald Ford (an Eagle Scout himself) to write the Foreword to my history of the Boy Scout book, his assistant told me if I wrote it and faxed it to the President, he would okay it and send it back with a photo. Done! I produced and published a coffee table book about the Marine Corps for the Office of Military Affairs at the Pentagon in a record forty-six days. When I finally went back to work, I had to remind myself—sometimes daily—of the difficult and complicated projects I had completed. It helped in rebuilding my confidence. Once again, I would become a book publishing addict. Everything I did represented publishing at its best.

With fatherhood we must rejoice in the victories that come along: the first time a child rides a bike without training wheels; the first day getting on the school bus; the first time on the honor roll, and of course the first date. Nothing was as significant in my life as my role as a father. No matter what the future held, I knew I'd nudged, encouraged and often pushed—with compassion and sternness—to aid in my son's TBI recovery. For months I had planted the seeds of wellness and emotional stability, and I was determined to be present for the harvest.

One morning, a year after the accident, as the fall maple leaves were turning red and yellow, I tucked my fashionable mother, my life mentoring father, and my beautiful wife into another white rented van to go watch Ry swim in the National Catholic Swimming Championship. We were leaving for South Bend a few days early to watch Ry practice and spend some time with him before the big meet. It was going to be a nice family vacation, and I was looking forward to exploring the beautiful campus of Notre Dame. I had developed a huge attachment to its scholarly reputation.

My father was excited too to visit the Notre Dame campus, while my mother and Lynn couldn't wait to hug their grandson and son. The feeling in the van was bright. We were full of optimism and joy. None of us had thought we would be there to celebrate Ry's first national championship meet. During the summer, he had attended two swim practices a day, increasing his muscle mass and stamina. During the last semester, his bruised brain still struggled with some of the class assignments, but his professors soon saw his writing brilliance shine through. A year ago, Ry was spending hours in physical therapy sessions, and now we were about to see him back in the water, chasing his dream once again. It was difficult not to press further on the gas in my excitement to get us there sooner.

My dad was especially jubilant at the prospect of watching Ry swim again. I loved to listen to my father talk about his student years at the University of Virginia. He reminded us that when he was a student it was males only, and it's a reminder of how times have changed. To me, the thought of being part of a college education on a campus devoid of women was primitive. I could not imagine it.

"Dad, what do you remember about your student years at UVA?" I asked. My dad started chuckling.

"We didn't have calculators or computers. We had to use our brains, with pen on paper to figure weight limits on bridges and how many tons of concrete and steel we needed to hold up that bridge," Dad answered with a lot of pride in his voice. "Once we figured all the variables, then we knew it was time to go out and drink most of the night."

We all had a laugh about that statement, as UVA is still famous for its tail-gate parties before football games.

In the late afternoon, we arrived on campus to witness hundreds of students crisscrossing on sidewalks, wearing their blue-and-gold athletic coats, Notre Dame logos embroidered on every breast pocket. After a fourteen-hour drive we were tired, but everyone wanted to go to the aquatic center to watch the last hour of Ry's practice. Once inside, we found seats on the bleachers and waved to Ry when he took a short break. I never got bored of watching my son turn laps. Today, I could not detect any weaknesses in his stroke or turns, and I was shocked at how much he'd improved since the last time I had watched him swim. He was smooth, falling into a perfect rhythm as Coach Welsh yelled, "Butt up, butt up." A sinking butt equals drag in the water and it will add time in a one hundred-meter freestyle race.

The smell of chlorine was strong and I'd forgotten how much I missed it. Later in the hotel, our clothes would remind us of the chemical aroma of a pool. Ry pulled himself up over the wall as the practice was ending. I could see by the expanse of his ripped muscles that his body had returned to its former shape. He would tell me later that he ended every swim practice by doing at least one hundred sit-ups.

Coach Welsh came over when he saw us and gave us hugs, telling my mother and father, "Ry is a special athlete. His butterfly stroke is about perfect and, in some practices, Ry looks like he is going to take flight. It's beautiful." I glanced over at Dad to see him beaming from ear to ear.

"How are his grades?" my mother chimed in.

I thought it was a strange question but perhaps normal for someone of her generation and considering the importance she placed on acquiring knowledge. "Mom, I don't think coach Welsh would know that," I said.

"Actually, I do," he answered, surprising me. "The student-athletes must maintain grade integrity, so the registrar sends their reports to the coaches." He patted my mother's arm and added, "You will be happy to know Ry is doing well. In fact, he is on track to make the Dean's List."

Hearing the words "Dean's List" was golden, in light of the information given to me a year ago by a Sheltering Arms counselor. "Your son's return to Notre Dame might be a stretch considering the damage to his brain's processing capacity."

At the time, the term "processing capacity" had little meaning. I had no landmark, no starting point, no knowledge of the idiosyncrasies of the human brain. But I did know that the brain is not an ornamental organ encircled by bone, skin and hair. Gradually, through conversations with Ry's doctors, I learned that the brain is a big, beautiful map that controls all aspects of one's life. Damaged brain cells could affect a person's ability to remember, recognize and perceive incoming information. Through it all, I wanted two things for my son: that he would be able to feel love and be able to thrive in the world. Coach Tim Welch's words meant more to me than he could imagine. It wasn't about grades or accolades. It meant my son was back.

***

After Ry's practice, as rain clouds gathered in the distance, we went to dinner at an Italian place Ry recommended. He let me know it was a bit pricey but I shrugged it off. What better time to have a celebration than when we could all be together?

We piled into the van, and when I closed the sliding door, the noise echoed, metal on metal. The sound momentarily took me back to what I imagined, was the noise my son's car made when it collided with the light pole. I could not pretend fear didn't still creep up, and cup my heart that something could happen to any one of us. I had learned that life was unpredictable, so we had to be grateful for every moment. Standing on the blacktop on the campus of Notre Dame was surreal. I took a second to pause looking out the van window and to celebrate our current life, while the others chatted away. My parents were healthy, my wife was in love with me, and my son had developed into a unique individual, walking his own path. I had been given so much. I felt like a little boy, enchanted in my new environment.

Parisi's Ristorante was family-owned; it said so on the door. The building was decorated like a Tuscan villa, with thick ivy vines growing on the walls. We didn't have a reservation and the manager was kind enough to seat our party in a private room that had not been booked. The room was much larger than we needed, but I found myself once again feeling grateful for the kindness of strangers.

As I sat down, I noticed the gold nameplate on the table, inscribed *Father Hesburgh*. He was the president of Notre Dame for more than forty years. I remember reading a quote on the back of a book written by him. "The best thing a father can do for his children is to love their mother." I looked over at Lynn and smiled. We had entered a new phase in our life, one without a child under our roof. Our emotions and day-to-day cares were now to be diverted to each other. The process of growing love was continual.

"Ry, what courses are you taking?" my mother asked, once again focusing on his studies.

"They loaded me up, Granny," Ry said. "With two-hour swim practices in the morning and afternoon and then five courses, some days I feel like a caged chicken. I have quantitative reasoning, which is a math course, the science of technology, which is like chemistry, a physics and biology course, and art and literature, which I love because I get to write. Then I have a one-credit course that they call the Moreau Experience. It's supposed to help first-year students acclimate to college life. Some students don't like it because we have to speak in class. It's really a religious course, because the topics come from the Holy Cross Education standards, developing the mind, heart, zeal, and family."

"Oh my," my mother answered. "When do you have time to eat?" She shook her head and peered over the menu. "Why would they make you take so many?"

"Well, Granny, since I missed my first semester last year, I'm taking an extra course. I want to graduate on time."

A short time later, after a couple of glasses of wine, our food arrived along with another bottle of Chianti. Over the speakers, Frank Sinatra sang, "I got you under my skin." There was a plate of warm bread and olive oil dipping sauce, which was passed around more than once. I looked around the table, seeing all smiles. I reached over, taking Lynn's hand and brought it to my lips." I love you," I said.

"I love you too." She smiled and poured herself some wine.

"Ry, what course do you like? Do you have a favorite professor?" I asked.

Ry shook some parmesan over his plate as he thought about the answer. Like all college students being bombarded with questions from family, he seemed more interested in the food than our curiosity. Still, as a polite kid, he took the time to patiently respond to our eager faces. "I love my Art and Literature class. Professor Nicholson taught at Harvard with Robert Frost. I can't wait to take his Beowulf course, but I have to be a sophomore."

He stabbed two raviolis and stuffed them his mouth. My child had been perpetually starving since he was thirteen. It was beautiful to see his ferocious appetite returned. Ry swallowed his food and continued, "We have to write two papers a week. But

I'm okay with that, although some days I get writer's block." He picked up his glass of milk and chugged it down. "With all the classwork and twice-a-day swim practices, I get tired." He shoveled in more ravioli and tore off a hunk of bread. "I need a lot of naps."

"Do you think there are some residual effects from your accident?" I asked

Ry didn't answer. He shrugged and took another bite of bread then changed the subject by saying, "Hey, Granny, are you going to finish that chicken parmigiana?"

I wondered if his silence meant he was uncomfortable with me bringing up the accident. Perhaps he had decided to leave it in the past and focus on his future. If so, I supported his decision and decided not to bring up the accident again. If he ever wished to talk about it, I would always be here for him, but I understood his desire to move on with his life.

***

The next morning, I called my parents in their hotel room to see if they were ready for some breakfast. The championship swim meet started that night, with Ry swimming the fifty-meter butterfly, one hundred-meter freestyle, and the four hundred-meter freestyle relay. I opened my door to walk to the van, and dozens of sparrows and juncos scrambled in every direction. I remembered I had bought some sunflower seeds the day before and reached into my coat pocket to pull out what remained of the bag. I opened it and scattered the seeds among my new friends. Other birds soon noticed the random chaos and joined the breakfast.

My heart was calm but my emotions were mixed. My brain

floated from being blank one second to feeling like a kayak in river rapids the next. I could not force or prevent my mind from thinking something terrible was just around the corner. We'd had a beautiful dinner the night before, and now I was wrestling with this awful sense of doom in my stomach. Was this how it was going to be forever?

Questions would not stop tumbling through my mind. It was driving me crazy. What if Ry fell on the ice this semester and became brain injured again? Although the window for seizures from his TBI had come and gone, statistically he was still at a higher risk than the average population. A wave of panic shook me. I went back to what Stephanie and Dr. Benoit had told me about being in the moment. Focus on the moment. I took several deep breaths and reminded myself that nothing in life is ever guaranteed. Not just for my family but for everyone. Humming a little song helped to redirect my thoughts while I continued to remind myself that life was a cycle of ongoing mysteries and human stories.

By the time everyone else made it out to the van, I had talked myself back into the present moment. I realized why Ry didn't answer the question the night before about whether the accident was causing his need for naps. It didn't matter. Just like it didn't matter what had set off my momentary lapse into panicked thinking. Both my son and I had learned that it did no good to focus on what had caused the problem; it was how we were going to deal with it now. That's how we moved forward. We couldn't stay stuck in the past, and we couldn't run around our troubles. We had to stop, face what was happening and walk straight through it. Or in Ry's case, swim through it.

Chapter 28

Hope is an Endless River

The butterfly stroke is unique unto itself. It requires a high fitness level, and reducing one's swim times in the butterfly requires daily practices for years. It's the butterfly stroke that is most dependent on rhythm in stroke mechanics and breath control while in the water. When a butterflier has rhythm, they have to establish good momentum in the recovery phase of the stroke—that's the moment in which the arms break clear of the water and begin movement toward their re-entry back into the water. It's the point of the arms into the water that the hips must be at their highest point of elevation as well. Placing the hips or butt in the right place at the right time is also critical to the rhythm. I have watched Ry's butterfly rhythms for twelve years. He was six when those rhythms first entered his body.

We took our seats in the Rolfs Center, and I was thrilled that my mother and father were there to witness their grandson swim in a college championship swim meet. They were getting an opportunity to take home memories of sounds, smells, and the excitement of the moment.

Just as we were taking our seats, Mom suddenly pointed to the opposite side of the pool. "I think that's Ry swinging his arms!" she said.

I had to laugh. My mother had seen Ry at hundreds of swim meets over the years, and he'd swung his arms every time, but this was Notre Dame. This was a national championship meet. This was a celebration. Ry's life had been restored. As a family we knew it. The swim team knew it. The dorm priest knew it. God had granted a wish. Redemption is not made to be a crumb.

"Yes, that's your grandson swinging his arms," I said with a big smile. I was just as excited as Mom but trying to play it cool—at least a little bit. My heart was racing and I could feel the adrenaline rush, just like I did at the end of a 10K. Joy pertains to everything in life.

At six thirty, the voice of the Notre Dame commentator began announcing the teams. "Let's welcome Boston College, Georgetown University, Marquette University, Villanova, Xavier College." Each team paraded out on the pool deck to receive a warm welcome from their fans. Ry waved to us, and we all stood up and shouted his name. "Go, Ry!"

The Georgetown team was clearly the one to beat. It seemed every swimmer was over six feet tall. They were huge and broad-shouldered, even more so than Ry. Notre Dame, being the home team, got to warm up first. Ry jumped in the water and began doing an easy freestyle. After what seemed to be ten minutes, my father asked, "How many practice laps are they going to do? They won't have any energy for the race."

"Dad, they practice twice a day, two hours in the morning and two hours in the afternoon. The warm-up may last thirty minutes. He looks smooth," I said, pointing to Ry in the water. "Notice there's barely a splash of water when his arms make their way back into the water. That's the rhythm."

When Ry had finished his warm-up, the meet was a few minutes away from starting. After his accident, he'd worked relentlessly to regain the speed and strength he'd lost. This was the most important meet of his life. It was his moment to prove he was back. If he was successful, no one would look at him any longer, with pity in their eyes, as "the kid who had been in the accident." If he failed, those looks would go on. I got up from my seat and walked to the edge of the railing, motioning for Ry to come over. I wanted one last pep talk with my son.

"What are you going to do tonight?" I asked.

"Win," he answered with a determined look on his face.

"How are you going to do that?"

The answer had been the same for over ten years. Today though, there was a new kind of determination. Ry was smack dab in the center of creating his future and he knew it. "Stay focused on my rhythm and be aggressive," Ry said as he smiled.

I reached behind his head and pulled him towards me, leaning into his ear. "Your discipline got you to this moment. Do you believe you can win?"

"Yes."

"When the pain cruises to the edges of your mind, welcome it. Then push through it, just like you've been doing all year. I love you." I turned to walk away, but Ry didn't let go of my hand.

Pulling me back toward him he said, "I'm here tonight because a lot of people were there for me. But mostly you, Dad. It was you who never left my side. I could never have done this without you."

"It's what fathers do," I said with a smile. I leaned in close and pointed to the other swimmers then continued. "Ry, look at each and every face of your competitors and know no one worked harder than you to be here. Now, go break records. Winning is not everything. But tonight, Ry, it is."

I squeezed the back of his neck and then walked back up the bleachers. Before getting to my seat, I turned back to take another look at my son. Seeing him standing with his teammates, preparing to climb onto the blocks, a prayer entered my mind and I whispered, "God, give him angel's wings to fly." It was only one of a few prayers I had said in years, and I felt it deep in my heart. In this moment, in a dome, surrounded by the scent of chlorine and an audience filled with love, I truly felt the magnitude of a higher power. I could only describe it as God's love.

After releasing the pain around Audrey and watching the miraculous recovery in my son, I had begun to see that God had not targeted me for tragedy. This was simply the unpredictability of life. I had learned by watching my son that obstacles in life are not meant to break us down; they are meant to make us stronger. It was only by losing Audrey that there was a space for Lynn and Ry to come into my life. I could see that now. Trusting in God once again helped me stay in the moment and let go of my fears. I knew I couldn't control everything around me. Whatever was going to happen today was going to happen.

The first event of the night was the one hundred-meter freestyle, which Ry had decided not to swim so he could save his energy for the one hundred-meter butterfly. The noise of the crowd fell away as the gun sounded to start the race. Coming off the blocks, every swimmer hit the water together. Their strokes were crisp and clean. Georgetown took the lead early and never fell behind. Notre Dame finished second.

The next event was the one hundred-meter butterfly, Ry's event. He jumped into the water for his warm-up laps. What an odyssey he had been on for the past twelve months.

"I am so nervous," Lynn said. "I'm shaking."

"So am I, Sweetie," I answered, suddenly realizing I'd been holding my breath. What would our emotional response be if he did poorly? Some of the top butterfliers in the country were here.

Was my confidence too high? Too low? I didn't know what to think. Is it human nature that we don't allow for the possibility we might fail, no matter how much we have prepared? I wondered how much of Ry's neuron network had been degraded after his accident.

"All swimmers for the one hundred-meter butterfly please come to the blocks," the announcer said. The stands had filled with more than a thousand spectators. The beep of the starter's signal was the swimmers' cue to stand on the blocks and wait for the gun. Everything from that moment forward becomes automatic and beautiful when the swimmer's rhythm is right.

The sound of the gun's blast nearly jolted me out of my seat. I couldn't get my nerves under control as I watched the swimmers dive off the blocks into the water. This was it. This was what my son had been fighting for all his life. Ry's lift off the blocks and his entry into the water was smooth, with minimal splash.

"Damn!" I shouted to no one in particular. "Everyone is even!" Ry's form looked great but he was not ahead of anyone.

My father and mother were standing, yelling, "Go, Ry! Go, Ry!" I wasn't sure if they even knew which lane he was in, but it didn't matter. Seeing my parents jumping and yelling was part of being in the moment. Being alive.

I looked at Lynn and said, "He needs to pick up his stroke."

"He's pacing himself," she responded with a mother's knowing smile.

"Maybe. His stroke looks flawless."

At the fifty-meter turn, Ry touched the wall first but only by a hand. He was doing the work but I was having the adrenaline rush. My heart rate skyrocketed as he pushed off the wall, but when his body emerged from under the water, he'd lost any lead he had. The Boston College swimmer had a slight edge. I began to scream, "Pick up the stroke, pick up the stroke!"

In practice, Ry had swum this a thousand times, right down to the stroke count and breath. He knew what was left in his tank. It's hard to hold the perfect stroke in the last fifty meters, so it becomes a mind game. Ry used to tell me that the slightest deviation in his form would affect the position of his head when he came up for air in between strokes. Is this what happens in the last minute of a race when exhaustion hits? If your lungs can't take in enough oxygen, the muscles are affected and you lose speed?

With twenty-five meters left, the Notre Dame students in the bleachers were standing and screaming, "Ry, Ry, Ry!"

I knew that if Ry was going to win, he had to redline. This was round fifteen of a title boxing match. There were no phonies at this level. My parents, Lynn and I joined the crowd chanting, "Ry, Ry, Ry!"

It seemed all eight swimmers touched the timing pads at the same time. I looked up at the scoreboard on the other side of the pool just as all thousand people did the same. Lane five flashed the winning time of 53.21, and the crowd erupted into a deafening roar. The cement floors under my feet began vibrating with all the jumping up and down. I squeezed Lynn and my mother and father as we added to the movement of the floor. My mother and Lynn cried rapturously.

The voice of the Notre Dame commentator began announcing the results. "In first place, with a new Notre Dame one hundred-meter butterfly record, Ry Beville, with a time of 53.21!" Ry had won by six tenths of a second ahead of the Boston College swimmer.

Ry's teammates rushed to the end of the pool as he pulled himself out of the water. Tim Welsh, the Notre Dame swim coach, reached him first and gave him an enormous bear hug while the rest of the team piled on. I saw Ry searching me out in the crowd, so I waved my hand over my head. When his eyes found us, he raised a fist, punching the air in victory. I had never seen such a wide smile on my son's face. I would cherish this scene on my deathbed.

Just a year before, I'd had a panic attack while staring at an X-ray of my son's injured brain. A parent's greatest fear, seeing their children hurting, was staring me right in the face. I couldn't run and I couldn't control the situation. I just had to sit in the present moment and accept the pain. Over the months that followed, I learned more and more to let go where I couldn't have control and embrace the small victories as they came.

I could not say for sure if all of my prayers had reached God's ears. Dr. Benoit told me that God lives in all of us and He gives us the power to heal, quoting an ancient Roman philosopher, Symmachus, "The heart of so great a mystery cannot ever be reached by following one road only." Did God heal my son? There was a lot of praying going on, at Notre Dame, at my parish, by Dr. Benoit, and Ry's friends. There was also medical science at play. What the last year had taught me was to get up every morning with a calm heart and a mind overflowing with hope.

That night, watching my son break a Notre Dame swim record, holding my wife's hand and witnessing the tears in my parents' eyes, told me that life's changes never end and hope is like an endless river.

My son was a living proof.

Epilogue

The following night, at Notre Dame's Rolfs Aquatic Center, Ry broke another Notre Dame swim record that had stood for almost ten years. Later, several of his poems were published in the peer-reviewed Notre Dame literary magazine. In his junior year, he was awarded a Fulbright Scholarship to travel to Japan to study Japanese literature. At the end of his senior year, he was Notre Dame's Rhodes Scholar nominee. He graduated on time and received a degree in creative writing and a second degree in Japanese. He earned his master's and Ph.D. from the University of California, Berkeley campus. He is now a professor of Japanese literature at a major university. He also teaches a course in Neurodiversity in Literature.

He is the founder and president of the Yokohama-based company Bright Wave Media, which publishes the quarterly journals *Japan Beer Times* and *Sake Today* and produces another digital media content related to Japan. He has authored the fictional novel *What Remains* and has published translations of two books of poetry by Nakahara Chuya.

Ry and his wife split their time between Japan and the Bay Area in California. They have two children, who fill their home with laughter and joy. He still loves crispy fried chicken.